RICHARD HARDING DAVIS

AMERICAN NEWSPAPERMEN 1790-1933

From a photograph Copyright by Pirie MacDonald

Richard Harding Davis

CHARLES BELMONT DAVIS, Editor

THE ADVENTURES AND LETTERS OF RICHARD HARDING DAVIS

BEEKMAN PUBLISHERS INC.

NEW YORK   1974

© *Copyright 1917 by Scribner, New York.*

Reprinted 1974 with permission of the Publisher

Manufactured in the United States of America

Library of Congress Cataloging in Publication Data

Davis, Richard Harding, 1864-1916.
    Adventures and letters of Richard Harding Davis.

    (American Newspapermen, 1790-1933)
    Reprint of the edition published by Scribner, New York.
    1. Davis, Richard Harding, 1864-1916--Correspondence. 2. Davis, Richard Harding, 1864-1916--Biography. I. Davis, Charles Belmont, 1866-1926, ed.
PS1523.A43   1974   070'.92'4 (B)   74-769
ISBN 0-8464-0024-3

CONTENTS

CHAPTER		PAGE
I.	THE EARLY DAYS	1
II.	COLLEGE DAYS	21
III.	FIRST NEWSPAPER EXPERIENCES	37
IV.	NEW YORK	44
V.	FIRST TRAVEL ARTICLES	67
VI.	THE MEDITERRANEAN AND PARIS	92
VII.	FIRST PLAYS	132
VIII.	CENTRAL AND SOUTH AMERICA	140
IX.	MOSCOW, BUDAPEST, LONDON	173
X.	CAMPAIGNING IN CUBA AND GREECE	186
XI.	THE SPANISH-AMERICAN WAR	227
XII.	THE BOER WAR	260
XIII.	THE SPANISH AND ENGLISH CORONATIONS	294
XIV.	THE JAPANESE-RUSSIAN WAR	297
XV.	MOUNT KISCO	313
XVI.	THE CONGO	321
XVII.	A LONDON WINTER	336
XVIII.	MILITARY MANŒUVRES	342
XIX.	VERA CRUZ AND THE GREAT WAR	354
XX.	THE LAST DAYS	408
	INDEX	413

ILLUSTRATIONS

Richard Harding Davis . . . . *Frontispiece*	
	FACING PAGE
R. H. D. as he looked when he first came to New York in 1890	46
With Joseph Jefferson at Marion, 1899	92
With John Drew at Marion, 1909	136
Three Gringos in Venezuela	142
In the Greco-Turkish War, 1897	204
Ethel Barrymore at seventeen	220
A consultation at General Wheeler's headquarters . .	248
With Colonel Roosevelt in Cuba	254
Kaffir boys at Ladysmith	276
Mr. Davis's "workshop" at Marion	292
At Marion	294
R. H. D. and John Fox in Manchuria, 1904	310
The terrace at Crossroads	314
In the Congo, 1907	328
Turner's House, Chelsea, 118 Cheyne Walk, where the Davises spent the winter of 1908–9	336
With Mr. and Mrs. Morris, Aiken, 1912	346
At Mt. Kisco	350

ILLUSTRATIONS

FACING PAGE

R. H. D. and Augustus Thomas filming "Soldiers of Fortune" in Santiago 352

Rurales at the Gap on the road to Mexico City . . 356

At Plattsburg 382

R. H. D. and Captain Gabriel Puaux of the General Headquarters Staff at the ruined village of Gerbéviller 386

Latest photograph of Richard Harding Davis . . . 400

Hope Davis 404

Mrs. R. H. Davis and Hope Davis 410

The passport and photograph which, though indorsed by Mr. Whitlock and Mr. Gibson, led to the arrest of Mr. Davis 412

Mr. Davis's ticket of leave 412

Mr. Davis's passport on his last trip to Europe, 1915–16 412

ADVENTURES AND LETTERS
OF
RICHARD HARDING DAVIS

CHAPTER I

THE EARLY DAYS

RICHARD HARDING DAVIS was born in Philadelphia on April 18, 1864, but, so far as memory serves me, his life and mine began together several years later in the three-story brick house on South Twenty-first Street, to which we had just moved. For more than forty years this was our home in all that the word implies, and I do not believe that there was ever a moment when it was not the predominating influence in Richard's life and in his work. As I learned in later years, the house had come into the possession of my father and mother after a period on their part of hard endeavor and unusual sacrifice. It was their ambition to add to this home not only the comforts and the beautiful inanimate things of life, but to create an atmosphere which would prove a constant help to those who lived under its roof—an inspiration to their children that should endure so long as they lived. At the time of my brother's death the fact was frequently commented upon that, unlike most literary folk, he had never known what it was to be poor and to suffer the pangs of hunger and failure. That he never suffered from the lack of a home was certainly as true as that in his work he knew but little of failure, for the first stories he wrote for the magazines brought him into a prominence and popularity that lasted until the end. But if Richard gained his success early in life and was blessed with a very lovely home to which he could always return, he was not brought up in a manner which in any way could be called lavish. Lavish he may have been in later years, but if he was it was with the money for which those who knew him best knew how very hard he had worked.

In a general way, I cannot remember that our life as boys differed in any essential from that of other boys. My brother went to the Episcopal Academy and his weekly report never failed to fill the whole house with an impenetrable gloom and ever-increasing fears as to the possibilities of his future. At school and at college Richard was, to say the least, an indifferent student. And what made this undeniable fact so annoying, particularly to his teachers, was that morally he stood so very high. To "crib," to lie, or in any way to cheat or to do any unworthy act was, I believe, quite beyond his understanding. Therefore, while his constant lack of interest in his studies goaded his teachers to despair, when it came to a question of stamping out wrongdoing on the part of the student body he was invariably found aligned on the side of the faculty. Not that Richard in any way resembled a prig or was even, so far as I know, ever so considered by the most reprehensible of his fellow students. He was altogether too red-blooded for that, and I believe the students whom he antagonized rather admired his chivalric point of honor even if they failed to imitate it. As a schoolboy he was aggressive, radical, outspoken, fearless, usually of the opposition and, indeed, often the sole member of his own party. Among the students at the several schools he attended he had but few intimate friends; but of the various little groups of which he happened to be a member his aggressiveness and his imagination usually made him the leader. As far back as I

THE EARLY DAYS 3

can remember, Richard was always starting something —usually a new club or a violent reform movement. And in school or college, as in all the other walks of life, the reformer must, of necessity, lead a somewhat tempestuous, if happy, existence. The following letter, written to his father when Richard was a student at Swarthmore, and about fifteen, will give an idea of his conception of the ethics in the case:

SWARTHMORE—1880.
DEAR PAPA:
I am quite on the Potomac. I with all the boys at our table were called up, there is seven of us, before Prex. for stealing sugar-bowls and things off the table. All the youths said, "O President, I didn't do it." When it came my turn I merely smiled gravely, and he passed on to the last. Then he said, "The only boy that doesn't deny it is Davis. Davis, you are excused. I wish to talk to the rest of them." That all goes to show he can be a gentleman if he would only try. I am a natural born philosopher so I thought this idea is too idiotic for me to converse about so I recommend silence and I also argued that to deny you must necessarily be accused and to be accused of stealing would of course cause me to bid Prex. good-by, so the only way was, taking these two considerations with each other, to deny nothing but let the good-natured old duffer see how silly it was by retaining a placid silence and so crushing his base but thoughtless behavior and machinations.
DICK.

In the early days at home—that is, when the sun shone—we played cricket and baseball and football in our very spacious back yard, and the programme of our sports was always subject to Richard's change without notice. When it rained we adjourned to the third-story front, where we played melodrama of simple plot but many thrills, and it was always Richard who wrote the plays, produced them, and played the principal part. As I recall these dramas of my early youth, the action was almost endless and, although the company comprised two charming misses (at least I know that they eventually grew into two very lovely women), there was no time wasted over anything so sentimental or futile as love-scenes. But whatever else the play contained in the way of great scenes, there was always a mountain pass—the mountains being composed of a chair and two tables—and Richard was forever leading his little band over the pass while the band, wholly indifferent as to whether the road led to honor, glory, or total annihilation, meekly followed its leader. For some reason, probably on account of my early admiration for Richard and being only too willing to obey his command, I was invariably cast for the villain in these early dramas, and the end of the play always ended in a hand-to-hand conflict between the hero and myself. As Richard, naturally, was the hero and incidentally the stronger of the two, it can readily be imagined that the fight always ended in my complete undoing. Strangulation was the method usually employed to finish me, and, whatever else Richard was at that tender age, I can testify to his extraordinary ability as a choker.

But these early days in the city were not at all the happiest days of that period in Richard's life. He took but little interest even in the social or the athletic side of his school life, and his failures in his studies troubled him sorely, only I fear, however, because it troubled his mother and father. The great day of the year to us was the day our schools closed and we started for our summer vacation. When Richard was less than a year old my mother and father, who at the time was convalescing from a long illness, had left Philadelphia on a search for a complete rest in the country. Their travels, which it seems were undertaken in the spirit of a voyage of discovery and adventure, finally led them to the old Curtis House at Point Pleasant on the New Jersey coast. But the Point Pleasant of that time had very little in common with the present well-known summer resort. In those days the place was reached after a long journey by rail followed by a three hours' drive in a rickety stage-coach over deep sandy roads, albeit the roads did lead through silent, sweet-smelling pine forests. Point Pleasant itself was then a collection of half a dozen big farms which stretched from the Manasquan River to the ocean half a mile distant. Nothing could have been more primitive or as I remember it in its pastoral loveliness much more beautiful. Just beyond our cottage the river ran its silent, lazy course to the sea. With the exception of several farmhouses, its banks were then unsullied by human habitation of any sort, and on either side beyond the low green banks lay fields of wheat and corn, and dense groves of pine and oak and chestnut trees. Between us and the ocean were more waving fields of corn, broken by little clumps of trees, and beyond these damp Nile-green pasture meadows, and then salty marshes that led to the glistening, white sand-dunes, and the great silver semicircle of foaming breakers, and the broad, blue sea. On all the land that lay between us and the ocean, where the town of Point Pleasant now stands, I think there were but four farmhouses, and these in no way interfered with the landscape or the life of the primitive world in which we played.

Whatever the mental stimulus my brother derived from his home in Philadelphia, the foundation of the physical strength that stood him in such good stead in the campaigns of his later years he derived from those early days at Point Pleasant. The cottage we lived in was an old two-story frame building, to which my father had added two small sleeping-rooms. Outside there was a vine-covered porch and within a great stone fireplace flanked by cupboards, from which during those happy days I know Richard and I, openly and covertly, must have extracted tons of hardtack and cake. The little house was called "Vagabond's Rest," and a haven of rest and peace and content it certainly proved for many years to the Davis family. From here it was that my father started forth in the early mornings on his all-day fishing excursions, while my mother sat on the sunlit porch and wrote novels and mended the badly rent garments of her very active sons. After a seven-o'clock breakfast at the Curtis House our energies never ceased until night closed in on us and from sheer exhaustion we dropped unconscious into our patch-quilted cots. All day long we swam or rowed, or sailed, or played ball, or camped out, or ate enormous meals—anything so long as our activities were ceaseless and our breathing apparatus given no rest. About a mile up the river there was an island—it's a very small, prettily wooded, sandy-beached little place, but it seemed big enough in those days. Robert Louis Stevenson made it famous by rechristening it Treasure Island, and writing the

THE EARLY DAYS

new name and his own on a bulkhead that had been built to shore up one of its fast disappearing sandy banks. But that is very modern history and to us it has always been "The Island." In our day, long before Stevenson had ever heard of the Manasquan, Richard and I had discovered this tight little piece of land, found great treasures there, and, hand in hand, had slept in a six-by-six tent while the lions and tigers growled at us from the surrounding forests.

As I recall these days of my boyhood I find the recollections of our life at Point Pleasant much more distinct than those we spent in Philadelphia. For Richard these days were especially welcome. They meant a respite from the studies which were a constant menace to himself and his parents; and the freedom of the open country, the ocean, the many sports on land and on the river gave his body the constant exercise his constitution seemed to demand, and a broad field for an imagination which was even then very keen, certainly keen enough to make the rest of us his followers.

In an extremely sympathetic appreciation which Irvin S. Cobb wrote about my brother at the time of his death, he says that he doubts if there is such a thing as a born author. Personally it so happened that I never grew up with any one, except my brother, who ever became an author, certainly an author of fiction, and so I cannot speak on the subject with authority. But in the case of Richard, if he was not born an author, certainly no other career was ever considered. So far as I know he never even wanted to go to sea or to be a bareback rider in a circus. A boy, if he loves his father, usually wants to follow in his professional footsteps, and in the case of Richard, he had the double inspiration of following both in the footsteps of his father and in those of his mother. For years before Richard's birth his father had been a newspaper editor and a well-known writer of stories and his mother a novelist and short-story writer of great distinction. Of those times at Point Pleasant I fear I can remember but a few of our elders. There were George Lambdin, Margaret Ruff, and Milne Ramsay, all painters of some note; a strange couple, Colonel Olcott and the afterward famous Madam Blavatsky, trying to start a Buddhist cult in this country; Mrs. Frances Hodgson Burnett, with her foot on the first rung of the ladder of fame, who at the time loved much millinery finery. One day my father took her out sailing and, much to the lady's discomfiture and greatly to Richard's and my delight, upset the famous authoress. At a later period the Joseph Jeffersons used to visit us; Horace Howard Furness, one of my father's oldest friends, built a summer home very near us on the river, and Mrs. John Drew and her daughter Georgie Barrymore spent their summers in a near-by hostelry. I can remember Mrs. Barrymore at that time very well—wonderfully handsome and a marvellously cheery manner. Richard and I both loved her greatly, even though it were in secret. Her daughter Ethel I remember best as she appeared on the beach, a sweet, long-legged child in a scarlet bathing-suit running toward the breakers and then dashing madly back to her mother's open arms. A pretty figure of a child, but much too young for Richard to notice at that time. In after-years the child in the scarlet bathing-suit and he became great pals. Indeed, during the latter half of his life, through the good days and the bad, there were very few friends who held so close a place in his sympathy and his affections as Ethel Barrymore.

Until the summer of 1880 my brother continued on at the Episcopal Academy. For some reason I was sent to a different school, but outside of our supposed hours of learning we were never apart. With less than two years' difference in our ages our interests were much the same, and I fear our interests of those days were largely limited to out-of-door sports and the theatre. We must have been very young indeed when my father first led us by the hand to see our first play. On Saturday afternoons Richard and I, unattended but not wholly unalarmed, would set forth from our home on this thrilling weekly adventure. Having joined our father at his office, he would invariably take us to a chop-house situated at the end of a blind alley which lay concealed somewhere in the neighborhood of Walnut and Third Streets, and where we ate a most wonderful luncheon of English chops and apple pie. As the luncheon drew to its close I remember how Richard and I used to fret and fume while my father in a most leisurely manner used to finish off his mug of musty ale. But at last the three of us, hand in hand, my father between us, were walking briskly toward our happy destination. At that time there were only a few first-class theatres in Philadelphia—the Arch Street Theatre, owned by Mrs. John Drew; the Chestnut Street, and the Walnut Street—all of which had stock companies, but which on the occasion of a visiting star acted as the supporting company. These were the days of Booth, Jefferson, Adelaide Neilson, Charles Fletcher, Lotta, John McCullough, John Sleeper Clark, and the elder

Sothern. And how Richard and I worshipped them all—not only these but every small-bit actor in every stock company in town. Indeed, so many favorites of the stage did my brother and I admire that ordinary frames would not begin to hold them all, and to overcome this defect we had our bedroom entirely redecorated. The new scheme called for a gray wallpaper supported by a maroon dado. At the top of the latter ran two parallel black picture mouldings between which we could easily insert cabinet photographs of the actors and actresses which for the moment we thought most worthy of a place in our collection. As the room was fairly large and as the mouldings ran entirely around it, we had plenty of space for even our very elastic love for the heroes and heroines of the footlights.

Edwin Forrest ended his stage career just before our time, but I know that Richard at least saw him and heard that wonderful voice of thunder. It seems that one day, while my mother and Richard were returning home, they got on a street-car which already held the great tragedian. At the moment Forrest was suffering severely from gout and had his bad leg stretched well out before him. My brother, being very young at the time and never very much of a respecter of persons, promptly fell over the great man's gouty foot. Whereat (according to my mother, who was always a most truthful narrator) Forrest broke forth in a volcano of oaths and for blocks continued to hurl thunderous broadsides at Richard, which my mother insisted included the curse of Rome and every other famous tirade in the tragedian's repertory which in any way fitted the occasion. Nearly forty years later my father became the president of the Edwin

Forrest Home, the greatest charity ever founded by an actor for actors, and I am sure by his efforts of years on behalf of the institution did much to atone for Richard's early unhappy meeting with the greatest of all the famous leather-lunged tragedians.

From his youth my father had always been a close student of the classic and modern drama, and throughout his life numbered among his friends many of the celebrated actors and actresses of his time. In those early days Booth used to come to rather formal luncheons, and at all such functions Richard and I ate our luncheon in the pantry, and when the great meal was nearly over in the dining-room we were allowed to come in in time for the ice-cream and to sit, figuratively, at the feet of the honored guest and generally, literally, on his or her knees. Young as I was in those days I can readily recall one of those lunch-parties when the contrast between Booth and Dion Boucicault struck my youthful mind most forcibly. Booth, with his deep-set, big black eyes, shaggy hair, and lank figure, his wonderfully modulated voice, rolled out his theories of acting, while the bald-headed, rotund Boucicault, his twinkling eyes snapping like a fox-terrier's, interrupted the sonorous speeches of the tragedian with crisp, witty criticisms or "asides" that made the rest of the company laugh and even brought a smile to the heavy, tragic features of Booth himself. But there was nothing formal about our relations with John Sleeper Clark and the Jefferson family. They were real "home folks" and often occupied our spare room, and when they were with us Richard and I were allowed to come to all the meals, and, even if unsolicited, freely express our views on the modern drama.

In later years to our Philadelphia home came Henry Irving and his fellow player Ellen Terry and Augustin Daly and that wonderful quartet, Ada Rehan, Mrs. Gilbert, James Lewis, and our own John Drew. Sir Henry I always recall by the first picture I had of him in our dining-room, sitting far away from the table, his long legs stretched before him, peering curiously at Richard and myself over black-rimmed glasses and then, with equal interest, turning back to the ash of a long cigar and talking drama with the famous jerky, nasal voice but always with a marvellous poise and convincing authority. He took a great liking to Richard in those days, sent him a church-warden's pipe that he had used as Corporal Brewster, and made much of him later when my brother was in London. Miss Terry was a much less formal and forbidding guest, rushing into the house like a whirlwind and filling the place with the sunshine and happiness that seemed to fairly exude from her beautiful magnetic presence. Augustin Daly usually came with at least three of the stars of his company which I have already mentioned, but even the beautiful Rehan and the nice old Mrs. Gilbert seemed thoroughly awed in the presence of "the Guv'nor." He was a most crusty, dictatorial party, as I remember him with his searching eyes and raven locks, always dressed in black and always failing to find virtue in any actor or actress not a member of his own company. I remember one particularly acrid discussion between him and my father in regard to Julia Marlowe, who was then making her first bow to the public. Daly contended that in a few years the lady would be absolutely unheard of and backed his opinion by betting a dinner for those present with my father that his judgment would prove correct. However, he was very kind to Richard and myself and frequently allowed us to play about behind the scenes, which was a privilege I imagine he granted to very few of his friends' children. One night, long after this, when Richard was a reporter in New York, he and Miss Rehan were burlesquing a scene from a play on which the last curtain had just fallen. It was on the stage of Daly's theatre at Thirtieth Street and Broadway, and from his velvet box at the prompt-entrance Daly stood gloomily watching their fooling. When they had finished the mock scene Richard went over to Daly and said, "How bad do you think I am as an actor, Mr. Daly?" and greatly to my brother's delight the greatest manager of them all of those days grumbled back at him: "You're so bad, Richard, that I'll give you a hundred dollars a week, and you can sign the contract whenever you're ready." Although that was much more than my brother was making in his chosen profession at the time, and in spite of the intense interest he had in the theatre, he never considered the offer seriously. As a matter of fact, Richard had many natural qualifications that fitted him for the stage, and in after-years, when he was rehearsing one of his own plays, he could and frequently would go up on the stage and read almost any part better than the actor employed to do it. Of course, he lacked the ease of gesture and the art of timing which can only be attained after sound experience, but his reading of lines and his knowledge of characterization was quite unusual. In proof of this I know of at least two managers who, when Richard wanted to sell them plays, refused to have him read them the manuscript on the ground that his reading gave the dialogue a value it did not really possess.

In the spring of 1880 Richard left the Episcopal Academy, and the following September went to Swarthmore College, situated just outside of Philadelphia. I fear, however, the change was anything but a success. The life of the big coeducational school did not appeal to him at all and, in spite of two or three friendships he made among the girls and boys, he depended for amusement almost wholly on his own resources. In the afternoons and on holidays he took long walks over the country roads and in search of adventure visited many farmhouses. His excuse for these calls was that he was looking for old furniture and china, and he frequently remained long enough to make sketches of such objects as he pretended had struck his artistic fancy. Of these adventures he wrote at great length to his mother and father, and the letters were usually profusely decorated with illustrations of the most striking incidents of the various escapades. Several of these Swarthmore experiences he used afterward in short stories, and both the letters and sketches he sent to his parents at the time he regarded in the light of preparation for his future work. In his studies he was perhaps less successful than he had been at the Episcopal Academy, and although he played football and took part in the track sports he was really but little interested in either. There were half-holidays on Wednesdays and Saturdays, and when my brother did not come to town I went to Swarthmore and we spent the afternoons in first cooking our lunch in a hospitable woods and then playing some games in the open that Richard had devised. But as I recall these outings they were not very joyous occasions, as Richard was extremely unhappy over his failures

THE EARLY DAYS

at school and greatly depressed about the prospects for the future.

He finished the college year at Swarthmore, but so unhappy had he been there that there was no thought in his mind or in that of his parents of his returning. At that time my uncle, H. Wilson Harding, was a professor at Lehigh University, and it was arranged that Richard should go to Bethlehem the following fall, live with his uncle, and continue his studies at Ulrich's Preparatory School, which made a specialty of preparing boys for Lehigh. My uncle lived in a charming old house on Market Street in Bethlehem, quite near the Moravian settlement and across the river from the university and the iron mills. He was a bachelor, but of a most gregarious and hospitable disposition, and Richard therefore found himself largely his own master, in a big, roomy house which was almost constantly filled with the most charming and cultivated people. There my uncle and Richard, practically of about the same age so far as their viewpoint of life was concerned, kept open house, and if it had not been for the occasional qualms his innate hatred of mathematics caused him, I think my brother would have been completely happy. Even studies no longer worried him particularly and he at once started in to make friendships, many of which lasted throughout his life. As is usual with young men of seventeen, most of these men and women friends were several times Richard's age, but at the period Richard was a particularly precocious and amusing youth and a difference of a few decades made but little difference —certainly not to Richard. Finley Peter Dunne once wrote of my brother that he "probably knew more waiters, generals, actors, and princes than any man who lived," and I think it was during the first year of his life at Bethlehem that he began the foundation for the remarkable collection of friends, both as to numbers and variety, of which he died possessed. Although a "prep," he made many friends among the undergraduates of Lehigh. He made friends with the friends of his uncle and many friends in both of the Bethlehems of which his uncle had probably never heard. Even at that early age he counted among his intimates William W. Thurston, who was president of the Bethlehem Iron Company, and J. Davis Brodhead, one of Pennsylvania's most conspicuous Democratic congressmen and attorneys. Those who knew him at that time can easily understand why Richard attracted men and women so much older than himself. He was brimming over with physical health and animal spirits and took the keenest interest in every one he met and in everything that was going on about him. And in the broadest sense he saw to it then, as he did throughout his life, that he always did his share.

During those early days at Bethlehem his letters to his family were full of his social activities, with occasional references to his work at school. He was always going to dinners or dances, entertaining members of visiting theatrical companies; and on Friday night my mother usually received a telegram, saying that he would arrive the next day with a party of friends whom he had inadvertently asked to lunch and a matinée. It was after one of these weekly visits that my mother wrote Richard the following:

My Darling Boy: Monday Night.

You went off in such a hurry that it took my breath at the last. You say coming down helps you. It certainly does me. It brings a real sunshine to Papa and me. He was saying that to-day. I gave Nolly a sort of holiday after her miseries last night. We went down street and got Papa a present for our wedding day, a picture, after all, and then I took Miss Baker some tickets for a concert. I saw her father who said he "must speak about my noble looking boy." I always thought him a genius but now I think him a man of penetration as well. Then Nolly and I went over to see the Russians. But they are closely boxed up and not allowed to-day to see visitors. So we came home cross and hungry. All evening I have been writing business letters.

Papa has gone to a reception and Charley is hard at work at his desk.

I answered Mr. Allen's letter this morning, dear, and told him you would talk to him. When you do, dear, talk freely to him as to me. You will not perhaps agree with all he says. But your own thoughts will be healthier for bringing them—as I might say, out of doors. You saw how it was by coming down here. Love of Christ is not a melancholy nor a morbid thing, dear love, but ought to make one more social and cheerful and alive.

I wish you could come home oftener. Try and get ahead with lessons so that you can come oftener. And when you feel as if prayer was a burden, stop praying and go out and try to put your Christianity into real action by doing some kindness—even speaking in a friendly way to somebody. Bring yourself into contact with new people—not John, Hugh, Uncle and Grandma, and try to act to them as Christ would have you act, and my word for it, you will go home with a new light on your own relations to Him and a new meaning for your prayers. You remember the prayer "give me a great thought to refresh me." I think you will find some great thoughts in human beings—they will help you to understand yourself and God, when you try to help them God makes you happy my darling.

Mama.

It was in this year that Richard enjoyed the thrill of seeing in print his first contribution to a periodical. The date of this important event, important, at least, to my brother, was February 1, the fortunate publication was *Judge*, and the effusion was entitled "The Hat and Its Inmate." Its purport was an overheard conversation between two young ladies at a matinée and the editors thought so well of it that for the privilege of printing the article they gave Richard a year's subscription to *Judge*. His scrap-book of that time shows that in 1884 *Life* published a short burlesque on George W. Cable's novel, "Dr. Sevier," and in the same year *The Evening Post* paid him $1.05 for an article about "The New Year at Lehigh." It was also in the spring of 1884 that Richard published his first book, "The Adventures of My Freshman," a neat little paper-covered volume including half a dozen of the short stories that had already appeared in *The Lehigh Burr*. In writing in a copy of this book in later years, Richard said: "This is a copy of the first book of mine published. My family paid to have it printed and finding no one else was buying it, bought up the entire edition. Finding the first edition had gone so quickly, I urged them to finance a second one, and when they were unenthusiastic I was hurt. Several years later when I found the entire edition in our attic, I understood their reluctance. The reason the book did not sell is, I think, because some one must have read it."

In the summer of 1882 Richard went to Boston, and in the following letter unhesitatingly expressed his opinion of that city and its people.

BOSTON, Wednesday.
July 1882.

DEAR FAMILY:—

I left Newport last night or rather this morning. I stopped at Beverly and called on Dr. Holmes. He talked a great deal about mama and about a great many other things equally lovely in a very easy, charming way. All I had to do was to listen and I was only too willing to do that. We got along splendidly. He asked me to stay to dinner but I refused with thanks, as I had only come to pay my respects and put off to Dr. Bartol's. Dr. Holmes accompanied me to the depot and saw me safely off. Of all the lovely men I ever saw Dr. Bartol is the one. He lives in a great, many roomed with as many gables, house. Elizabethan, of course, with immense fireplaces, brass and dark woods, etchings and engravings, with the sea and rocks immediately under the window and the ocean stretching out for miles, lighthouses and more Elizabethan houses half hid on the bank, and ships and small boats pushing by within a hundred rods of the windows. I stayed to dinner there and we had a very jolly time. There were two other young men and another maiden besides Miss Bartol. They talked principally about the stage; that is, the Boston Stock Company, which is their sole thought and knowledge of the drama. The Dr. would strike off now and then to philosophizing and moralizing but his daughter would immediately sit upon him, much to my disgust but to the evident relief of the rest. His wife is as lovely as he is but I can't give it to you all now. Wait until I get home.

The young lady, the youths and myself came up to Boston together and had as pleasant a ride, as the heat would allow. I left them at the depot and went up to the Parker House and then to the Art Museum. The statuary is plaster, the coins are copies, and by the way, I found one exactly like mine, which, if it is genuine is worth, "well considerable", as the personage in charge remarked. The pictures were simply vile, only two or three that I recognized and principally Millet and some charcoal sketches of Hunt's, who is the Apostle of Art here. The china was very fine but they had a collection of old furniture and armor which was better than anything else. Fresh from or rather musty from these antiques, who should I meet but the cheerful Dixey and Powers. We had a very jolly talk and I enjoyed it immensely, not only myself but all the surrounding populace, as Dixey would persist in showing the youthful some new "gag," and would break into a clog or dialect much to the delectation of the admiring Bostonians. I am stranded here for to night and will push on to Newport to-morrow. I'll go see the "babes" to night, as there is nothing else in the city that is worth seeing that I haven't investigated. I left the Newburyportians in grief with regret. I met lots of nice people and every one was so very kind to me, from the authoresses to the serving maids. Good-bye.

DICK.

CHAPTER II

COLLEGE DAYS

IN the fall of 1882 Richard entered Lehigh, but the first year of his college life varied very little from the one he had spent in the preparatory school. During that year he had met most of the upper classmen, and the only difference was that he could now take an active instead of a friendly interest in the life and the sports of the college. Also he had formed certain theories which he promptly proceeded to put into practical effect. Perhaps the most conspicuous of these was his belief that cane-rushes and hazing were wholly unnecessary and barbarous customs, and should have no place in the college of his day. Against the former he spoke at college meetings, and wrote long letters to the local papers decrying the custom. His stand against hazing was equally vehement, and he worked hand in hand with the faculty to eradicate it entirely from the college life. That his stand was purely for a principle and not from any fear of personal injury, I think the following letter to his father will show:

BETHLEHEM, February 1882.

DEAR DAD:

You may remember a conversation we had at Squan about hazing in which you said it was a very blackguardly thing and a cowardly thing. I didn't agree with you, but when I saw how it really was and how silly and undignified it was, besides being brutal, I thought it over and changed my mind completely, agreeing with you in every respect. A large number of our class have been hazed, taking it as a good joke, and have been laughed at by the whole college. I talked to the boys about it, and said what I would do and so on, without much effect. Wednesday a junior came to me, and told me I was to be hazed as I left the Opera House Friday night. After that a great many came to me and advised and warned me as to what I should do. I decided to get about fifty of our class outside and then fight it out; that was before I changed my mind. As soon as I did I regretted it very much, but, as it turned out, the class didn't come, so I was alone, as I wished to be. You see, I'd not a very good place here; the fellows looked on me as a sort of special object of ridicule, on account of the hat and cane, walk, and so on, though I thought I'd got over that by this time. The Opera House was partly filled with college men, a large number of sophomores and a few upper class men. It was pretty generally known I was going to have a row, and that brought them as much as the show. Poor Ruff was in agony all day. He supposed I'd get into the fight, and he knew he'd get in, too, sooner or later. If he did he'd be held and not be able to do anything, and then the next day be blamed by the whole college for interfering in a class matter. He hadn't any money to get into the show, and so wandered around outside in the rain in a great deal more excited state than I was. Howe went all over town after putting on his old clothes, in case of personal damage, in search of freshmen who were at home out of the wet. As I left the building a man grabbed me by my arm, and the rest, with the seniors gathered around; the only freshman present, who was half scared to death, clung as near to me as possible. I withdrew my arm and faced them. "If this means hazing," I said, "I'm not with you. There's not enough men here to haze me, but there's enough to thrash me, and I'd rather be thrashed than hazed." You see, I wanted them to understand exactly how I looked at it, and they wouldn't think I was simply hotheaded and stubborn. I was very cool about it all. They broke in with all sorts of explanations; hazing was the last thing they had thought of. No, indeed, Davis, old fellow, you're mistaken. I told them if that was so, all right, I was going home. I saw several of my friends in the crowd waiting for me, but as I didn't want them to interfere, I said nothing, and they did not recognize me. When among the crowd of sophomores, the poor freshman made a last effort, he pulled me by the coat and begged me to come with him. I said no, I was going home. When I reached the next corner I stopped. "I gave you fair warning, keep off. I tell you I'll strike the first man, the first one, that touches me." Then the four who had been appointed to seize me jumped on me, and I only got one good blow in before they had me down in the gutter and were beating me on the face and head. I put my hands across my face, and so did not get any hard blows directly in the face. They slipped back in a moment, and when I was ready I scrambled up pretty wet and muddy, and with my face stinging where they had struck. It had all been done so quickly, and there was such a large crowd coming from the theatre, that, of course, no one saw it. When I got up there was a circle all around me. They hadn't intended to go so far. The men, except those four who had beaten me, were rather ashamed and wished they were out of it. I turned to Emmerich, a postgraduate, and told him to give me room. "Now," I said, "you're not able to haze me, and I can't thrash twelve of you, but I'll fight any one man you bring out." I asked for the man that struck me, and named another, but there was no response. The upper classmen, who had just arrived, called out that was fair, and they'd see it fair. Goodnough, Purnell and Douglas, who don't like me much, either. Ruff was beside me by this time. He hadn't seen anything of it, and did not get there until he heard me calling for a fair chance and challenging the class for a man. I called out again, the second time, and still no one came, so I took occasion to let them know why I had done as I did in a short speech to the crowd. I said I was a peaceable fellow, thought hazing silly, and as I never intended to haze myself, I didn't intend any one to haze me. Then I said again, "This is the third time, will one of your men fight this fair? I can't fight twelve of you." Just then two officers who had called on some mill-hands, who are always dying for a fight, and a citizen to help them, burst into the crowd of students, shouldering them around like sheep until they got to me, when one of them put his arm around me, and said, "I don't know anything about this crowd, but I'll see you're protected, sir. I'll give 'em fair play." One officer got hold of Ruff and pretty near shook him to pieces until I had to interfere and explain. They were for forming a body-guard, and were loud in their denunciations of the college, and declaring they'd see me through if I was a stranger to 'em.

Two or three of the sophomores, when they saw how things were going, set up a yell, but Griffin struck out and sent one of them flying one way and his hat another, so the yells ended. Howe and Murray Stuart took me up to their rooms, and Ruff went off for beefsteak for my eye, and treated the crowd who had come to the rescue, at Dixon's, to beer. The next day was Saturday, and as there was to be a meeting of the Athletic Association, of course, I wanted to show up. The fellows all looked at my eye pretty hard and said nothing. I felt pretty sure that the sympathy was all with me.

Four men are elected from the college to be on the athletic committee. They can be nominated by any one, though generally it is done by a man in their own class. We had agreed the day before to vote for Tolman for our class, so when the president announced nominations were in order for the freshmen class, Tolman was instantly nominated. At the same time one of the leading sophomores jumped up and nominated Mr. Davis, and a number of men from the same class seconded it. I knew every one in the college knew of what had happened, and especially the sophomores, so I was, of course, very much surprised. I looked unconscious, though, and waited. One of the seniors asked that the nominees should stand up, as they didn't know their names only their faces. As each man rose he was hissed and groaned down again. When I stood up the sophomores burst into a yell and clapped and stamped, yelling, "Davis! Davis! vote for D!" until I sat down. As I had already decided to nominate Tolman, I withdrew my name from the nominees, a movement which was received by loud cries of "No! No!" from the sophs. So, you see, Dad, I did as you said, as I thought was right, and came out well indeed. You see, I am now the hero of the hour, every one in town knows it, and every one congratulates me, and, "Well done, me boy," as Morrow '83 said, seems to be the idea, one gets taken care of in this world if you do what's the right thing, if it is only a street fight. In fact, as one of the seniors said, I've made five friends where I had one before. The sophs are ashamed and sorry, as their conduct in chapel, which was more marked than I made it, shows. I've nothing to show for it but a red mark under the eye, and so it is the best thing that could possibly have happened. Poor Ruff hugged me all the way home, and I've started out well in a good way, I think, though not a very logical one.

Uncle says to tell you that my conduct has his approval throughout.

DICK.

To which letter my father promptly replied:

PHILADELPHIA. February 25th, 1882.

DEAR OLD BOY:

I'm glad the affair ended so well. I don't want you to fight, but if you have to fight a cuss like that do it with all your might, and don't insist that either party shall too strictly observe the Markis O' Queensbury rules. Hit first and hardest so that thine adversary shall beware of you.

DAD.

At that time the secret societies played a very important part in the college life at Lehigh, and while I do not believe that Richard shared the theory of some of the students that they were a serious menace to the social fabric, he was quite firm in his belief that it was inadvisable to be a member of any fraternity. In a

COLLEGE DAYS

general way he did not like the idea of secrecy even in its mildest form, and then, as throughout his life, he refused to join any body that would in any way limit his complete independence of word or action. In connection with this phase of his college life I quote from an appreciation which M. A. De W. Howe, one of Richard's best friends both at college and in afterlife, wrote for *The Lehigh Burr* at the time of my brother's death:

"To the credit of the perceptive faculty of undergraduates, it ought to be said that the classmates and contemporaries of Richard Harding Davis knew perfectly well, while he and they were young together, that in him Lehigh had a son so marked in his individuality, so endowed with talents and character that he stood quite apart from the other collegians of his day. Prophets were as rare in the eighties as they have always been, before and since, and nobody could have foreseen that the name and work of Dick Davis would long before his untimely death, indeed within a few years from leaving college, be better known throughout the world than those of any other Lehigh man. We who knew him in his college days could not feel the smallest surprise that he won himself quickly a brilliant name, and kept a firm hold upon it to the last.

"What was it that made him so early a marked man? I think it was the spirit of confidence and enthusiasm which turned every enterprise he undertook into an adventure,—the brave and humorous playing of the game of life, the true heart, the wholesome body and soul of my friend and classmate. He did not excel in studies or greatly, in athletics. But in his own field, that of writing, he was so much better than the rest of us that no one of his fellow-editors of the *Epit-*

ome or *Burr* needed to be considered in comparison with him. No less, in spite of his voluntary non-membership in the fraternities of his day, was he a leader in the social activities of the University. The 'Arcadian Club' devoted in its beginnings to the 'pipes, books, beer and gingeralia' of Davis's song about it and the 'Mustard and Cheese' were his creations. In all his personal relationships he was the most amusing and stimulating of companions. With garb and ways of unique picturesqueness, rarer even in college communities a generation ago than at present, it was inevitable that he sometimes got himself laughed at as well as with. But what did it all matter, even then? To-day it adds a glow of color to what would be in any case a vivid, deeply valued memory.

"It is hard to foresee in youth what will come most sharply and permanently in the long run. After all these years it is good to find that Davis and what his companionship gave one hold their place with the strongest influences of Lehigh."

But Richard was naturally gregarious and at heart had a great fondness for clubs and social gatherings. Therefore, having refused the offer of several fraternities that did him the honor to ask him to become a member, it was necessary for him to form a few clubs that held meetings, but no secrets. Perhaps the most successful of these were "The Mustard and Cheese," a dramatic club devoted to the presentation of farces and musical comedies, and The Arcadia Club, to the fortnightly meetings of which he devoted much time and thought. The following letter to his father will give some idea of the scope of the club, which, as in the case of "The Mustard and Cheese," gained a permanent and important place in the social life of Lehigh.

DEAR DAD:

We have started the best sort of a club up here which I am anxious to tell you of. It consists of a spread, net price of which will be about 30 cents each, every two or three weeks. Only six fellows belong and those the best of the College. Purnell, Haines and myself founded it. I chose Charley, Purnell, Reeves, Haines and Howe. We will meet Saturday nights at 9 so as not to interfere with our work, and sing, read, eat and box until midnight. It is called the "Pipe and Bowl," and is meant to take the place that The Hasty Pudding, Hammer and Tongs and Mermaid do at other colleges. Two of us are to invite two outsiders in turn each meeting. We will hope to have Dad a member, honorary, of course, when we can persuade him to give us a night off with his company. We want to combine a literary feature and so will have selected readings to provoke discussions after the pipes are lit. The men are very enthusiastic about it and want to invite Mr. Allen and you and every one that they can make an honorary member of immediately.

It was first as an associate editor and afterward as editor-in-chief of the college paper, *The Lehigh Burr*, that Richard found his greatest pleasure and interest during his three years at Lehigh. In addition to his editorial duties he wrote a very great part of every issue of the paper, and his contributions included short stories, reports of news events, editorials, and numerous poems.

As, after his life at college, Richard dropped verse as a mode of expression, I reprint two of the poems which show him in the lighter vein of those early days.

A COMMENCEMENT IDYL

"I'm a Freshman who has ended his first year,
    But I'm new;
And I do whate'er the Juniors, whom I fear,
    Bid me do.
    Under sudden showers I thrive;
    To be bad and bold I strive,
    But they ask—'Is it alive?'
    So they do.

I'm a Sophomore who has passed off his exams,
    Let me loose!
With a mark as high as any other man's,
    As obtuse
    I'm fraternal. I am Jolly.
    I am seldom melancholy
    And to bone I think is folly,
    What's the use?

I'm a Junior whom exams. have left forlorn,
    Flunked me dead;
So I'll keep the town awake 'till early morn;
    Paint it red.
    At class-meetings I'm a kicker,
    Take no water with my liquor,
    And a dumb-bell's not thicker
    Than my head.

I'm a Senior whose diploma's within reach,
    Eighty-four.
On Commencement Day you'll hear my maiden-speech;
    I will soar!
    I got through without condition;
    I'm a mass of erudition;
    Do you know of a position!"

OUR STREET

"Our street is still and silent,
    Grass grows from curb to curb,

No baker's bells
With jangling knells
  Our studious minds disturb.
No organ grinders ever call,
  No hucksters mar our peace;
For traffic shuns our neighborhood
  And leaves us to our ease.

But now it lives and brightens,
  Assumes a livelier hue;
The pavements wide,
On either side,
  Would seem to feel it too.
You might not note the difference,
  The change from grave to gay,
But I can tell, and know full well,
  Priscilla walks our way."

Shortly after his return to college Richard celebrated his nineteenth birthday, and received these letters from his father and mother:

                                April 17th, 1883.

MY DEAR BOY:

When I was thinking what I could give to you to-morrow, I remembered the story of Herder, who when he was old and weak and they brought him food and wine asked for "a great thought to quicken him."

So I have written some old sayings for you that have helped me. Maybe, this year, or some other year, when I am not with you, they may give you, sometimes, comfort and strength.

      God bless you my son—
        YOUR OLD MOTHER
            who loves you dearly—dearly.

THE PHILADELPHIA INQUIRER
PHILADELPHIA, April 17th, 1883.

MY DEAR BOY:

You are to be nineteen years old on Wednesday. After two years more you will be a man. You are so manly and good a boy that I could not wish you to change in any serious or great thing. You have made us very happy through being what you have been, what you are. You fill us with hope of your future virtue and usefulness.

To be good is the best thing of all; it counts for more than anything else in the world. We are very grateful that you have even in youth been wise enough to choose the right road. You will find it not easy to keep upon it always, but remember if you do get off struggle back to it. I do not know but I think God loves the effort to do as well as the act done.

I congratulate you my dear son, on your new birthday. I wish you health, happiness and God's loving care. May he bless you my son forever. I enclose a trifle for your pleasure. My love to you always, but God bless you dear Dick.

DAD.

In the fall of 1885, Richard decided to leave Lehigh and go to John Hopkins University, where he took a special course in such studies as would best benefit him in the career which he had now carefully planned. During this year in Baltimore Richard's letters show that he paid considerable attention to such important subjects as political economy and our own labor problems, but they also show that he did not neglect football or the lighter social diversions. In a short space of time he had made many friends, was very busy going to dinners and dances, and had fallen in love with an entirely new set of maids and matrons. Richard had already begun to send contributions to the magazines, and an occasional acceptance caused him the satisfaction common to all beginners. It was in regard to one of these early contributions that my mother wrote Richard the following letter:

PHILADELPHIA
January 1887.

DEAR BOY:
What has become of *The Current?* It has not come yet. If it has suspended publication be sure and get your article back. You must not destroy a single page you write. You will find every idea of use to you hereafter.

Sometimes I am afraid you think I don't take interest enough in your immediate success now with the articles you send. But I've had thirty years experience and I know how much that sort of success depends on the articles suiting the *present* needs of the magazine, and also on the mood of the editor when he reads it.

Besides—except for your own disappointment—I know it would be better if you would not publish under your own name for a little while. Dr. Holland —who had lots of literary shrewdness both as writer and publisher—used to say for a young man or woman to rush into print was sure ruin to their lasting fame. They either compromised their reputations by inferior work or they made a great hit and never played up to it, afterwards, in public opinion.

Now my dear old man this sounds like awfully cold comfort. But it is the wisest idea your mother has got. I confess I have *great* faith in you—and I try to judge you as if you were not my son. I think you are going to take a high place among American authors, but I do not think you are going to do it by articles like that you sent to *The Current*. The qualities which I think will bring it to you, you don't seem to value at all. They are your dramatic eye. I mean your quick perception of character and of the way character shows itself in looks, tones, dress, etc., and in your keen sympathy—with all kinds of people— Now, these are the requisites for a novelist. Added to that your humour.

You ought to make a novelist of the first class. But you must not expect to do it this week or next. A lasting, real success takes time, and patient, steady work. Read Boz's first sketches of "London Life" and compare them with "Sydney Carton" or "David Copperfield" and you will see what time and hard work will do to develop genius.

I suppose you will wonder why I am moved to say all this? It is, I think, because of your saying "the article sent to *St. Nicholas* was the best you would be able to do for years to come" and I saw you were going to make it a crucial test of your ability. That is, forgive me, nothing but nonsense. Whatever the article may be, you may write one infinitely superior to it next week or month. Just in proportion as you feel more deeply, or notice more keenly, and as you acquire the faculty of expressing your feelings or observations more delicately and powerfully which faculty must come into practice. It is not inspiration—it never was that—without practice, with any writer from Shakespeare down.

Understand me. I don't say, like Papa, stop writing. God forbid. I would almost as soon say stop breathing, for it is pretty much the same thing. But only to remember that you have not yet conquered your art. You are a journeyman not a master workman, so if you don't succeed, it does not count. The future is what I look to, for you. I had to stop my work to say all this, so good-bye dear old chum.

Yours,
MOTHER.

If anything worried Richard at all at this period, I think it was his desire to get down to steady newspaper work, or indeed any kind of work that would act as the first step of his career and by which he could pay his own way in the world. It was with this idea uppermost in his mind in the late spring of 1886, and without any particular regret for the ending of his college career, that he left Baltimore and, returning to his home in Philadelphia, determined to accept the first position that presented itself. But instead of going to work at once, he once more changed his plans and decided to sail for Santiago de Cuba with his friend William W. Thurston, who as president of the Bethlehem Steel Company, was deeply interested in the iron mines of that region. Here and then it was that Richard first fell in love with Cuba—a love which in later years became almost an obsession with him. Throughout his life whenever it was possible, and sometimes when it seemed practically impossible, my brother would listen to the call of his beloved tropics and, casting aside all responsibilities, would set sail for Santiago. After all it was quite natural that he should feel as he did about this little Cuban coast town, for apart from its lazy life, spicy smells, waving palms and Spanish cooking, it was here that he found the material for his first novel and greatest monetary success, "Soldiers of Fortune." Apart from the many purely pleasure trips he made to Santiago, twice he returned there to work—once as a correspondent during the Spanish-American War, and again when he went with Augustus Thomas to assist in the latter's film version of the play which years before Thomas had made from the novel.

CHAPTER III

FIRST NEWSPAPER EXPERIENCES

In the late summer of 1886 Richard returned from Cuba and settled down in Philadelphia to write an article about his experiences at Santiago and to look for regular newspaper work. Early in September he wrote his mother:

September, 1886.
Dear Mother:

I saw the *Record* people to-day. They said there was not an opening but could give me "chance" work, that is, I was to report each day at one and get what was left over. I said I would take it as I would have my mornings free to write the article and what afternoons I did not have newspaper work besides. This is satisfactory. They are either doing all they can to oblige Dad or else giving me a trial trip before making an opening. The article is progressing but slowly. To paraphrase Talleyrand, what's done is but little and that little is not good. However, since your last letter full of such excellent "tips" I have re-written it and think it is much improved. I will write to Thurston concerning the artist to-morrow. He is away from B. at present. On the whole the article is not bad.

Your boy,

Dick.

Richard's stay on *The Record*, however, was short-lived. His excuse for the brevity of the experience was given in an interview some years later. "My

City Editor didn't like me because on cold days I wore gloves. But he was determined to make me work, and gave me about eighteen assignments a day, and paid me $7. a week. At the end of three months he discharged me as incompetent."

From *The Record* Richard went to *The Press*, which was much more to his liking, and, indeed it was here that he did his first real work and showed his first promise. For nearly three years he did general reporting and during this time gained a great deal more personal success than comes to most members of that usually anonymous profession. His big chance came with the Johnstown flood, and the news stories he wired to his paper showed the first glimpse of his ability as a correspondent. Later on, disguised as a crook, he joined a gang of yeggmen, lived with them in the worst dives of the city, and eventually gained their good opinion to the extent of being allowed to assist in planning a burglary. But before the actual robbery took place, Richard had obtained enough evidence against his crook companions to turn them over to the police and eventually land them in prison. It was during these days that he wrote his first story for a magazine, and the following letter shows that it was something of a milestone in his career.

PHILADELPHIA.
August, 1888.

DEAR FAMILY:

The *St. Nicholas* people sent me a check for $50 for the "pirate" story. It would be insupportable affectation to say that I was not delighted. Jennings Crute and I were waiting for breakfast when I found the letter. I opened it very slowly, for I feared they would bluff me with some letter about illustrations or

FIRST NEWSPAPER EXPERIENCES 39

revision, or offering me a reduced subscription to the magazine. There was a letter inside and a check. I read the letter before I looked at the check, which I supposed would be for $30, as the other story was valued at $20. The note said that a perfect gentleman named Chichester would be pleased if I would find enclosed a check for $50. I looked at Jenny helplessly, and said, "It's for fifty, Jenny." Crute had an insane look in his eyes as he murmured "half a hundred dollars, and on your day off, too." Then I sat down suddenly and wondered what I would buy first, and Crute sat in a dazed condition, and abstractedly took a handful of segars out of the box dear old Dad gave me. As I didn't say anything, he took another handful, and then sat down and gazed at the check for five minutes in awe. After breakfast I calculated how much I would have after I paid my debts. I still owe say $23, and I have some shoes to pay for and my hair to cut. I had a wild idea of going over to New York and buying some stocks, but I guess I'll go to Bond's and Baker's instead.

I'm going down street now to see if Drexel wants to borrow any ready money—on the way down I will make purchases and pay bills so that my march will be a triumphal procession.

I got a story on the front page this morning about an explosion at Columbia Avenue Station—I went out on it with another man my senior in years and experience, whom Watrous expected to write the story while I hustled for facts. When we got back I had all the facts, and what little he had was incorrect—so I said I would dispense with his services and write the story myself. I did it very politely, but it queered the man before the men, and Watrous grew very sarcastic at his expense. Next time Andy will know better and let me get my own stories alone.

Your Millionaire Son,
Dick.

I'm still the "same old Dick"; not proud a bit.

This was my mother's reply:

Thursday.
August 1888.

Dear Dick:

Your letter has just come and we are all delighted. Well done for old *St. Nicholas!* I thought they meant to wait till the story was published. It took me back to the day when I got $50. for "Life in the Iron Mills." I carried the letter half a day before opening it, being so sure that it was a refusal.

I had a great mind to read the letter to Davis and Cecile who were on the porch but was afraid you would not like it.

I did read them an extremely impertinent enclosure which was so like the letter I sent yesterday. That I think you got it before writing this.

. . . Well I am glad about that cheque! Have you done anything on Gallagher? That is by far the best work you've done—oh, by far—Send that to Gilder. In old times *The Century* would not print the word "brandy." But those days are over.

Two more days—dear boy—

Your　　Mother.

In addition to his work on *The Press*, Richard also found time to assist his friend, Morton McMichael, 3d, in the editing of a weekly publication called *The*

Stage. In fact with the exception of the services of an office boy, McMichael and Richard were *The Stage.* Between them they wrote the editorials, criticisms, the London and Paris special correspondence, solicited the advertisements, and frequently assisted in the wrapping and mailing of the copies sent to their extremely limited list of subscribers. During this time, however, Richard was establishing himself as a star reporter on *The Press*, and was already known as a clever newsgatherer and interviewer. It was in reply to a letter that Richard wrote to Robert Louis Stevenson enclosing an interview he had had with Walt Whitman, that Stevenson wrote the following letter—which my brother always regarded as one of his greatest treasures:

Why, thank you so much for your frank, agreeable and natural letter. It is certainly very pleasant that all you young fellows should enjoy my work and get some good out of it and it was very kind in you to write and tell me so. The tale of the suicide is excellently droll, and your letter, you may be sure, will be preserved. If you are to escape unhurt out of your present business you must be very careful, and you must find in your heart much constancy. The swiftly done work of the journalist and the cheap finish and ready made methods to which it leads, you must try to counteract in private by writing with the most considerate slowness and on the most ambitious models. And when I say "writing"—O, believe me, it is rewriting that I have chiefly in mind. If you will do this I hope to hear of you some day.

Please excuse this sermon from
Your obliged
ROBERT LOUIS STEVENSON.

In the spring of 1889 Richard as the correspondent of the Philadelphia *Telegraph*, accompanied a team of Philadelphia cricketers on a tour of Ireland and England, but as it was necessary for him to spend most of his time reporting the matches played in small university towns, he saw only enough of London to give him a great longing to return as soon as the chance offered. Late that summer he resumed his work on *The Press*, but Richard was not at all satisfied with his journalistic progress, and for long his eyes had been turned toward New York. There he knew that there was not only a broader field for such talent as he might possess, but that the chance for adventure was much greater, and it was this hope and love of adventure that kept Richard moving on all of his life.

On a morning late in September, 1889, he started for New York to look for a position as reporter on one of the metropolitan newspapers. I do not know whether he carried with him any letters or that he had any acquaintances in the journalistic world on whose influence he counted, but, in any case, he visited a number of offices without any success whatever. Indeed, he had given up the day as wasted, and was on his way to take the train back to Philadelphia. Tired and discouraged, he sat down on a bench in City Hall Park, and mentally shook his fist at the newspaper offices on Park Row that had given him so cold a reception. At this all-important moment along came Arthur Brisbane, whom Richard had met in London when the former was the English correspondent of *The Sun*. Brisbane had recently been appointed editor of *The Evening Sun*, and had already met with a rather spectacular success. On hearing the object of Richard's visit to New York, he promptly offered him a position on his staff and Richard as promptly accepted. I remember that the joyous telegram he sent to my mother, telling of his success, and demanding that the fatted calf be killed for dinner that night was not received with unalloyed happiness. To my mother and father it meant that their first-born was leaving home to seek his fortune, and that without Richard's love and sympathy the home could never be quite the same. But the fatted calf was killed, every one pretended to be just as elated as Richard was over his good fortune, and in two days he left us for his first adventure.

The following note to his mother Richard scribbled off in pencil at the railway-station on his way to New York:

I am not surprised that you were sad if you thought I was going away for good. I could not think of it myself. I am only going to make a little reputation and to learn enough of the business to enable me to live at home in the centre of the universe with you. That is truth. God bless you.

DICK.

CHAPTER IV

NEW YORK

Of the many completely happy periods of Richard's life there were few more joyous than the first years he spent as a reporter in New York. For the first time he was completely his own master and paying his own way—a condition which afforded him infinite satisfaction. He was greatly attached to Brisbane and as devoted to the interests of *The Evening Sun* as if he had been the editor and publisher. In return Brisbane gave him a free rein and allowed him to write very much what and as he chose. The two men were constantly together, in and out of office hours, and planned many of the leading features of the paper which on account of the brilliancy of its news stories and special articles was at that time attracting an extraordinary amount of attention. Richard divided his working hours between reporting important news events, writing specials (principally about theatrical people), and the Van Bibber stories, nearly all of which were published for the first time in *The Evening Sun*. These short tales of New York life soon made a distinct hit, and, while they appeared anonymously, it was generally known that Richard was their author. In addition to his newspaper work my brother was also working on short stories for the magazines, and in 1890 scored his first real success in this field, with "Gallegher," which appeared in *Scribner's*. This was shortly followed by "The Other Woman," "Miss

Catherwaite's Understudy," "A Walk up the Avenue," "My Disreputable Friend, Mr. Raegen," "An Unfinished Story," and other stories that soon gave him an established reputation as a writer of fiction. But while Richard's success was attained in a remarkably short space of time and at an extremely early age, it was not accomplished without an enormous amount of hard work and considerable privation. When he first went to New York his salary was but thirty dollars a week, and while he remained on *The Evening Sun* never over fifty dollars, and the prices he received for his first short stories were extremely meagre. During the early days on *The Evening Sun* he had a room in a little house at 108 Waverly Place, and took his meals in the neighborhood where he happened to find himself and where they were cheapest. He usually spent his week-ends in Philadelphia, but his greatest pleasure was when he could induce some member of his family to visit him in New York. I fear I was the one who most often accepted his hospitality, and wonderful visits they were, certainly to me, and I think to Richard as well. The great event was our Saturday-night dinner, when we always went to a little restaurant on Sixth Avenue. I do not imagine the fifty-cent table d'hôte (*vin compris*) the genial Mr. Jauss served us was any better than most fifty-cent table-d'hôte dinners, but the place was quaint and redolent of strange smells of cooking as well as of a true bohemian atmosphere. Those were the days when the Broadway Theatre was given over to the comic operas in which Francis Wilson and De Wolfe Hopper were the stars, and as both of the comedians were firm friends of Richard, we invariably ended our evening at the Broadway. Sometimes we occupied a box as the guests of the management, and at other times we went behind the scenes and sat in the star's dressing-room. I think I liked it best when Hopper was playing, because during Wilson's régime the big dressing-room was a rather solemn sort of place, but when Hopper ruled, the room was filled with pretty girls and he treated us to fine cigars and champagne. Halcyon nights those, and then on Sunday morning we always breakfasted at old Martin's on University Place—eggs à la Martin and that wonderful coffee and pain de ménage. And what a wrench it was when I tore myself away from the delights of the great city and scurried back to my desk in sleepy Philadelphia. Had I been a prince royal Richard could not have planned more carefully than he did for these visits, and to meet the expense was no easy matter for him. Indeed, I know that to pay for all our gayeties he usually had to carry his guitar to a neighboring pawn-broker where the instrument was always good for an eight-dollar loan. But from the time Richard first began to make his own living one of the great pleasures of his life was to celebrate, or as he called it, to "have a party." Whenever he had finished a short story he had a party, and when the story had been accepted there was another party, and, of course, the real party was when he received the check. And so it was throughout his life, giving a party to some one whom a party would help, buying a picture for which he had no use to help a struggling artist, sending a few tons of coal to an old lady who was not quite warm enough, always writing a letter or a check for some one of his own craft who had been less fortunate than he—giving to every beggar that he met, fearing that among all the thousand fakers he might refuse one worthy

R. H. D. as he looked when he first came to New York in 1890.

case. I think this habit of giving Richard must have inherited from his father, who gave out of all proportion to his means, and with never too close a scrutiny to the worthiness of the cause. Both men were too intensely human to do that, but if this great desire on the part of my father and brother to help others gave the recipients pleasure I'm sure that it caused in the hearts of the givers an even greater happiness. The following letters were chosen from a great number which Richard wrote to his family, telling of his first days on *The Evening Sun,* and of his life in New York.

NEW YORK *Evening Sun*—1890

DEAR MOTHER:

Today is as lovely and fresh as the morning, a real spring day, and I feel good in consequence. I have just come from a couple of raids, where we had a very lively time, and some of them had to pull their guns. I found it necessary to punch a few sports myself. The old sergeant from headquarters treats me like a son and takes the greatest pride in whatever I do or write. He regularly assigns me now to certain doors, and I always obey orders like the little gentleman that I am. Instead of making me unpopular, I find it helps me with the sports, though it hurts my chances professionally, as so many of them know me now that I am no use in some districts. For instance, in Mott and Pell streets, or in the Bowery, I am as safe as any precinct detective. I tell you this to keep you from worrying. They won't touch a man whom they think is an agent or an officer. Only it spoils my chances of doing reportorial-detective work. For instance, the captain of the Bowery district refused me a detective the other morning to take the Shippens around the

Chinese and the tougher quarters because he said they were as safe with me as with any of the other men whose faces are as well known. To-night I am going to take a party to the headquarters of the fire department, where I have a cinch on the captain, a very nice fellow, who is unusually grateful for something I wrote about him and his men. They are going to do the Still Alarm act for me.

These clippings all came out in to-day's paper. The ladies in the Tombs were the Shippens, of course; and Mamie Blake is a real girl, and the story is true from start to finish. I think it is a pathetic little history.

Give my love to all. I will bring on the story I have finished and get you to make some suggestions. It is quite short. Since *Scribner's* have been so civil, I think I will give them a chance at the great prize. I am writing a comic guide book and a history of the Haymarket for the paper; both are rich in opportunities. This weather makes me feel like another person. I will be so glad to get home. With lots of love and kisses for you and Nora.

Dick-O.

New York—1890.
Dear Chas:

Brisbane has suggested to me that the Bradley story would lead anyone to suppose that my evenings were spent in the boudoirs of the horizontales of 34th Street and has scared me somewhat in consequence. If it strikes you and Dad the same way don't show it to Mother. Dad made one mistake by thinking I wrote a gambling story which has made me nervous. It is hardly the fair thing to suppose that a man must have an intimate acquaintance with

NEW YORK

whatever he writes of intimately. A lot of hunting people, for instance, would not believe that I had written the "Traver's Only Ride" story because they knew I did not hunt. Don't either you or Dad make any mistake about this.

DICK.

As a matter of fact they would not let me in the room, and I don't know whether it abounded in signed etchings or Bougereau's nymphs.

NEW YORK—1890.
DEAR FAMILY:

Today has been more or less feverish. In the morning's mail I received a letter from Berlin asking permission to translate "Gallegher" into German, and a proof of a paragraph from *The Critic* on my burlesque of Rudyard Kipling, which was meant to please but which bored me. Then the "Raegen" story came in, making nine pages of the *Scribner's*, which at ten dollars a page ought to be $90. Pretty good pay for three weeks' work, and it is a good story. Then at twelve a young man came bustling into the office, stuck his card down on the desk and said, "I am S. S. McClure. I have sent my London representative to Berlin and my New York man to London. Will you take charge of my New York end?"

If he thought to rattle me he was very much out of it, for I said in his same tone and manner, "Bring your New York representative back and send me to London, and I'll consider it. As long as I am in New York I will not leave *The Evening Sun*."

"Edmund Gosse is my London representative," he said; "you can have the same work here. Come out and take lunch."

I said, "Thank you, I can't; I'll see you on Tuesday."

"All right," he said. "I'll come for you. Think of what I say. I'll make your fortune. Bradford Merrill told me to get you. You won't have anything to do but ask people to write novels and edit them. I'll send you abroad later if you don't like New York. Can you write any children's stories for me?"

"No," I said, "see you Tuesday."

This is a verbal report of all and everything that was said. I consider it a curious interview. It will raise my salary here or I go. What do *you* think?

DICK.

NEW YORK—1890.

DEAR FAMILY:

The more I thought of the McClure offer the less I thought of it. So I told him last night I was satisfied where I was, and that the $75 he offered me was no inducement. Brisbane says I will get $50 about the first of October, which is plenty and enough for a young man who intends to be good to his folks. I cannot do better than stay where I am, for it is understood between Brisbane and Laffan that in the event of the former's going into politics I shall take his place, which will suit very well until something better turns up. Then there is the chance of White's coming back and my going to Lunnon, which would please me now more for what I think I could make of it than what I think others have made of it. If I had gone to Mc-Clure I would have been shelved and side-tracked, and I am still in the running, and learning every day. Brisbane and I have had our first serious difficulty over Mrs. R——, who is staying with Mrs. "Bill." There is at present the most desperate rivalry, and we discuss each other's chances with great anger. He counts on his transcontinental knowledge, but my short stories hit very hard, and he is not in it when I sing "Thy Face Will Lead Me On" and "When Kerrigan Struck High C." She has a fatal fondness for Sullivan, which is most unfortunate, as Brisbane can and does tell her about him by the half hour. Yesterday we both tried to impress her by riding down in front of the porch and showing off the horses and ourselves. Brisbane came off best, though I came off quickest, for my horse put his foot in a hole and went down on his knees, while I went over his head like the White Knight in "Alice." I would think nothing of sliding off a roof now. But I made up for this mishap by coming back in my grey suit and having it compared with the picture in *The Century*. It is a very close fight, and, while Brisbane is chasing over town for photographs of Sullivan, I am buying books of verses of which she seems to be fond. As soon as she gets her divorce one of us is going to marry her. We don't know which. She is about as beautiful a woman as I ever saw, and very witty and well-informed, but it would cost a good deal to keep her in diamonds. She wears some the Queen gave her, but she wants more.

DICK.

NEW YORK—1890.
DEAR MOTHER (LATE MA):
I am well and with lots to do. I went up to see Hopper the other night, which was the first time in three months that I have been back of a theater, and it was like going home. There is a smell about the

painty and gassy and dusty place that I love as much as fresh earth and newly cut hay, and the girls look so pretty and bold lying around on the sets, and the men so out of focus and with such startling cheeks and lips. They were very glad to see me and made a great fuss. Then I've been to see Carmencita dance, which I enjoyed remarkably, and I have been reading Rudyard Kipling's short stories, and I think it is disgusting that a boy like that should write such stories. He hasn't left himself anything to do when he gets old. He reminds me of Bret Harte and not a bit of Stevenson, to whom some of them compare him.

I am very glad you liked the lady in mid-air story so much, but it wasn't a bit necessary to add the *Moral* from a *Mother*. I saw it coming up before I had read two lines; and a very good moral it is, too, with which I agree heartily. But, of course, you know it is not a new idea to me. Anything as good and true as that moral cannot be new at this late date. I went to the Brooklyn Handicap race yesterday. It is one of the three biggest races of the year, and a man stood in front of me in the paddock in a white hat. Another man asked him what he was "playing."

"Well," he said, "I fancy Fides myself."

"Fides!" said his friend, "why, she ain't in it. She won't see home. Raceland's the horse for your money; she's favorite, and there isn't any second choice. But Fides! Why, she's simply impossible. Raceland beat *her* last Suburban."

"Yes, I remember," said the man in the white hat, "but I fancy Fides."

Then another chap said to him, "Fides is all good enough on a dust track on a sunny, pleasant day, but she can't run in the mud. She hasn't got the staying powers. She's a pretty one to look at, but she's just a 'grandstand' ladies' choice. She ain't in it with Raceland or Erica. The horse *you* want is not a pretty, dainty flyer, but a stayer, that is sure and that brings in good money, not big odds, but good money. Why, I can name you a dozen better'n Fides."

"Still, somehow, I like Fides best," said the obstinate man in the white hat.

"But Fides will take the bit in her mouth and run away, or throw the jock or break into the fence. She isn't steady. She's all right to have a little bet on, just enough for a flyer, but she's not the horse to plunge on. If you're a millionaire with money to throw away, why, you might put some of it up on her, but, as it is, you want to put your money where it will be sure of a 'place,' anyway. Now, let me mark your card for you?"

"No," said the man, "what you all say is reasonable, I see that; but, somehow, I rather fancy Fides best."

I've forgotten now whether Fides won or not, and whether she landed the man who just fancied her without knowing why a winner or sent him home broke. But, in any event, that is quite immaterial, the story simply shows how obstinate some men are as regards horses and—other uncertain critters. I have no doubt but that the Methodist minister's daughter would have made Hiram happy if he had loved her, but he didn't. No doubt Anne ——, Nan ——, Katy —— and Maude —— would have made me happy if they would have consented to have me and I had happened to love them, but I fancied Fides.

But now since I have scared you sufficiently, let me add for your peace of mind that I've not enough money to back any horses just at present, and before I put any money up on any one of them for the Matrimonial stakes, I will ask you first to look over the card and give me a few pointers. I mayn't follow them, you know, but I'll give you a fair warning, at any rate.

"You're my sweetheart, I'm your beau."

DICK.

NEW YORK, May 29, 1890.

This is just a little good night note to say how I wish I was with you down at that dear old place and how much I love you and Nora who is getting lovelier and sweeter and prettier everyday and I know a pretty girl when I see 'em, Fides, for instance. But I won't tease you about that any more.

I finished a short silly story to night which I am in doubt whether to send off or not. I think I will keep it until I read it to you and learn what you think.

Mr. Gilder has asked me to stay with them at Marion, and to go to Cambridge with Mrs. Gilder and dear Mrs. Cleveland and Grover Cleveland, when he reads the poem before D. K. E.

I have bought a book on decorations, colored, and I am choosing what I want, like a boy with a new pair of boots.

Good-night, my dearest Mama.

DICK.

In addition to his regular work on *The Evening Sun*, my brother, as I have already said, was devoting a great part of his leisure moments to the writing of short stories, and had made a tentative agreement with a well-known magazine to do a series of short sketches of New York types. Evidently fearful that Richard was writing too much and with a view to pecuniary gain, my mother wrote the following note of warning:

PHILADELPHIA, 1890.
DEAR DICK:

I wouldn't undertake the "types." For one thing, you will lose prestige writing for ——'s paper. For another, I dread beyond everything your beginning to do hack work for money. It is the beginning of decadence both in work and reputation for you. I know by my own and a thousand other people. Begin to write because it "is a lot of money" and you stop doing your best work. You make your work common and your prices will soon go down. George Lewes managed George Eliot wisely.

He stopped her hack work. Kept her at writing novels and soon one each year brought her $40,000. I am taking a purely mercenary view of the thing. There is another which you understand better than I— Mind your Mother's advice to you—now and all the time is "do only your best work—even if you starve doing it." But you won't starve. You'll get your dinner at Martin's instead of Delmonico's, which won't hurt you in the long run. Anyhow, $1000. for 12,500 words is not a great price.

That was a fine tea you gave. I should like to have heard the good talk. It was like the regiment of brigadier generals with no privates.

Your
MOTHER.

This is a letter written by my father after the publication of Richard's story "A Walk up the Avenue."

Richard frequently spoke of his father as his "kindest and severest critic."

PHILADELPHIA, July 22nd, 1890.
10.30 P. M.

MY DEAR BOY:

You can do it; you have done it; it is all right. I have read *A Walk up the Avenue*. It is far and away the best thing you have ever done—Full of fine subtle thought, of rare, manly feeling.

I am not afraid of Dick the author. He's all right. I shall only be afraid—when I am afraid—that Dick the man will not live up to the other fellow, that he may forget how much the good Lord has given him, and how responsible to the good Lord and to himself he is and will be for it. A man entrusted with such talent should carry himself straighter than others to whom it is denied. He has great duties to do; he owes tribute to the giver.

Don't let the world's temptations in any of its forms come between you and your work. Make your life worthy of your talent, and humbly by day and by night ask God to help you to do it.

I am very proud of this work. It is good work, with brain, bone, nerve, muscle in it. It is human, with healthy pulse and heartsome glow in it. Remember, hereafter, you have by it put on the bars against yourself preventing you doing any work less good. You have yourself made your record, you can't lower it. You can only beat it.

Lovingly,
DAD.

In the latter part of December, 1890, Richard left *The Evening Sun* to become the managing editor of

Harper's Weekly. George William Curtis was then its editor, and at this time no periodical had a broader or greater influence for the welfare of the country. As Richard was then but twenty-six, his appointment to his new editorial duties came as a distinct honor. The two years that Richard had spent on *The Evening Sun* had been probably the happiest he had ever known. He really loved New York, and at this time Paris and London held no such place in his affections as they did in later years. And indeed there was small reason why these should not have been happy years for any young man. At twenty-six Richard had already accomplished much, and his name had become a familiar one not only to New Yorkers but throughout the country. Youth and health he had, and many friends, and a talent that promised to carry him far in the profession he loved. His new position paid him a salary considerably larger than he had received heretofore, and he now demanded and received much higher terms for his stories. All of which was well for Richard because as his income grew so grew his tastes. I have known few men who cared less for money than did my brother, and I have known few who cared more for what it could buy for his friends and for himself. Money to him, and, during his life he made very large sums of it, he always chose to regard as income but never capital. A bond or a share of stock meant to him what it would bring that day on the Stock Exchange. The rainy day which is the bugaboo for the most of us, never seemed to show on his horizon. For a man whose livelihood depended on the lasting quality of his creative faculties he had an infinite faith in the future, and indeed his own experience seemed to show that he was justified in this belief. It could not have been very long after his start as a fiction writer that he received as high a price for his work as any of his contemporaries; and just previous to his death, more than twenty years later, he signed a contract to write six stories at a figure which, so far as I know, was the highest ever offered an American author. In any case, money or the lack of it certainly never caused Richard any worriment during the early days of which I write. For what he made he worked extremely hard, but the reputation and the spending of the money that this same hard work brought him caused him infinite happiness. He enjoyed the reputation he had won and the friends that such a reputation helped him to make; he enjoyed entertaining and being entertained, and he enjoyed pretty much all of the good things of life. And all of this he enjoyed with the naïve, almost boyish enthusiasm that only one could to whom it had all been made possible at twenty-six. Of these happy days Booth Tarkington wrote at the time of my brother's death:

"To the college boy of the early nineties Richard Harding Davis was the 'beau ideal of *jeunesse dorée*,' a sophisticated heart of gold. He was of that college boy's own age, but already an editor—already publishing books! His stalwart good looks were as familiar to us as were those of our own football captain; we knew his face as we knew the face of the President of the United States, but we infinitely preferred Davis's. When the Waldorf was wondrously completed, and we cut an exam. in Cuneiform Inscriptions for an excursion to see the world at lunch in its new magnificence, and Richard Harding Davis came into the Palm Room —then, oh, then, our day was radiant! That was the top of our fortune; we could never have hoped for so much. Of all the great people of every continent, this was the one we most desired to see."

Richard's intimate friends of these days were Charles Dana Gibson, who illustrated a number of my brother's stories, Robert Howard Russell, Albert La Montagne, Helen Benedict, now Mrs. Thomas Hastings, Ethel Barrymore, Maude Adams, E. H. Sothern, his brother, Sam, and Arthur Brisbane. None of this little circle was married at the time, its various members were seldom apart, and they extracted an enormous amount of fun out of life. I had recently settled in New York, and we had rooms at 10 East Twenty-eighth Street, where we lived very comfortably for many years. Indeed Richard did not leave them until his marriage in the summer of 1899. They were very pleasant, sunny rooms, and in the sitting-room, which Richard had made quite attractive, we gave many teas and supper-parties. But of all the happy incidents I can recall at the Twenty-eighth Street house, the one I remember most distinctly took place in the hallway the night that Richard received the first statement and check for his first book of short stories, and before the money had begun to come in as fast as it did afterward. We were on our way to dinner at some modest resort when we saw and at once recognized the long envelope on the mantel. Richard guessed it would be for one hundred and ninety dollars, but with a rather doubting heart I raised my guess to three hundred. And when, with trembling fingers, Richard had finally torn open the envelope and found a check for nine hundred and odd dollars, what a wild dance we did about the hall-table, and what a dinner we had that night! Not at the modest restaurant as originally intended, but at Delmonico's! It was during these days that Seymour Hicks and his lovely wife Ellaline Terriss first visited America, and they and Richard formed a mutual attachment that lasted until his death.

Richard had always taken an intense interest in the drama, and at the time he was managing editor of *Harper's Weekly* had made his first efforts as a playwright. Robert Hilliard did a one-act version of Richard's short story, "Her First Appearance," which under the title of "The Littlest Girl" he played in vaudeville for many years. E. H. Sothern and Richard had many schemes for writing a play together, but the only actual result they ever attained was a one-act version Sothern did at the old Lyceum of my brother's story, "The Disreputable Mr. Raegen." It was an extremely tense and absorbing drama, and Sothern was very fine in the part of Raegen, but for the forty-five minutes the playlet lasted Sothern had to hold the stage continuously alone, and as it preceded a play of the regulation length, the effort proved too much for the actor's strength, and after a few performances it was taken off. Although it was several years after this that my brother's first long play was produced he never lost interest in the craft of playwriting, and only waited for the time and means to really devote himself to it.

BOSTON, January 22nd, 1891.

DEAR FAMILY:—

This is just to say that I am alive and sleepy, and that my head is still its normal size, although I have at last found one man in Boston who has read one of my stories, and that was Barrymore from New York. The Fairchilds' dinner was a tremendous affair, and I was conquered absolutely by Mr. Howells, who

NEW YORK

went far, far out of his way to be as kind and charming as an old man could be. Yesterday Mrs. Whitman gave a tea in her studio. I thought she meant to have a half dozen young people to drink a cup with her, and I sauntered in in the most nonchalant manner to find that about everybody had been asked to meet me. And everybody came, principally owing to the "Harding Davis" part of the name for they all spoke of mother and so very dearly that it made me pretty near weep. Everybody came from old Dr. Holmes who never goes any place, to Mrs. "Jack" Gardner and all the debutantes. "I was on in that scene." In the evening I went with the Fairchilds to Mrs. Julia Ward Howe's to meet the S——s but made a point not to as he was talking like a cad when I heard him and Mrs. Fairchild and I agreed to be the only people in Boston who had not clasped his hand. There were only a few people present and Mrs. Howe recited the Battle Hymn of the Republic, which I thought very characteristic of the city. To-day I posed again and Cumnock took me over Cambridge and into all of the Clubs where I met some very nice boys and felt very old. Then we went to a tea Cushing gave in his rooms and to night I go to Mrs. Deland's. But the mornings with the Fairchilds are the best.

DICK.

In the spring of 1891 my mother and sister, Nora, went abroad for the summer, and the following note was written to Richard just before my mother sailed:

DEAR DICK:

This is just to give my dearest love to you my darling. Some day at sea when I cannot hear you nor see you, whenever it is that you get it—night or morning—you may be sure that we are all loving and thinking of you.

Keep close to the Lord. Your Lord who never has refused to hear a prayer of yours.

Just think that I have kissed you a thousand times.
MOTHER.

FRANKLIN SQUARE, NEW YORK.
June, 1891.

DEAR MOTHER:

Your letters are a great delight to me but I think you are going entirely too quickly. You do not feel it now but you are simply hurrying through the courses of your long dinner so rapidly that when dessert comes you will not be up to it. A day or two's rest and less greed to see many things would be much more fun I should think, and you will enjoy those days more to look back to when you wandered around some little town by yourselves and made discoveries than those you spent doing what you feel you ought to do. Excuse this lecture but I know that when I got to Paris I wanted to do nothing but sit still and read and let "sights" go— You will soon learn not to duplicate and that one cathedral will answer for a dozen. And I am disappointed in your mad desire to get to Edinboro to get letters from home, as though you couldn't get letters from me every day of your life and as if there were not enough of you together to keep from getting homesick. I am ashamed of you. But that is all the scolding I have to do for I do not know what has given me more pleasure than your letters and Nora's especially. They tell me the best news in the world and that is, that you are all getting as much happiness out of it as I have prayed you would. I may go over in September myself. But I would only go to London. Now, then for Home news. I have sold the "Reporter Who Made Himself King" to *McClure's* for $300. to be published in the syndicate in August. I have finished "Her First Appearance" and Gibson is doing the illustrations, three. I got $175. for it.

I am now at work on a story about Arthur Cumnock, Harvard's football captain who was the hero of Class Day. It will come out this week and will match Lieut. Grant's chance. In July I begin a story called the "Traveller's Tale" which will be used in the November *Harper*. That is all *I* am doing.

So far the notices of "Gallegher" have been very good, I mean the English ones.

I went up to Class Day on Friday and spent the day with Miss Fairchild and Miss Howells and with Mr. H. for chaperone. He is getting old and says he never deserved the fuss they made over him. We had a pretty perfect day although it threatened rain most of the time. We wandered around from one spread to another meeting beautifully dressed girls everywhere and "lions" and celebrities. Then the fight for the roses around the tree was very interesting and picturesque and arena like and the best of all was sitting in the broad window seats of the dormitories with a Girl or two, generally "a" girl and listening to the glee club sing and watching the lanterns and the crowds of people as beautiful as Redfern could make them.

Half of Seabright was burnt down last week but not my half, although the fire destroyed all the stores and fishermen's houses and stopped only one house away from Pannachi's, where I will put up. I am very well and content and look forward to much pleasure this summer at Seabright and much work. I find I have seldom been so happy as when working hard and fast as I have been forced to do these last two weeks and so I will keep it up. Not in such a way as to hurt me but just enough to keep me happy.

DICK.

NEW YORK, August 1891.

From *The Pall Mall Budget Gazette.*

"The Americans are saying, by the way, that they have discovered a Rudyard Kipling of their own. This is Mr. Richard Harding Davis, a volume of whose stories has been published this week by Mr. Osgood. Mr. Davis is only twenty-six, was for sometime on the staff of the New York *Evening Sun*. He is now the editor of *Harper's Weekly*."

That is me. I have also a mother and sister who once went to London and what do you think they first went to see, *in London*, mind you. They got into a four wheeler and they said "cabby drive as fast as you can," not knowing that four wheelers never go faster than a dead march—"to—" where do you think? St. Paul's, the Temple, the Abbey, their lodgings, the Houses of Parliament—the Pavilion Music Hall—the Tower—no to none of these—"To the Post Office." That is what my mother and sister did! After this when they hint that they would like to go again and say "these muffins are not English muffins" and "do you remember the little Inn at Chester, ah, those were happy days," I will say, "And do you remember the Post Office in Edinburgh and London. We have none such in America." And as they only go abroad to get letters they will hereafter go to Rittenhouse Square and I will write letters to them from London. All this shows that a simple hurriedly written letter from Richard Harding Davis is of more value than all the show places of London. It makes me quite *proud.* And so does this:

" 'Gallegher' is as good as anything of Bret Harte's, although it is in Mr. Davis's own vein, not in the borrowed vein of Bret Harte or anybody else. 'The Cynical Miss Catherwaight' is very good, too, and 'Mr. Raegen' is still better."

But on the other hand, it makes me tired, and so does *this:*

" 'The Other Woman' is a story which offends good taste in more than one way. It is a blunder to have written it, a greater blunder to have published it, and a greater blunder *still* to have republished it."

I suppose now that Dad has crossed with Prince George and Nora has seen the Emperor, that you will be proud too. But you will be prouder of your darling boy Charles, even though he does get wiped out at Seabright next week and you will be even prouder when he writes great stories for *The Evening Sun.*

RICHARD.

The Players,
16 Gramercy Park.
November 24th, 1891.

DEAR FAMILY:

I had a great day at the game and going there and coming back. I met a great many old football men and almost all of them spoke of the "Out of the Game" story. Cumnock, Camp, Poe, Terry and lots more whose names mean nothing to you, so ignorant are you, were there and we had long talks.

I went to see Cleveland yesterday about a thing of which I have thought much and talked less and that was going into politics in this country. To say he discouraged me in so doing would be saying the rain is wet. He seemed to think breaking stones as a means of getting fame and fortune was quicker and more genteel. I also saw her and the BABY. She explained why she had not written you and also incidentally why she *had* written Childs. I do not know as what Cleveland said made much impression upon me—although I found out what I could expect from him—that is nothing here but apparently a place abroad if I wanted it. But he thought Congress was perfectly feasible but the greatest folly to go there.

DICK.

CHAPTER V

FIRST TRAVEL ARTICLES

For Richard these first years in New York were filled to overflowing with many varied interests, quite enough to satisfy most young men of twenty-seven. He had come and seen and to a degree, so far as the limitation of his work would permit, had conquered New York, but Richard thoroughly realized that New York was not only a very small part of the world but of his own country, and that to write about his own people and his own country and other people and other lands he must start his travels at an early age, and go on travelling until the end. And for the twenty-five years that followed that was what Richard did. Even when he was not on his travels but working on a novel or a play at Marion or later on at Mount Kisco, so far as it was possible he kept in touch with events that were happening and the friends that he had made all over the globe. He subscribed to most of the English and French illustrated periodicals and to one London daily newspaper which every day he read with the same interest that he read half a dozen New York newspapers and the interest was always that of the trained editor at work. Richard was not only physically restless but his mind practically never relaxed. When others, tired after a hard day's work or play, would devote the evening to cards or billiards or chatter, Richard would write letters or pore over some strange foreign magazine, consult maps, make notes, or read the stories of his contemporaries. He practically read every American magazine from cover to cover—advertisements were a delight to him, and the finding of a new writer gave him as much pleasure as if he had been the fiction editor who had accepted the first story by the embryo genius. The official organs of our army and navy he found of particular interest. Not only did he thus follow the movements of his friends in these branches of the service but if he read of a case wherein he thought a sailor or a soldier had been done an injustice he would promptly take the matter up with the authorities at Washington, and the results he obtained were often not only extremely gratifying to the wronged party but caused Richard no end of pleasure.

According to my brother's arrangement with the Harpers, he was to devote a certain number of months of every year to the editing of *The Weekly*, and the remainder to travel and the writing of his experiences for *Harper's Monthly*. He started on the first of these trips in January, 1892, and the result was a series of articles which afterward appeared under the title of "The West from a Car Window."

January, 1892.

(Some place in Texas)

I left St. Louis last night, Wednesday, and went to bed and slept for twelve hours. To-day has been most trying and I shall be very glad to get on dry land again. The snow has ceased although the papers say this is the coldest snap they have had in San Antonio in ten years. It might have waited a month for me I think. It has been a most dreary trip from a car window point of view. Now that the snow has gone, there is mud and ice and pine trees and colored people, but no cowboys as yet. They talk nothing but Chili and war and they make such funny mistakes. We have a G. A. R. excursion on the train, consisting of one fat and prosperous G. A. R. the rest of the excursion having backed out on account of Garza who the salient warriors imagine as a roaring lion seeking whom he may devour. One old chap with white hair came on board at a desolate station and asked for "the boys in blue" and was very much disgusted when he found that "that grasshopper Garza" had scared them away— He had tramped five miles through the mud to greet a possible comrade and was much chagrined. The excursion shook hands with him and they took a drink together. The excursion tells me he is a glass manufacturer, an owner of a slate quarry and the best embalmer of bodies in the country. He says he can keep them four years and does so "for specimens" those that are left on his hands and others he purchases from the morgue. He has a son who is an actor and he fills me full of the most harrowing tales of Indian warfare and the details of the undertaking business. He is *so* funny about the latter that I weep with laughter and he cannot see why— Joe Jefferson and I went to a matinee on Wednesday and saw Robson in "She stoops to Conquer." The house was absolutely packed and when Joe came in the box they yelled and applauded and he nodded to them in the most fatherly, friendly way as though to say "How are you, I don't just remember your name but I'm glad to see you—" It was so much sweeter than if he had got up and bowed as I would have done.

San Antonio

I knew more about Texas than the Texans and when they told me I would find summer here I smiled knowingly— That is all the smiling I have done— Did you ever see a stage set for a garden or wood scene by daylight or Coney Island in March—that is what the glorious, beautiful baking city of San Antonio is like. There is mud and mud and mud—in cans, in the gardens of the Mexicans and snow around the palms and palmettos— Does the sun shine anywhere? Are people ever warm— It is raw, ugly and muddy, the Mexicans are merely dirty and not picturesque. I am greatly disappointed. But I have set my teeth hard and I will go on and see it through to the bitter end— But I will not write anything for publication until I can take a more cheerful view of it. I already have reached the stage where I admit the laugh is on me— But there is still London to look forward to and this may get better when the sun comes out— I went to the fort to-day and was most courteously received. But they told me I should go on to Laredo, if I expected to see any campaigning— There is no fighting nor is any expected but they say they will give me a horse and I can ride around the chaparral as long as I want. I will write you from Laredo, where I go to-morrow, Saturday—

Dick.

At Laredo Richard left the beaten track of the traveller, and with Trooper Tyler, who acted as his guide, joined Captain Hardie in his search for Garza. The famous revolutionist was supposed to be in hiding this side of the border, and the Mexican Government had asked the United States to find him and return him to the officials of his own country.

In Camp, February 2nd.

DEAR MOTHER:—

We have stopped by the side of a trail for a while and I will take the chance it gives me to tell you what I have been doing. After Tyler and I returned to camp, we had a day of rest before Captain Hardie arrived. He is a young, red-moustached, pointed-bearded chap with light blue eyes, rough with living in the West but most kind hearted and enthusiastic. He treats me as though I were his son which is rather absurd as he is only up to my shoulder. It is so hot I cannot make the words go straight and you must not mind if I wander. We are hugging a fence for all the shade there is and the horses and men have all crawled to the dark side of it and are sleeping or swearing at the sun. It is about two o'clock and we have been riding since half-past seven. I have had a first rate time but I do not see that there has been much in it to interest any one but myself and where *Harper Brothers* or the "gentle reader" comes in, I am afraid I cannot see, and if I cannot see it I fear he will be in a bad way. It has pleased and interested me to see how I could get along under difficult circumstances and with so much discomfort but as I say I was not sent out here to improve my temper or my health or to make me more content with my good things in the East. If we could have a fight or something that would excuse and make a climax for all this marching and reconnoitering and discomfort the story would have a suitable finale and a raison d'être. However, I may get something out of it if only to abuse the

Government for their stupidity in chasing a jack rabbit with a brass band or by praising the men for doing their duty when they know there is no duty to be done. This country is more like the ocean than anything else and drives one crazy with its monotony and desolation. And to think we went to war with Mexico for it— To-day is my tenth day with the troops in the camp and in the field and I will leave them as soon as this scout is over which will be in three days at the most. Then I will go to Corpus Christi and from there to the ranches but I will wait until I get baths, hair cuts and a dinner and cool things to drink— One thing has pleased me very much and that is that I, with Tyler and the Mexican Scout made the second best riding record of the troop since they have been in the field this winter. The others rode 115 miles in 32 hours, four of them under the first Sergeant, after revolutionists, and we made 110 miles in 33 hours. The rest of the detachment made 90 miles and our having the extra thirty to our credit was an accident. On the 31st Hardie sent out the scout and two troopers, of which Tyler was one, to get a trail and as I had been resting and loafing for three days, I went out with them. We left at eight after breakfast and returned at seven, having made thirty miles. When we got in we found that a detachment was going out on information sent in while we were out. Tyler was in it and so we got fresh horses and put out at nine o'clock by moonlight. That was to keep the people in the ranch from knowing we were going out. We rode until half-past three in the morning and then camped at the side of the road until half-past six, when we rode on until five in the afternoon. The men who were watching to see me give up grew more and more interested as the miles rolled out and the First Sergeant was very fearful for his record for which he has been recommended for the certificate of merit. The Captain was very much pleased and all the men came and spoke to me. It must have been a good ride for Tyler who is a fifth year man was so tired that he paid a man to do his sentry duty. We slept at Captain Hunter's camp that last night and we both came on this morning, riding thirty miles up to two o'clock to-day. From here we go on into the brush again. I am very proud of that riding record and of my beard which is fine. I will finish this when we get near a post-office.

DICK.

February 4th— We rode forty miles through the brush but saw nothing of Garza, who was supposed to be in it. But we captured 3 revolutionists, one of whom ran away but the scout got him. Hardie, Tyler, who is his orderly, and the scout and I took them in because the rest of the column was lagging in the rear and the Lieutenant got bally hooly for it. Tyler disarmed one and I took away the other chaps things. Then we took a fourth in and let them all go for want of evidence and after some of the ranch men had identified them.

CORPUS CHRISTI, February 6.

We ended our scout yesterday, and camped at Captain Hunter's last night— Mother can now rest her soul in peace as I have done with scoutings and have replaced the free and easy belt and revolver for the black silk suspenders and the fire badge of civilization. I am still covered with 11 days dirt but will get lots of good things to eat and drink and smoke at Corpus Christi to night, where I will stay for two days. I am writing this on the car and a ranger is shooting splinters out of the telegraph poles from the window in front and has a New York drummer in a state of absolute nervous prostration. I met the Rangers last night as we came into camp and find them quite the most interesting things yet. They are just what I expected to find here and have not disappointed me. Everything else is either what we know it to be and know all about or else is disappointingly commonplace. I mean we know certain things are picturesque and I find them so but they have been "done" to death and new material seems so scarce. I am sometimes very fearful of the success of the letters— However, the Rangers I simply loved. They were gentle voiced and did not swear as the soldiers do and some of them were as handsome men as I ever saw and *so big*. And such children. They showed me all their tricks at the request of the Adjutant General, who looks upon them as his special property. They shot four shots into a tree with a revolver, going at full gallop, hit a mark with both hands at once, shot with the pistol upside down and the Captain put eight shots into a board with a Winchester, while I was putting two into the field around it. We got along very well indeed and they were quite keen for me to go back and chase Garza. They are sure they have him now. I gave the Captain permission to put four shots into my white helmet. He only put two and the rest of the company thinking their reputations were at stake whipped out their guns and snatched up their rifles and blazed away until they danced the hat all over the ranch. Then remorse overcame them and they proposed taking up a collection to get me a sombrero, which I stopped. So Nora's hat is gone but I am going to get another and save myself from sunstroke again. The last part of the ride was enlivened by the presence of three Mexican murderers handcuffed and chained with iron bands around the neck, that is Texas civilization isn't it—

I have had my dinner and a fine dinner it was with fresh fish and duck and oysters and segars which I have not had for a week. I am finishing this at Constantine's and will be here for two days to write things and will then go on to King's ranch and from there to San Antonio, where I will also rest a week. I will just about get through my schedule in the ten weeks at this rate. I had a good time in the bush and am enjoying it very much though it is lonely now and then— Still, it is very interesting and if the stories amount to anything I will be pleased but I am constantly wondering how on earth Chas stood it as he did. He is a hero to me for I have some hope of getting back and he had not— He is a sport— How I will sleep to night—a real bed and sheets and pajamas, after the ground and the same clothes for eleven days. Lots of love.

DICK.

While Richard was travelling in the West, his second volume of short stories, "Van Bibber and Others," was published. The volume was dedicated to my father, who wrote Richard the following letter:

PHILADELPHIA, February 15, 1892.

MY DEAR OWN DICK:

I have not been the complete letter writer I should have been, as I told you on Saturday, but I know you will understand. Your two good letters came this evening, one to Mamma and one to Nora. They were a good deal to us all, most, of course, to your dear mother and sister, who have a fond, foolish fancy or love for you—strange—isn't it? Yes, dear boy, I liked the new story very, very much. It was in your best book and in fine spirit, and I liked, too, the dedication of the book—its meaning and its manner. I am glad to be associated with my dear boy and with his work even in that brief way. You may not yet thought about it after this fashion, but I have thought a good deal about it. Reports come to me of you from many sources, and they are all good, and they all reflect honor upon me— Upon me as I'm getting ready to salute the world, as our French friends say. It is very pleasant to me as I think it over to feel and to know that my boy has honored my name, that he has done something good and useful in the world and for the world. I have something more than pride in you. I am grateful to you. If this is a little prosie, dear old fellow, forgive it. It is late at night and I am a little tired, and being tired stupid. You saw *The Atlantic* notice of your work. I wish you could have heard Nora on the author of it, who would not have been happy in his mind if he had unhappily heard her. She went for that Heathen Chinee like a wild cat. No disrespect to her, but, all the same, like a wild cat. To me it was interesting. I did not agree with it, but here and there I saw the flash of truth even in the adverse praise. I should have had more respect for the author's opinion if he had liked that vital speck, Raegen. If he could not see the divine, human spark in that—a flash from Calvary, what is the use of considering him? My greatest pride in you, that which has added some sweetness and joy to my life, has been the recognition that something of the divine element was given you, and that your voice rang out sweet and pure at a time when other voices were sounding the fascinations of impurity. That, like Christ, you taught humanity. Don't be afraid of being thought "fresh," fear to be thought "knowing." Life isn't much worth at best,—it is worth nothing at all unless some good be done in it—the more, the better. Don't make it too serious either. Enjoy it as you go, but after a fashion that will bring no reproach to your manhood. Don't be afraid to preach the truth and above all the religion of humanity. Good night, dear boy. I'm a little tired to night. With great love,

DAD.

ANADARKO—February 26th, 1892.
DEAR FAMILY:—

I could not write you before as I have been traveling from pillars to posts, (a joke), in a stage, night and day. I went to Fort Reno from Oklahoma City where they drove me crazy almost with town lots and lot sites and homestead holdings. It was all raw and mean, and greedy for money and a man is much better off in every way in a tenement on Second Avenue than the "owner of his own home" in one of these mushroom cities—So I think. I went to Fort Reno by stage and it seemed to me that I was really in the West for the first time— The rest has been as much like the oil towns around Pittsburgh as anything else. But here there are rolling prairie lands with millions of prairie dogs and deep cañons and bluffs of red clay that stand out as clear as a razor hollowed and carved away by the water long ago. And the grass is as high as a stirrup and the trees very plentiful after the plains of Texas. The men at Fort Reno were the best I have met, indeed I am just a little tired of trying to talk of things of interest to the Second Lieutenant's intellect. But I had to leave there because I had missed the beef issue and had to see it and as it was due here I pushed on. This post is very beautiful but the men are very young and civil appointments mainly, which means that they have not been to West Point but had fathers and have friends with influence and they are fresh. But the scenery around the post is delightfully wild and big and there is an Indian camp at the foot of the hill on which the fort is stuck. Mother, instead of going to Europe, should come here and see her Indians. Only if she did she would bring a dozen or more of the children back with her. They are the brightest spot in my trip and I spend the mornings and afternoons trying to get them to play with me. They are very shy and pretty and beautifully barbaric and wear the most gorgeous trappings. The women, the older ones, are the ugliest women I ever saw. But the men are fine. I never saw such color as they give to the landscape and one always thinks they have dressed up just to please you. I have spent most of my time and money in buying things from them but they are very dear because the Indians take long to make them and do not like to part with them. I have had rough times lately but I think I would be content to remain in the west six months if I could. It is the necessity of leaving places I like and pushing on to places I don't, I dislike. Reno was fine with a band and lots of fine fellows. This post is not so queer but they are so young— It makes a great bit of color though with the yellow capes of the cavalry and the soldiers wig-waging red and white flags at other soldiers eight miles away on other mountains and the Indians in yellow buckskin and blankets and their faces painted too. I went to the beef issue to-day—it was not a pretty sight and most barbarous and cruel. I also went to a council at which the chiefs were protesting against the cutting down of their rations which is Commissioner Morgan's doing and which it is expected will lead to war— We went in out of curiosity and without knowing it was a Council and were very much ashamed when one of the Chiefs rose and said he was glad to see the officers present as they were the best friends the Indians had and the only men they could respect in times of peace as a friend, or in times of war as an enemy. At which we took off our hats and sat it through. Mother's blood would rise if she could hear the stories they tell, and they are so dignified and polite. They have an Indian troop here, like the one described in *The Weekly*, which you should read and the Captain told them I was a great Chief from the East, whereat all the soldiers who were of noble lineage claimed their privilege of shaking hands with me, which had a demoralizing effect upon the formation and the white privates were either convulsed with mirth or red with indignation. But you cannot treat them like white men who do not know their ancestors— Dad's letter was the best I have ever got from him and he had always better write when he is tired. I will always keep it.   DICK.

DENVER—March 7, 1892.
DEAR FAMILY:
I arrived in Denver Friday night and realized that I was in a city again where the more you order people

about the more they do for you, being civilized and so understanding that you mean to tip them. I found my first letter on the newsstand and was very much pleased with it, and with the way they put it out. The proof was perfect and if there had been more pictures I would have been entirely satisfied, as it was I was very much pleased. My baggage had not come, so covered with mud and dust and straw from the stages and generally disreputable I went to see a burlesque, and said "Front row, end seat," just as naturally as though I was in evening dress and high hat— and then I sank into a beautiful deep velvet chair and saw Amazon marches and ladies in tights and heard the old old jokes and the old old songs we know so well and sing so badly. The next morning I went for my mail and the entire post office came out to see me get it. It took me until seven in the evening to finish it, and I do not know that it will ever be answered. The best of it was that you were all pleased with my letters. That put my mind at rest. Then there was news of deaths and marriages and engagements and the same people doing the same things they did when I went away. I did not intend to present any letters as I was going away that night to Creede, but I found I could not get any money unless some one identified me so I presented one to a Mr. Jerome who all the bankers said they would be only too happy to oblige. After one has been variously taken for a drummer, photographer and has been offered so much a line to "write up" booming towns, it is a relief to get back to a place where people know you.—I told Mr. Jerome I had a letter of introduction and that I was Mr. Davis and he shook hands and then looked at the letter and said "Good Heavens are you that Mr. Davis" and then rushed off and brought back the entire establishment brokers, bankers and mine owners and they all sat around and told me funny stories and planned more things for me to do and eat than I could dispose of in a month.

I am now en route to Creede. Creede when you first see it in print looks like creede but after you have been in Denver or Colorado even for one day it reads like C R E E D E. All the men on this car think they are going to make their fortunes, and toward that end they have on new boots and flannel shirts, and some of them seeing *my* beautiful clothing and careful array came over and confided to me that they were really not so tough as they looked and had never worn a flannel shirt before. This car is typical of what they told me I would find at Creede. There are rich mine owners who are pointed out by the conductor as the fifth part owner of the "Pot Luck" mine, and dudes in astrakan fur coats over top boots and new flannel shirts, and hardened old timers with their bedding and tin pans, who have prospected all over the state and women who are smoking and drinking.

I feel awfully selfish whenever I look out of the car window. Switzerland which I have never seen is a spot on the map compared to this. The mountains go up with snow on one side and black rows of trees and rocks on the other, and the clouds seem packed down between them. The sun on the snow and the peaks peering above the clouds is all new to me and so very beautiful that I would like to buy a mountain and call it after my best girl. I will finish this when I get to Creede. I expect to make my fortune there.

DICK.

CREEDE, March 7.

A young man in a sweater and top boots met me at the depot and said that I was Mr. Davis and that he was a young man whose life I had written in "There was 90 and 9." He was from Buffalo and was editing a paper in Creede. He said I was to stop with him—Creede is built of new pine boards and lies between two immense mountains covered with pines and snow. The town is built in the gulley and when the spring freshets come will be a second Johnstown. Faber, the young man, took me to the Grub State Cabin where I found two most amusing dudes and thoroughbred sports from Boston, Harvard men living in a cabin ten by eight with four bunks and a stove, two banjos and H O P E. They own numerous silver mines, lots, and shares, but I do not believe they have five dollars in cash amongst them. They have a large picture of myself for one of the *ornaments* and are great good fellows. We sat up in our bunks until two this morning talking and are planning to go to Africa and Mexico and Asia Minor together.—Lots of love.

DICK.

Very happy indeed to be back in his beloved town, Richard returned to New York late in March, 1892, and resumed his editorial duties. But on this occasion his stay was of particularly short duration, and in May, he started for his long-wished-for visit to London. The season there was not yet in full swing, and after spending a few days in town, journeyed to Oxford, where he settled down to amuse himself and collect material for his first articles on English life as he found it. In writing of this visit to Oxford, H. J. Whigham, one of Richard's oldest friends, and who afterward served with him in several campaigns, said:

"When we first met Richard Harding Davis he was living, to all practical purposes, the life of an undergraduate at Balliol College, Oxford. Anyone at all conversant with the customs of universities, especially with the idiosyncrasies of Oxford, knows that for a person who is not an undergraduate to share the life of undergraduates on equal terms, to take part in their adventures, to be admitted to their confidence is more difficult than it is for the camel to pass through the eye of a needle or for the rich man to enter heaven. It was characteristic of Davis that although he was a few years older than the average university "man" and came from a strange country and, moreover, had no official reason for being at Oxford at all, he was accepted as one of themselves by the Balliol undergraduates, in fact, lived in Balliol for at least a college term, and happening to fall in with a somewhat enterprising generation of Balliol men he took the lead in several escapades which have been written into Oxford history. There is in the makeup of the best type of college undergraduate a wonderful spirit of adventure, an unprejudiced view of life, an almost Quixotic feeling for romance, a disdain of sordid or materialistic motives, which together make the years spent at a great university the most golden of the average man's career. These characteristics Davis was fortunate enough to retain through all the years of his life. The same spirit that took him out with a band of Oxford youths to break down an iron barrier set by an insolent landowner across the navigable waters of Shakespeare's Avon carried him, in after years, to the battlefields where Greece fought against the yoke of Turkey, to the insurrecto camps of Cuba, to the dark horrors of the Congo, to Manchuria, where gallant Japan beat back the overwhelming power of Russia, to Belgium, where he saw the legions of Germany trampling over the prostrate bodies of a small people. Romance was never dead while Davis was alive."

That Richard lost no time in making friends at Oxford as, indeed, he never failed to do wherever he went, the following letters to his mother would seem to show:

Oxford—May, 1892.
Dear Family:

I came down here on Saturday morning with the Peels, who gave an enormous boating party and luncheon on a tiny little island. The day was beautiful with a warm brilliant sun, and the river was just as narrow and pretty as the head of the Squan river, and with old walls and college buildings added. We had the prettiest Mrs. Peel in our boat and Mrs. Joseph Chamberlain, who was Miss Endicott and who is very sweet and pretty. We raced the other punts and rowboats and soon, after much splashing and exertion, reached the head of the river. Then we went to tea in New College and to see the sights of the different colleges now on the Thames. The barges of the colleges, painted different colors and gilded like circus band-wagons and decorated with coats of arms and flying great flags, lined the one shore for a quarter of a mile and were covered by girls in pretty frocks and under-grads in blazers. Then the boats came into sight one after another with the men running alongside on the towpath. This was one of the most remarkable sights of the country so far. There were over six hundred men coming six abreast, falling and stumbling and pushing, shouting and firing pistols. It sounded like a cavalry charge and the line seemed endless. The whole thing was most theatrical and effective. Then we went to the annual dinner of the Palmerston Club, where I made a speech which was, as there is no one else to tell you, well received, "being frequently interrupted with applause," from both the diners and the ladies in the gallery. It was about Free Trade and the way America was misrepresented in the English papers, and composed of funny stories which had nothing to do with the speech. I did not know I was going to speak until I got there, and considering the fact, as Wilson says, that your uncle was playing on a strange table with a crooked cue he did very well. The next morning we breakfasted with the Bursar of Trinity and had luncheon with the Viscount St. Cyres to meet Lord and Lady Coleridge. St. Cyres is very shy and well-bred, and we would have had a good time had not the M. P.'s present been filled with awe of the Lord Chief Justice and failed to draw him out. As it was he told some very funny stories; then we went to tea with Hubert Howard, in whose rooms I live and am now writing, and met some stupid English women and shy girls. Then we dined with the dons at New College, so-called because it is eight hundred years old. We sat at a high table in a big hall hung with pictures and lit by candles. The under-grads sat beneath in gowns and rattled pewter mugs. We all wore evening dress and those that had them red and white fur collars. After dinner we left the room according to some process of selection, carrying our napkins with us. We entered a room called the Commons, where we drank wines and ate nuts and raisins. It was all very solemn and dull and very dignified. Outside it was quite light although nine o'clock. Then we marched to another room where there were cigars and brandy and soda, but Arthur Pollen and I had to go and take coffee with the Master of Balliol, the only individual of whom Pollen stands in the least awe. He was a dear old man who said, "O yes, you're from India," and on my saying "No, from America"; he said, "O yes, it's the other one." I found the other one was an Indian princess in a cashmere cloak and diamonds, who looked so proud and lovely and beautiful that I wanted to take her out to one of the seats in the quadrangle and let her weep on my shoulder. How she lives among these cold people I cannot understand. We were all to go to a concert in the chapel, and half of the party started off, but the Master's wife said, "Oh, I am sure the Master expects them to wait for him in the hall. It is always done." At which all the women made fluttering remarks of sympathy and the men raced off to bring the others back. Only the Indian girl and I remained undisturbed and puzzled. The party came back, but the Master saw them and said, "Well, it does not matter, but it is generally done." At which we all felt guilty. When we got to the chapel everybody stood up until the Master's party sat down, but as it was broken in the middle of the procession, they sat down, and then, seeing we had not all passed, got up again, so that I felt like saying, "As you were, men," as they do out West in the barracks. Then Lord Coleridge in taking off his overcoat took off his undercoat, too, and stood unconscious of the fact before the whole of Oxford. The faces of the audience which packed the place were something wonderful to see; their desire to laugh at a tall, red-faced man who looks like a bucolic Bill Nye struggling into his coat, and then horror at seeing the Chief Justice in his shirt-sleeves, was a terrible effort—and no one would help him, on the principle, I suppose, that the Queen of Spain has no legs. He would have been struggling yet if I had not, after watching him and Lady Coleridge struggling with him, for a full minute, taken his coat and firmly pulled the old gentleman into it, at which he turned his head and *winked*.

I will go back to town by the first to see the Derby and will get into lodgings there. *I am having a very good time and am very well.* The place is as beautiful as one expects and yet all the time startling one with its beauty.
DICK.

When the season at Oxford was over Richard returned to London and took a big sunny suite of rooms in the Albany. Here he settled down to learn all he could of London, its ways and its people. In New York he had already met a number of English men and women distinguished in various walks of life, and with these as a nucleus he soon extended his circle of friends until it became as large as it was varied. In his youth, and indeed throughout his life, Richard had the greatest affection for England and the English. No truer American ever lived, but he thought the United States and Great Britain were bound by ties that must endure always. He admired British habits, their cosmopolitanism and the very simplicity of their mode of living. He loved their country life, and the swirl of London never failed to thrill him. During the last half of his life Richard had perhaps as many intimate friends in London as in New York. His fresh point of view, his very eagerness to understand theirs, made them welcome him more as one of their own people than as a stranger.

LONDON, June 3, 1892.

DEAR FAMILY:

I went out to the Derby on Wednesday and think it is the most interesting thing I ever saw over here. It is *so* like these people never to have seen it. It seems to be chiefly composed of costermongers and Americans. I got a box-seat on a public coach and went out at ten. We rode for three hours in a procession of donkey shays, omnibuses, coaches, carriages, vans, advertising wagons; every sort of conveyance stretching for sixteen miles, and with people lining the sides to look on. I spent my time when I got there wandering around over the grounds, which were like Barnum's circus multiplied by thousands. It was a beautiful day and quite the most remarkable sight of my life. Much more wonderful than Johnstown, so you see it must have impressed me. We were five hours getting back, the people singing all the way and pelting one another and saying funny impudent things.

My rooms are something gorgeous. They are on the first floor, looking into Piccadilly from a court, and they are filled with Hogarth's prints, old silver, blue and white china, Zulu weapons and fur rugs, and easy chairs of India silk. You never saw such rooms! And a very good servant, who cooks and valets me and runs errands and takes such good care of me that last night Cust and Balfour called at one to get some supper and he would not let them in. Think of having the Leader of the House of Commons come to ask you for food and having him sent away. Burdett-Coutts heard of my being here in the papers and wrote me to dine with him tonight. I lunched with the Tennants today; no relation to Mrs. Stanley, and it was informal and funny rather. The Earl of Spender was there and Lord Pembroke and a lot of women. They got up and walked about and changed places and seemed to know one another better than we do at home. I think I will go down to Oxford for Whitsuntide, which is a heathen institution here which sends everyone away just as I want to meet them.

I haven't written anything yet. I find it hard to do so. I think I would rather wait until I get home for the most of it. Chas. will be here in less than a week now and we will have a good time. I have planned it out for days. He must go to Oxford and meet those boys, and then, if he wishes, on to Eastnor, which I learn since my return is one of the show places of England. I am enjoying myself, it is needless to say, very much, and am well and happy.   DICK.

During these first days in England Richard spent much of his time at Eastnor, Lady Brownlow's place in Lincolnshire, and one of the most beautiful estates in England. Harry Cust, to whom my brother frequently refers in his letters, was the nephew of Lady Brownlow, and a great friend of Richard's. At that time Cust was the Conservative nominee for Parliament from Lincolnshire, and Richard took a most active part in the campaign. Happily, we were both at Lady Brownlow's during its last few tense days, as well as on the day the votes were counted, and Cust was elected by a narrow margin. Of our thrilling adventures Richard afterward wrote at great length in "Our English Cousins."

LONDON, July 6, 1892.
DEAR MOTHER:

On the Fourth of July, Lady Brownlow sent into town and had a big American flag brought out and placed over the house, which was a great compliment, as it was seen and commented on for miles around. Cushing of Boston, a very nice chap and awfully handsome, is there, too. The same morning I went out to photograph the soldiers, and Lord William Frederick, who is their colonel, charged them after me whenever I appeared. It seems he has a sense of humor and liked the idea of making an American run on the Fourth of July from Red-coats. I doubt if the five hundred men who were not on horseback thought it as funny. They chased me till I thought I would die. The Conservative member for the county got in last night and we rejoiced greatly, as the moral effect will help Harry Cust greatly. His election takes place next Monday. The men went in to hear the vote declared after dinner, and so did two of the girls, who got Lady Brownlow's consent at dinner, and then dashed off to change their gowns before she could change her mind. As we were intent on seeing the fun and didn't want them, we took them just where we would have gone anyway, which was where the fighting was. And they showed real sporting blood and saw the other real sort. There were three of us to each girl, and it was most exciting, with stones flying and windows crashing and cheers and groans. A political meeting or election at home is an afternoon tea to the English ones. When we came back the soldiers were leaving the Park to stop the row, and as we flew past, the tenants ran to the gate and cheered for the Tory victory in "good old lopes." When we got to the house the servants ran cheering all over the shop and rang the alarm bell and built fires, and we had a supper at one-fifteen. What they will do on the night of Cust's election, I cannot imagine—

burn the house down probably. Cushing and I enjoy it immensely. We know them well enough now to be as funny as we like without having them stare. They are nice when you know them, but you've *got* to know them first. I had a great dinner at Farrar's. All the ecclesiastical lights of England in knee-breeches were there, and the American Minister and Phillips Brooks. It was quite novel and fun. Lots of love. I have all the money I want.

DICK.

With Cust properly elected, Richard and I returned to the Albany and settled down to enjoy London from many angles. Although my brother had been there but a few weeks his acquaintances among the statesmen, artists, social celebrities, and the prominent actors of the day was quite as extraordinary as his geographical and historical knowledge of the city. We gave many jolly parties, and on account of Richard's quickly acquired popularity were constantly being invited to dinners, dances, and less formal but most amusing Bohemian supper-parties. During these days there was little opportunity for my brother to do much writing, but he was very busy making mental notes not only for his coming book on the English people, but for a number of short stories which he wrote afterward in less strenuous times. We returned to New York in August, and Richard went to Marion to rest from his social activities, and to work on his English articles.

CHAPTER VI

THE MEDITERRANEAN AND PARIS

IT was, I think, the year previous to this that my mother and father had deserted Point Pleasant as a place to spend their summer vacations in favor of Marion, on Cape Cod, and Richard and I, as a matter of course, followed them there. At that time Marion was a simple little fishing village where a few very charming people came every summer and where the fishing was of the best. In all ways the life was most primitive, and happily continued so for many years. In these early days Grover Cleveland and his bride had a cottage there, and he and Joseph Jefferson, who lived at Buzzard's Bay, and my father went on daily fishing excursions. Richard Watson Gilder was one of the earliest settlers of the summer colony, and many distinguished members of the literary and kindred professions came there to visit him. It was a rather drowsy life for those who didn't fish—a great deal of sitting about on one's neighbor's porch and discussion of the latest novel or the newest art, or of one's soul, and speculating as to what would probably become of it. From the first Richard formed a great affection for the place, and after his marriage adopted it as his winter as well as his summer home. As a workshop he had two rooms in one of the natives' cottages, and two more charming rooms it would be hard to imagine. The little shingled cottage was literally covered with honeysuckle, and inside there were the old wall-papers,

With Joseph Jefferson at Marion, 1899.

THE MEDITERRANEAN AND PARIS

the open hearths, the mahogany furniture, and the many charming things that had been there for generations, and all of which helped to contribute to the quaint peaceful atmosphere of the place. Dana Gibson had a cottage just across the road, and around the corner Gouverneur Morris lived with his family. At this time neither of these friends of Richard, nor Richard himself, allied themselves very closely to the literary colony and its high thoughts, but devoted most of their time to sailing about Sippican Harbor, playing tennis and contributing an occasional short story or an illustration to a popular magazine. But after the colony had taken flight, Richard often remained long into the fall, doing really serious work and a great deal of it. At such times he had to depend on a few friends who came to visit him, but principally on the natives to many of whom he was greatly attached. It was during these days that he first met his future wife, Cecil Clark, whose father, John M. Clark of Chicago, was one of the earliest of the summer colonists to build his own home at Marion. A most charming and hospitable home it was, and it was in this same house where we had all spent so many happy hours that Richard was married and spent his honeymoon, and for several years made his permanent home. Of the life of Marion during this later period, he became an integral part, and performed his duties as one of its leading citizens with much credit to the town and its people. For Marion Richard always retained a great affection, for there he had played and worked many of his best years. He had learned to love everything of which the quaint old town was possessed, animate and inanimate, and had I needed any further proof of how deeply the good people of

Marion loved Richard, the letters I received from many of them at the time of his death would show.

In the early fall of 1892 Richard returned to his editorial work on *Harper's Weekly*, and one of the first assignments he gave was to despatch himself to Chicago to report the Dedication Exercises of the World's Fair. That the trip at least started out little to my brother's liking the following seems to show. However, Richard's moods frequently changed with the hour, and it is more than possible that before the letter was sent he was enjoying himself hugely and regarding Chicago with his usual kindly eyes.

The Chicago Club,
October 2, 1892.

DEAR FAMILY:

Though lost to sight I am still thinking of you sadly. It seems that I took a coupé after leaving you and after living in it for a few years I grew tired and got out on the prairie and walked along drinking in the pure air from the lakes and reading Liebig's and Cooper's advs. After a brisk ten mile walk I reentered my coupé and we in time drew up before a large hotel inhabited by a clerk and a regular boarder. I am on the seventh floor without a bathroom or electric button—I merely made remarks and then returned to town in a railroad train which runs conveniently near. After gaining civilization I made my way through several parades or it may have been the same one to the reviewing stand. My progress was marked by mocking remarks by the police who asked of each other to get on to my coat and on several occasions I was mistaken by a crowd of some thousand people for the P——e of W——s, and tumultuously cheered. At last I found an inspector of police on horseback, who agreed to get me to the stand if it took a leg. He accordingly charged about 300 women and clubbed eight men—I counted them—and finally got me in. He was very drunk but he was very good to me.

DICK.

Once back from Chicago Richard divided his time between his desk at Franklin Square, his rooms on Twenty-eighth Street, and in quickly picking up the friendships and the social activities his trip to England had temporarily broken off. Much as he now loved London, he was still an enthusiastic New Yorker, and the amount of work and play he accomplished was quite extraordinary. Indeed it is difficult to understand where he found the time to do so much. In addition to his work on *Harper's* he wrote many short stories and special articles, not only because he loved the mere writing of them, but because he had come to so greatly enjoy the things he could buy with the money his labors now brought him. His pleasures had increased as steadily as the prices he could now command for his stories, and in looking back on those days it is rather remarkable when one considers his age, the temptations that surrounded him, and his extraordinary capacity for enjoyment, that he never seems to have forgotten the balance between work and play, and stuck to both with an unswerving and unceasing enthusiasm. However, after four months of New York, he decided it was high time for him to be off again, and he arranged with the Harpers to spend the late winter and the spring in collecting material for the two sets of articles which afterward appeared in book form under the titles of "The Rulers of the

Mediterranean" and "About Paris." He set sail for Gibraltar the early part of February, 1893, and the following letters describe his leisurely progress about the Mediterranean ports.

NEW YORK, February 3, 1893.

DEAREST MOTHER:

This is a little present for you and a goodby. Your packing-case is what I need and what I shall want, and I love it because you made it. But as *you* say, we understand and do not have to write love letters; you have given me all that is worth while in me, and I love you so that I look forward already over miles and miles and days and months, and just see us sitting together at Marion and telling each other how good it is to be together again and holding each other's hands. I don't believe you really know how *happy* I am in loving you, dear, and in having you say nice things about me. God bless you, dearest, and may I never do anything to make you feel less proud of your wicked son.

DICK.

Off Gibraltar,
February 12, 1893.

DEAR MOTHER:

Today is Sunday. We arrive at Gibraltar at five tomorrow morning and the boat lies there until nine o'clock. Unless war and pestilence have broken out in other places, I shall go over to Tangiers in a day or two, and from there continue on my journey as mapped out when I left. I have had a most delightful trip and the most enjoyable I have ever taken by sea. These small boats are as different from the big twin-screw steamers as a flat from a Broadway hotel.

THE MEDITERRANEAN AND PARIS 97

Everyone gets to know everything about everyone else, and it has been more like a yacht than a passenger steamer. When I first came on board I thought I would not find in any new old country I was about to visit anything more foreign than the people, and I was right, but they are most amusing and I have learned a great deal. They are different from any people I know, and are the Americans we were talking about. The ones of whom I used to read in *The Atlantic* and *Blackwood's*, as traveling always and sinking out of sight whenever they reached home. They, with the exception of a Boston couple, know none of my friends or my haunts, and I have learned a great deal in meeting them. It has been most *broadening* and the change has been *such* a rest. I had no idea of how tired I was of talking about the theater of Arts and Letters and Miss Whitney's début and my Soul. These people are simple and unimaginative and bourgeois to a degree and as kind-hearted and apparent as animal alphabets. I do not think I have had such a complete change or rest in years, and I am sure I have not laughed so much for as long. Of course, the idea of a six months' holiday is enough to make anyone laugh at anything, but I find that besides that I was a good deal harassed and run down, and I am glad to cut off from everything and start fresh. I feel miserably selfish about it all the time.

These Germans run everything as though you were the owner of the line. The discipline is like that of the German Army or of a man-of-war, everything moves by the stroke of a bell, and they have had dances and speeches and concerts and religious services and lectures every other minute. Into all of these I have gone with much enthusiasm. We have at the captain's table Dr. Field, the editor of *The Evangelist*, John Russell, a Boston Democrat, who was in Congress and who has been in public life for over forty years. A Tammany sachem, who looks like and worships Tweed, and who says what I never heard an American off the stage say: "That's me. That's what I do," he says. "When I have insomnia, I don't believe in your sleeping draughts. I get up and go round to Jake Stewart's on Fourteenth Street and eat a fry or a porterhouse steak and then I sleep good— that's me." There is also a lively lady from Albany next to me and her husband, who tells anecdotes of the war just as though it had happened yesterday. Indeed, they are all so much older than I that all their talk is about things I never understood the truth about, and it is most interesting. I really do not know when I have enjoyed my meal time so much. The food is very good, although queer and German, and we generally take two hours to each sitting. Dr. Field is my especial prey and he makes me laugh until I cry. He is just like James Lewis in "A Night Off," and is always rubbing his hands and smacking his lips over his own daring exploits. I twist everything he says into meaning something dreadful, and he is instantly explaining he did not really see a bullfight, but that he walked around the outside of the building. I have promised to show him life with a capital L, and he is afraid as death of me. But he got back at me grandly last night when he presented a testimonial to the captain, and referred to the captain's wife and boy whom he is going to see after a two years' absence, at which the captain wept and everybody else wept. And Field, seeing he had made a point, waved his arms and cried, "I have never

THE MEDITERRANEAN AND PARIS

known a man who amounted to anything who had not a good wife to care for—except *you*—" he shouted, pointing at me, "and no woman will ever save *you*." At which the passengers, who fully appreciated how I had been worrying him, applauded loudly, and the Doctor in his delight at having scored on me forgot to give the captain his testimonial.

There are two nice girls on board from Chicago and a queer Southern girl who paints pictures and sings and writes poetry, and who is traveling with an odd married woman who is an invalid and who like everyone else on board has apparently spent all her life away from home. I have spent my odd time in writing the story I told Dad the night before I sailed and I think it in some ways the best, quite the best, I have written. I read it to the queer girl and her queer chaperon and they weep whenever they speak of it, which they do every half hour. All the passengers apparently laid in a stock of "Gallegher" and "The West" before starting, and young women in yachting caps are constantly holding me up for autographs and favorite quotations. Yesterday we passed the Azores near enough to see the windows in the houses, and we have seen other islands at different times, which is quite refreshing. Tomorrow I shall post this and the trip will be over. It has been a most happy start. I am not going to write letters often, but am going head over ears into this new life and let the old one wait awhile. You cannot handle Africa and keep up your fences in New York at the same time. I am now going out to talk to the Boston couple, or to propose a lion hunt to Dr. Field.

Since I wrote that last I have seen *Portugal*. It made me seem suddenly very far away from New York.

Portugal is a high hill with a white watch tower on it flying signal flags. It is apparently inhabited by one man who lives in a long row of yellow houses with red roofs, and populated by sheep who do grand acts of balancing on the side of the hill. There is also a Navy of a brown boat with a leg-of-mutton sail and a crew of three men in the boat—not to speak of the dog. It is a great thing to have a traveled son. None of you ever saw Portugal, yah!

I am now in Gibraltar. It is a large place and there does not seem to be room in this letter, in which to express my feelings about Moors in bare legs and six thousand Red-coats and to hear Englishmen speak again. When I woke up Gibraltar was a black silhouette against the sky, but toward the south there was a low line of mountains with a red sky behind them, dim and mysterious and old, and that was Africa. Then Spain turned up all amethyst and green, and the Mediterranean as blue as they tell you it is. They wouldn't let me take my gun into Gibraltar. They know my reputation for war.

DICK.

GIBRALTAR.
February 14th, 1893.

DEAR MOTHER:

The luck of the British Army which I am modestly fond of comparing with my own took a vacation yesterday as soon as I had set foot on land. In the first place Egypt had settled down to her sluggish Nile like calm and cholera had quarantined the ship I wanted to take to Algiers, shutting off Algiers and what was more important Tunis. The Governor was ill shutting off things I wanted and his adjutant was boorish and proud and haughty. Then I determined

THE MEDITERRANEAN AND PARIS 101

to go to Spain but found I had arrived just one day too late for the last of the three days of the Mardi Gras and too early for bull fights. Had I taken Saavedra's letters I should have gone to Madrid and met the Queen and other proud folks. So on the whole I was blue. But I have now determined to take a boat for Tangier at once where I have letters to the Duke de Tnas who is the Master of the Hounds there and a great sport and they say it is very amusing and exciting. In a fortnight I shall go to Malta. I called on Harry Cust's brother and told him who I was and he took me in and put me at the head of the table of young subalterns in grand uniforms and we had marmalade and cold beef and beer and I was happy to the verge of tears to hear English as she is spoke. Then we went to a picnic and took tea in a smuggler's cave and all the foxterriers ran over the table cloth and the Captain spilt hot water over his white flannels and jumped around on one leg. After which we played a handkerchief game sitting in a row and pelting the girls with a knotted handkerchief and then fighting for it— During one of these scrimmages Mulvaney, two others and Learoyd came by and with eyes front and hands at their caps marched on with stolid countenances, but their officers were embarrassed. It is hard to return a salute with your face in the sand and a stout American sitting on your neck and pulling your first lieutenant's leg. I am now deeply engaged for dinners and dances and teas and rides and am feeling very cheerful again. I am also very well thank you and have no illnesses of any sort. You told me to be sure and put that in— As you see, I have cut out half of my trip to avoid the cholera, so you need not worry about *that*. To-day I am going over the ramparts as much as they will allow and to-morrow I go to Tangier where I expect to have some boar hunting. I would suggest your getting *The Evangelist* in a week or two as Dr. Field's letters cover all I have seen. I do not tell you anything about the place because you will read that in the paper to the H. W. but I can assure you the girls are very pretty and being garrison girls are not as shy as those at home in England. I am the first American they ever met they assure me every hour and we get on very well notwithstanding.

You can imagine what it is like when Spaniards, Moors and English Soldiers are all crowded into one long street with donkeys and geese and priests and smugglers and men in polo clothes and soldiers in football suits and sailors from the man-of-war. Of course, the Rock is the best story of it all. It is a fair green smiling hill not a fortress at all. No more a fortress to look at than Fairmont Park water works, but the joke of it is that under every bush there is a gun and every gun is painted green and covered with hanging curtains of moss and every promenade is undermined and the bleakest face of the rock is tunnelled with rooms and halls. Every night we are locked in and the soldiers carry the big iron keys clanking through the streets. It is going to make interesting reading.

DICK.

GIBRALTAR. February 23rd, 1893.

DEAR MOTHER:

Æneas who "ran the round of so many chances" in this neighborhood was a stationary stay at home to what I have to do. If I ever get away from the Rock I shall be a traveller of the greatest possible experience.

I came here intending to stay a week and to write my letter on Gib. and on Tangier quietly and peacefully like a gentleman and then to go on to Malta. I love this place and there is something to do and see every minute of the time but what happened was this: All the boats that ever left here stopped running, broke shafts, or went into quarantine or just sailed by, and unless I want to spend two weeks on the sea in order to have one at Malta, which is only a military station like this, I must go off to-morrow with my articles unwritten, my photos undeveloped and my dinner calls unpaid. I am now waiting to hear if I can get to Algiers by changing twice from one steamer to another along the coast of Spain. It will be a great nuisance but I shall be able to see Algiers and Tunis and Malta in the three weeks which would have otherwise been given to Malta alone. And Tunis I am particularly keen to see. While waiting for a telegram from Spain about the boats, I shall tell you what I have been doing. Everybody was glad to see me after my return from Tangier. I dined with the Governor on Monday, in a fine large room lined with portraits of all the old commanders and their coats-of-arms like a little forest of flags and the Governor's daughter danced a Spanish dance for us after it was over. Miss Buckle, Cust's fiancée, dances almost as well as Carmencita, all the girls here learn it as other girls do the piano. On Tuesday Cust and Miss B. and another girl and I went over into Spain to see the meet and we had a short run after a fox who went to earth, much to my relief, in about three minutes and before I had been thrown off. There are no fences but the ground is one mass of rocks and cactus and ravines down which these English go with an ease that makes me tremble with admiration. We had not come out to follow, so we, being quite soaked through and very hungry, went to an inn and it was such an inn as Don Quixote used to stop at, with the dining-room over the stable and a lot of drunken muleteers in the court and beautiful young women to wait on us. It is a beautiful country Spain, with every sort of green you ever dreamed of. We had omelettes and native wine and black bread and got warm again and then trotted home in the rain and got wet again, so we stopped at the guard house on the outside of the rock and took tea with the officer in charge and we all got down on our knees around his fire and he hobbled around dropping his eyeglasses in his hot water and very much honored and exceedingly embarrassed. I amused myself by putting on all the uniforms he did not happen to have on and the young ladies drank tea and thawed. This is the most various place I ever came across. You have mountains and seashore and allamandas like Monte Carlo in their tropical beauty and soldiers day and night marching and drilling and banging brass bands, and tennis and guns firing so as to rattle all the windows, and picnics and teas. I am engaged way ahead now but I must get off tomorrow. On Washington's birthday I gave a luncheon because it struck me as the most inappropriate place in which one could celebrate the good man's memory and the Governor would not think of coming at first, but I told him I was not a British subject and that if I could go to his dinner he could come to my lunch, so that, or the fact that the beautiful Miss Buckle was coming decided him to waive etiquette and he came with his A. D. C. and his daughter and officers and girls came and I had American flags and English flags and a portrait of

Washington and of the Queen and I ransacked the markets for violets and banked them all up in the middle. It was fine. I turned the hotel upside down and all the servants wore their best livery and everybody stood up in a row and saluted His Excellency and I made a speech and so did his Excellency and the chef did himself proud. I got it up in one morning. Helen Benedict could not have done it better.

I had a funny adventure the morning I left Tangier— There was a good deal of talk about Field (confound him) and my getting into the prison and *The Herald* and *Times* correspondents were rather blue about it and some of the English residents said that I had not been shown the whole of the prison, that the worst had been kept from us. Field who only got into the prison because I had worked at it two days, said there was an additional ward I had not seen. I went back into this while he and the guard were getting the door open to go out and saw nothing, but to make sure that the prison was as I believed an absolute square, I went back on the morning of my departure and climbed a wall and crawled over a house top and photographed the top of the prison. Then a horrible doubt came to me that this house upon which I was standing and which adjoined the prison might be the addition of which the English residents hinted. There was an old woman in the garden below jumping up and down and to whom I had been shying money to keep her quiet. I sent the guide around to ask her what was the nature of the building upon which I had trespassed and which seemed to worry her so much— He came back to tell me that I was on the top of a harem and the old woman thought I was getting up a flirtation with the gentleman's wives. So I dropped back again.

It will be a couple of months at least before my first story comes out in *The Weekly*. I cannot judge of them but I think they are up to the average of the Western stories, the material is much richer I know, but I am so much beset by the new sights that I have not the patience or the leisure I had in the West— Then there were days in which writing was a relief, now there is so much to see that it seems almost a shame to waste it.

By the grace of Providence I cannot leave here until the 28th, much to my joy and I have found out that I can do better by going direct to Malta and then to Tunis, leaving Algiers which I did not want to see out of it—Hurrah. I shall now return to the calm continuation of my story and to writing notes which Chas will enjoy.

DICK.

GIBRALTAR—February 1893.
DEAR MOTHER:

Morocco as it is is a very fine place spoiled by civilization. Not nice civilization but the dregs of it, the broken down noblemen of Spain and cashiered captains of England and the R—— L——'s of America. They hunt and play cricket and gamble and do nothing to maintain what is best in the place or to help what is worst. I love the Moors and the way they hate the Christian and the scorn and pride they show. They seem to carry all the mystery and dignity of Africa and of foreign conquests about them, and they are wonderfully well made and fine looking and self-respecting. The color is very beautiful, but the foreign element spoils it at every turn. One should really go inland but I shall not because I mean to do that when I reach Cairo. Everybody goes inland from here and Bonsal

THE MEDITERRANEAN AND PARIS 107

has covered it already. He is a great man here among all classes.

I have bought two long guns and three pistols three feet long and a Moorish costume for afternoon teas. I shall look fine. My guide's idea of pleasing me is to kick everybody out of the way which always brings down curses on me so I have to go back and give them money and am so gradually becoming popular and much sought after by blind beggars. You can get three pounds of copper for a franc and it lasts all day throwing it right and left all the time. I made a great tear in Bonsal's record today by refusing to pay a snake charmer all he wanted and then when he protested I took one of the snakes out of his hands and swung it around my head to the delight of the people. I wanted to show him he was a fakir to want me to pay for what I would do myself. It was a large snake about four feet long. Then my horse and another horse got fighting in the principal street in the city standing up on their hind legs and boxing like men and biting and squealing. It was awful and I got mine out of the way and was trod on and had my arm nearly pulled off and the crowd applauded and asked my guide whether I was American or English. They do not like the English. So with the lower classes I may say that I am having a social success.

DICK.

Off Malta—March 1, 1893.

DEAR MOTHER:

I have been having a delightful voyage with moonlight all night and sunlight all day. Africa kept in sight most of the time and before that we saw beautiful mountains in Spain covered with snow and red in the sunset. There were a lot of nice English people going out to India to meet their husbands and we have "tiffin" and "choota" and "curry," so it really seemed oriental. The third night out we saw Algiers sparkling like Coney Island. I play games with myself and pretend I am at my rooms reading a story which is very hard to pretend as I never read in my rooms and then I look up and exclaim "Hello, I'm not in New York, that's Algiers." The thing that has impressed me most is how absolutely small the world is and how childishly easy it is to go around it. You and Nora *must* take this trip; as for me I think Willie Chanler is the most sensible individual I have yet met.

All the fascination of King Solomon's Mines seems to be behind those great mountains and this I may add is a bit of advance work for mother, an entering wedge to my disappearing from sight for years and years in the Congo. Which, seriously, I will not do; only it is disappointing to find the earth so small and so easily encompassed that you want to go on where it is older, and new. The worst of it is that it is hard leaving all the nice people you meet and then must say good-bye to. The young ladies and Capt. Buckle and Cust came down to see me off and Buckle brought me a photo four feet long of Gib, an official one which I had to smuggle out with a great show of secrecy and now I shall be sorry to leave these people. Just as I wrote that one of the officers going out to join his regiment came to the door and blushing said the passengers were getting up a round robin asking me to stop on and go to Cairo.

Since writing the above lots of things have happened. I bid farewell to everyone at Malta and yet

THE MEDITERRANEAN AND PARIS

in four hours I was back again bag and baggage and am now on my way to Cairo. Tunis and the Bey are impossible. As soon as I landed at Malta I found that though I could go to Tunis I could not go away without being quarantined for ten days and if I remained in Malta I must stay a week. On balancing a week of Egypt against a week of Malta I could not do it so I put back to this steamer again and here I am. Tomorrow we reach Brindisi and we have already passed Sicily and had a glimpse of the toe of Italy and it is the coldest sunny Italy that I ever imagined. I am bitterly disappointed about Tunis. I have no letters to big people in Cairo only subalterns but I shall probably get along. I always manage somehow with my "artful little Ikey ways." It was most gratifying to mark my return to this boat. One young woman danced a Kangaroo dance and the Captain wept and all the stewards stood in a line and grinned. I sing Chevalier's songs and they all sit in the dining room below and forget to lay out the plates and last night some of the Royal Berkshire with whom I dined at Malta came on board and after hearing the Old Kent Road were on the point of Mutiny and refused to return to barracks. Great is the Power of Chevalier and great is his power for taking you back to London with three opening bars. Malta was the queerest place I ever got into. It was like a city, country and island made of cheese, mouldy cheese, and fresh limburger cheese with holes in it. You sailed right up to the front door as it were and people were hanging out of the windows smoking pipes and looking down on the deck as complacently as though having an ocean steamer in the yard was as much a matter of course as a perambulator. There were also women with black hoods which they wear as a penance because long ago the ladies of Malta got themselves talked about. I was on shore about five hours and saw some interesting things and with that and Brindisi and the voyage I can make a third letter but Tunis is writ on my heart like Calais.

Today Cleveland is inaugurated and I took all the passengers down at the proper time and explained to them that at that moment a great man was being made president and gave them each an American cocktail to remember it by and in which to toast him I am getting to be a great speech maker and if there are any more anniversaries in America I shall be a second Depew.

It is late but it is still the season here and it will be gay, but what I want to do now is to go off on a little trip inland although Cairo is the worst of all for it is surrounded by deserts and nothing to shoot but antelope and foxes and those I *scorn*. I want Zulus and lions. I shall be greatly disappointed if I do not have something to do outside of Cairo for I have had no adventures at all. It is just as civilized as Camden only more exciting and beautiful although Camden is exciting when you have to get there and back in time for the last edition. From what I have already seen I am ready to spend a month in Cairo and then confess to knowing nothing of it. But we shall see. There may be a W A R or a lion hunt or something yet if there is not I shall come back here again. I must fire that Winchester off at least once just for all the trouble it has given me at custom houses. Something exciting must happen or I shall lose faith in the luck of the British army which marches shoulder to shoulder with mine. If I don't have any adventures

I shall write essays on art after this like Mrs. Van. Love and lots of it.

DICK.

CAIRO, March 11, 1893.

DEAR MOTHER:

In a famous book this line occurs, "He determined to go to that hotel in Cairo where they were to have spent their honeymoon," or words like that. He is now at that hotel and you can buy the famous book across the street. It is called "Gallegher." So—in this way everything comes to him who waits and he comes to it. "Gallegher" is not the only thing you buy in Egypt. You ride to the Pyramids on a brake with a man in a white felt hat blowing a horn, and the bugler of the Army of Occupation is as much in evidence as the priest who calls them to prayer from the minaret. I left the people I liked on the *Sultey* last Thursday in the Suez Canal and came on here in a special train. It is very cold here, and it is not a place where the cold is in keeping with the surroundings. You see people in white helmets and astrakan overcoats. It is an immense city and intensely interesting, especially the bazaars, but you feel so ignorant about it all that it rather angers you. I wish I was not such a very bad hand at languages. That is *one thing* I cannot do, that and ride. I need it very much, traveling so much, and I shall study very hard while I am in Paris. Our consul-general here is a very young man, and he showed me a Kansas paper when I called on him, which said that I was in the East and would probably call on "Ed" L. He is very civil to me and gives me his carriages and outriders with gold clothes and swords whenever I will take them.

It is so beastly cold here that it spoils a lot of things, and there are a lot of Americans who say, "I had no idea you were so young a man," and that, after being five years old for a month and playing children's games with English people who didn't know or care anything about you except that you made them laugh, is rather trying. I am disappointed so far in the trip because it has developed nothing new beyond the fact that going around the world is of no more importance than going to breakfast, and I am selfish in my sight-seeing and want to see things others do not. And if you even do see more than those who are not so fortunate and who have to remain at home, still you are so ignorant in comparison with those who have lived here for years and to whom the whole of Africa is a speculation in land or railroads, it makes you feel like such a faker and as if it were better to turn correspondent for the N. Y. *Herald*, Paris edition, and send back the names of those who are staying at the hotels. That is really all you can speak with authority about. When you have Gordon and Stanley dishes on the bill-of-fare, you feel ashamed to say you've been in Egypt. Anyway, I am a faker and I don't care, and I proved it today by being photographed on a camel in front of the Pyramids, and if that wasn't impertinence I do not know its name. I accordingly went and bought a lot of gold dresses for Nora as a penance.

As a matter of fact, unless I get into the interior for a month and see something new, I shall consider the trip a failure, except as a most amusing holiday for one, and that was not exactly what I wanted or all I wanted. After this I shall go to big cities only and stay there. Everybody travels and everybody

THE MEDITERRANEAN AND PARIS 113

sees as much as you do and says nothing of it, certainly does not presume to write a book about it. Anyway, it has been great fun, so I shall put it down to that and do some serious work to make up for it. I'd rather have written a good story about the Inauguration than about Cairo.

I am well, as usual, and having a fine loaf, only I don't think much of what I have written—that's all.
DICK.

CAIRO, March 19th, 1893.
DEAR MOTHER:

I went up the Pyramids yesterday and I am very sore today. It sounds easy because so many people do it, but they do it because they don't know. I have been putting it off, and putting it off, until I felt ashamed to such a degree that I had to go. Little had never been either, so we went out together and met Stanford White and the Emmetts there, and we all went up. I would rather go into Central Africa than do it again. I am getting fat and that's about it—and I had to half pull a much fatter man than myself who pretended to help me. I finally told them I'd go alone unless the fat man went away, so the other two drove him off. Going down is worse. It's like looking over a precipice all the time. I was so glad when I got down that I sang with glee. I hate work like that, and to make it worse I took everybody's picture on top of the Pyramid, and forgot to have one of them take me, so there is no way to prove I ever went up. Little and I hired two donkeys and called them "Gallegher" and "Van Bibber" and raced them. My donkey was so little that they couldn't see him—only his ears. Gallegher won. The donkey-boys called it Von Bebey, so I don't think it will help the sale of the book.

Today we went to call on the Khedive. It was very informal and too democratic to suit my tastes. We went through a line of his bodyguard in the hall, and the master of ceremonies took us up several low but wide stairways to a hall. In the hall was a little fat young man in a frock coat and a fez, and he shook hands with us, and walked into another room and we all sat down on chairs covered with white muslin. I talked and Little talked about me and the Khedive pretended to be very much honored, and said the American who had come over after our rebellion had done more for the officers in his army than had anyone else, meaning the English. He did not say that because we were Americans, but because he hates the English. He struck me as being stubborn, which is one side of stupidity and yet not stupid, and I occasionally woke him to bursts of enthusiasm over the Soudanese. His bursts were chiefly "Ah." Little seemed to amuse him very much, and Little treated him exactly like a little boy who needed to be cheered up. I think in one way it was the most curious contrast I ever saw. "Ed" Little of Abilene, Kansas, telling the ruler of Egypt not to worry, that he had plenty of years in which to live and that he would get ahead of them all yet. Those were not his words, but that was the tone, he was perfectly friendly and sincere about it.

This place appeals to me as about the best place with which to get mixed up with that I know, and I've gone over a great many maps since I left home and know just how small the world is. So, I sent the Khedive my books after having asked his permission, and received the most abject thanks. And as Cromer called on me, I am going to drop around on him with a few of them. Some day there will be fine things going on here, and there is only one God, and Lord Cromer is his Prophet in this country. They think that Mohammed is but they are wrong. He is a very big man. The day he sent his ultimatum to the Khedive telling him to dismiss Facta Pasha and put back Riaz Pasha, he went out in full view of the Gezerik drive and played lawn tennis. Any man who can cable for three thousand more troops to Malta and stop a transport full of two thousand more at Aden with one hand, and bang tennis balls about with the other, is going in the long run to get ahead of a stout little boy in a red fez. It is getting awfully hot here, almost hot enough for me, and I can lay aside my overcoat by ten o'clock in the morning. Everyone else has been in flannels and pith helmets, but as they had to wear overcoats at night I could not see the advantage of the costume.

DICK.

I open this to say that *all* of your letters have just come, so I have intoxicated myself with them for the last hour and can go over them again tomorrow. I cannot tell you, dearest, what a delight your letters are and how I enjoy the clippings. I think of you all the time and how you would love this Bible land and seeing the places where Pharaoh's daughter found Moses, and hearing people talk of St. Paul and the plagues of Egypt and Joseph and Mary just as though they had lived yesterday. I have seen two St. Johns already, with long hair and melancholy wild eyes and bare breasts and legs, with sheepskin covering, eating figs and preaching their gospel. Yesterday two men came running into town and told one of the priests that they had seen the new moon in a certain well, and the priest proclaimed a month of fasting, and the men who pulled us up the Pyramid had to rest because they had not eaten or drunk all day. At six a sheik called from the village and all the donkey-boys and guides around the Sphinx ran to get water and coffee and food. Think of that—of two men running through the street to say that they had seen the new moon in a well, when every shop sells Waterbury watches and the people who passed them were driving dogcarts with English coachmen in top-boots behind. Is there any other place as incongruous as this, as old and as new?

DICK.

ATHENS, March 30, 1893.

DEAR MOTHER:

I am now in Athens, how I got here is immaterial. Suffice it to say that never in all my life was I so ill as I was in the two days crossing from Alexandria to Piraeus, which I did with two other men in *the same cabin* more ill than I and praying and swearing and groaning all the time. "It was awful."

> "I have crossed in many ships upon the seas
>   And some of them were good and some were not;
>   In German, P & O's and Genoese,
>   But the Khedive's was the worst one of the lot.
>   We never got a moment's peace in her
>   For everybody'd howl or pray or bellow;
>   She threw us on our heads or on our knees,
>   And turned us all an unbecoming yellow."

Athens is a small town but fine. It is chiefly yellow houses with red roofs, and mountains around it, which

THE MEDITERRANEAN AND PARIS 117

remind you of pictures you have seen when a youth. Also olive trees and straight black pines and the Acropolis. There is not much of it left as far as I can see from the city, but what there is is enough to make you wish you had brushed up your Greek history. I have now reached the place where Pan has a cave, where the man voted against Aristides because he was humanly tired of hearing him called the Just and where the Minotaur ate young women.

What was in the Isle of Crete but the rock from which the father of Theseus threw himself—is still here! Also the hill upon which Paul stood and told the Athenians they were too superstitious. You can imagine my feelings at finding all of these things are true. After this I am going to the North Pole to find Santa Claus and so renew my youth.

I regret to say that it is raining very hard and Athens is not set for a rainstorm. It is also cold but as I have not been warm since I crossed the North River with Chas. amid cakes of ice that is of no consequence. When I come here again I come in the summer. The good old rule that it is cold in winter and warm in summer is a good enough rule to follow. You have only to travel to find out how universally cold winter is. The last night I was in Cairo, I got in a carriage and drove out alone to the Pyramids. It was beautiful moonlight. I got a donkey and rode up around them and then walked over to the Sphinx. I had never understood or seen it before. It was the creepiest and most impressive thing I ever had happen to me, I do believe. There was no one except the two donkey-boys and myself and the Sphinx. All about was the desert and above it the purple sky and the white stars and the great negro's head in front of you with its paws stretched out, and the moonlight turning it into shadows and white lines. I think I stood there so long that I got sort of dizzy. It was just as if I had been the first man to stumble across it, and I felt that I was way back thousands of years and that the ghosts of Cæsar and Napoleon and Cleopatra and the rest were in the air. That was worth the entire trip to me. This place promises to be most exciting, the New York artists are all here, they are the most jauntily dull people I ever met. Do you know what I mean? They are very nice but so stupid. I don't let them bother me. Who was the chap who wrote about the bottle of Malvoisie? because I got a bottle of it for *breakfast* and it is *no good*. It is like sweet port. But on account of the poem and its being *vin du pays* I got it.

Dear Mother, I wish you were here now and enjoying all these beautiful things. I got you a present in Cairo that will amuse you. Had I stayed on in Cairo I should have had much and many marks of distinction from the English. Lady Gower-Browne, who found out from them that I had called and that they had done nothing except to be rude, raised a great hue and cry and everything changed. What she said of me I don't know but it made a most amusing difference. General Walker galloped a half mile across the desert to give me his own copy of the directions for the sham battle, and I was to have met Cromer at dinner tête-à-tête, and General Kitchener sent apologies by two other generals and all the subalterns called on me in a body. That was the day before I left. I don't know what Lady Gower-Browne said, but it made a change which I am sorry I could not avail myself of as I want politics as well as memories.

THE MEDITERRANEAN AND PARIS 119

The next time I come I shall go to even fewer places and see more people.

If the Harpers don't look out our interests will clash. I look at it like this. I can always see the old historical things and take my children up the Nile, but I want now to make friends with the Mammon of unrighteousness and the men of the hour. I may want to occupy an hour or two myself some day and they can help me. If America starts in annexing islands she will need people to tell her how it is generally done and it is generally done, I find, by the English. I may give up literature and start annexing things like Alexander and Cæsar and Napoleon. They say there will be another crisis in Cairo in a month or so. If that be true I am all right and solid with both parties. But it has got to be worth while of course or I won't go back. There is a king living in a fine palace across the square from my window, one of his officers is now changing the guard in the rain. I hope to call on the king because I like his guard. They wear petticoats and toes turned up in front. Don't you mind what I say about liking politics and don't think I am not enjoying the show things. I have a capacity for both that is so far unsatisfied, and I am now going out in the rain to try and find the postoffice. Lots of love.

DICK.

I am well and have been well (except sea sick) since February 4th.

P. S.—A funeral is just passing the window with the corpse exposed to view as is the quaint custom here, to add to its horror they rouge the face of the corpse and everybody kisses it. In the Greek church they burn candles for people and the number of candles I have burnt for you would light St. Paul's, and you ought to be good with so much wax being expended all over Athens for you. You buy candles instead of tipping the verger or putting it in the poor box, or because you are superstitious and think it will do some good, as I do.

Orient Express. Somehwere in Bulgaria on
the way to London.
April 14th, 1893.

DEAR MOTHER:

Tuesday I wrote you a letter in the club at Constantinople telling you how glad I would be to get out of that City on April 17th on the Orient Express which only leaves twice a week on Thursdays and Mondays. So any one who travels by the Orient is looked upon first as a millionaire and second, if he does not break the journey at Vienna, as a greater traveller than Col. Burnaby on his way to Khiva. Imagine a Kansas City man breaking the journey to New York. After I wrote you that letter I went in the next room and read of the Nile Expedition in search of Gordon—this went through three volumes of *The Graphic* and took some time, so that when I had reached the picture which announced the death of Gordon it was half past five and I had nothing more to do for four days— It was raining and cold and muddy and so I just made up my mind I would get up and get out and I jumped about for one hour like a kangaroo and by seven I was on the Orient with two Cook men to help me and had shaken my fist at the last minaret light of that awful city. So, now it is all over and it is done— I have learned a great deal in an imperfect way of the juxtaposition of certain countries and of the ease with which one can travel without speaking any known languages and of the absolute necessity for speaking one, French. I am still disappointed about the articles but selfishly I have made a lot out of the trip. You have no idea how hard it is not to tell about strange things and yet you know people do not care half as much for them as things they know all about— No matter, it is done and with the exception of the last week it was F I N E.

"I'm going back to London, to 'tea' and long frock coats
   I'm done with Cook and seeing sights
   I'm done with table d'hôtes
   So clear the track you signal man
   From Sofia to Pless, I'm going straight for London
   On the Orient Express.

I'm going straight for London
O'er Bulgaria's heavy sands
To Rotten Row and muffins, soles,
Chevalier and Brass Bands
Ho' get away you bullock man
You've heard the whistle blowed
There's a locomotive coming down the Grand Trunk Road."

This is a great country and I want to ask all the natives if they know "Stenie" Bonsal. They are all his friends and so are the "Balkans," and all the little Balkans. Nobody wears European clothes here. They are all as foreign and native and picturesque as they can be, the women with big silver plates over their stomachs and the men in sheepskin and tights and the soldiers are grand. We have been passing all day between snow covered mountains and between herds of cattle and red roofed, mud villages and long lakes of ice and snow— It is a beautiful day and I am very happy. (Second day out) 15th— We are now in Hungary and just outside of Buda Pesth "the wickedest city in the world," still in spite of that fact I am going on. I am very glad I came this way— The peasants and soldiers are most amusing and like German picture-papers with black letter type— I shall stop a day in Paris now that I have four extra days.

DICK.

In sight of Paris—April 16—1893.
DEAREST MOTHER:

This has been the most beautiful day since February 4th. It is the first day in which I have been warm. All through I have had a varnish of warmth every now and again but no real actual internal warmth— I am now in sight of Paris and it is the 16th of April, in the eleven weeks which have elapsed since the 4th of February I have been in Spain, France, Italy, Germany, Austria, Hungary, Serbia, Bulgaria, Turkey, Greece, Egypt and Morocco. I have sat on the Rock of Gibraltar, sailed on the Nile and the Suez Canal and crossed through the Dardanelles, over the Balkans, the steppes of Hungary and the Danube and Rhine. I have seen the sphinx by moonlight, the Parthenon and the Eiffel Tower and in two days more I shall have seen St. Paul's. What do you think I should like to see best now? *YOU*. I have been worrying of late as to whether or not I should not come home now and leave Paris for another time because it seems so rough on you to leave you without either of your younger sons for so long. But I have thought it over a great deal and I think it better that I should do

Paris now and leave myself clear for the rest of the year. I promise you one thing however that I shall not undertake to stay away so long again; it is too long and one grows out of things. But nothing I feel will be so easy or so amusing as Paris and I intend to get through with it soon and trot home to you by the middle of August *at the very latest.* So, please write me a deceitful letter and say you do not miss me at all and that my being so near as Paris makes a great difference and that I am better out of the way and if Chas goes to London I shall be near him in case he forgets to put on his overshoes or involves us in a war with G. B. Now, mother dear, do write me a cheerful letter and say that you do not mind waiting until the middle of August for me and when I come back this time I shall make a long stay with you at Marion and tell you lots of things I have not written you and I shall not go away again for ever so long and if I do go I shall only stay a little while. You have no idea how interesting this rush across the continent has been. I started in snow and through marshes covered with ice and long horned cattle and now we are in such a beautiful clean green land with green fields and green trees and flowering bushes which you can smell as the train goes by. I now think that instead of being a café-chantant singer I should rather be an Austrian baron and own a castle on a hill with a red roofed village around it. I have spent almost all of the trip sitting on the platform and enjoying the sight of the queer peasants and the soldiers and old villages. Tonight I shall be in "Paris, France" as Morton used to say and I shall get clean and put on my dress clothes but whether I shall go see Yvette Guilbert or Rusticana again I do not know. Perhaps

I shall just paddle around the fountain in the Place de la Concorde and make myself thoroughly at home. With a great deal of love to Dad and Nora and Chas and all.

Dick.

At the time that Richard's first travel articles appeared some of his critics took umbrage at the fact that he was evidently under the delusion that he had discovered London, Gibraltar, Athens, Paris, and the other cities he had visited, and that no one else had ever written about them. As a matter of fact no one could have been more keenly conscious of what an oft-told tale were the places that he had chosen to describe. If Richard took it for granted that the reader was totally unacquainted with the peoples of these cities and their ways, it was because he believed that that was the best way to write a descriptive article, always had believed it, and believed it so long as he wrote. And whatever difference of opinion may have existed among the critics and the public as to Richard's fiction, I think it is safe to say that as a reporter his work of nearly thirty years stood at least as high as that of any of his contemporaries or perhaps as that of the reporters of all time. As an editor, when he gave out an assignment to a reporter to write an article on some well-worn subject and the reporter protested, Richard's answer was the same: "You must always remember that that story hasn't been written until *you* write it." And when he suggested to an editor that he would like to write an article on Broadway, or the Panama Canal, or the ruins of Rome and the editor disapproved, Richard's argument was: "It hasn't been done until *I* do it." And it was not because he believed for a moment that he could do it better or as well as it had been done. It was simply because he knew the old story was always a good story, that is, if it was seen with new eyes and from a new standpoint. At twenty-eight he had written a book about England and her people, and the book had met with much success both in America and England. At twenty-nine, equally unafraid, he had "covered" the ancient cities that border the Mediterranean, and now Paris lay before him! This thought—indeed few thoughts—troubled Richard very much in those days of his early successes. He had youth, friends, a marvellous spirit of adventure, and besides there are many worse fates than being consigned to spending a few months in Paris, having a thoroughly joyous time, taking a few mental notes, and a little later on transferring them to paper in the quiet of a peaceful summer home at Marion.

Chief among his friends in Paris at this time was Charles Dana Gibson, who was living in a charming old house in the Latin Quarter, and where the artist did some of his best work and made himself extremely popular with both the Parisians and the American colony. In addition to Gibson there were Kenneth Frazier, the portrait-painter, and Tina, Newton, and James Eustis, the daughter and sons of James B. Eustis, who at that time was our ambassador to France, a most genial and kindly host, who made much of Richard and his young friends.

PARIS, May 5, 1893.
DEAR MOTHER:
It is a narrow street with apartment houses of gray stone and iron balconies along either side of it. The sun sets at one end of the street at different times dur-

ing the day and we all lean out on the balconies to look. On the house, one below mine, on the other side of our street, is a square sign that says:

ALFRED DE MUSSET
EST MORT DANS CETTE MAISON

A great many beautiful ladies with the fashionable red shade of hair still call there, as they used to do when the proper color was black and it was worn in a chignon and the Second Empire had but just begun. While they wait they stretch out in their carriages and gaze up at the balconies until they see me, and as I wear a gold and pink silk wrapper and not much else, they concentrate all their attention on the wrapper and forget to drop a sigh for the poet. There are two young people on the sixth floor opposite, who come out on the balcony after dinner and hold on to each other and he tells her all about the work of the day. Below there is a woman who sews nothing but black dresses, and who does that all day and all night by the light of a lamp. And below the concierge stands all day in a lace cap and black gown and blue, and looks up the street and down the street like the woman in front of Hockley's. *But* on the floor opposite mine there is a beautiful lady in a pink and white wrapper with long black hair and sleepy black eyes. She does not take any interest in my pink wrapper, but contents herself with passing cabs and stray dogs and women with loaves of bread and bottles in their hands who occasionally stray into our street. At six she appears in another gown and little slippers and a butterfly for a hat and says "Good-by" to the old concierge and trips off to dinner. Lots of love to all.

DICK.

PARIS, May 11th, 1893.

DEAR MOTHER:

I am still somewhat tentative as regards my opinion of the place, what it will bring me in the way of material I cannot tell. So far, "Paris Decadent" would be a good title for anything I should write of it. It is not that I have seen only the worst side of it but that that seems to be so much the most prominent. They worship the hideous Eiffel Tower and they are a useless, flippant people who never sleep and yet do nothing while awake. To-morrow I am going to a pretty inn surrounded by vines and trees to see a prize fight with all the silly young French men and their young friends in black and white who ape the English manners and customs even to "la box." To night at the Ambassadeurs the rejected lover of some actress took a gang of bullies from Montmartre there and hissed and stoned her. I turned up most innocently and greatly bored in the midst of it but I was too far away to pound anybody— I collected two Englishmen and we went in front to await her re-appearance but she had hysterics and went off in a cab and so we were not given a second opportunity of showing them they should play fair. It is a typical incident of the Frenchman and has made me wrathy. The women watching the prize fight will make a good story and so will the arms of the red mill, "The Moulin Rouge" they keep turning and turning and grinding out health and virtue and souls.

I dined to night with the C——s and P——s, the Ex-Minister and disagreed with everybody and found them all very middle class as to intellect. An old English lady next to me said apropos of something "that is because you are not clever like Mr. —— and do not have to work with your brains." To which I said, "I did not mind not being clever as my father was a many times millionaire," at which she became abjectly polite. Young Rothenstein is going to do a picture of me to-morrow morning. There is nothing much more to tell except that a horse stood on his fore legs in the Bois the other day and chucked me into space. I was very sore but I went on going about as it was the Varnishing day at the new salon and I wished to see it. I am over my stiffness now and if "anybody wants to buy a blooming bus" I have one for sale and five pairs of riding breeches and two of ditto boots. No more riding for me— The boxing bag is in good order now and I do not need for exercise. The lady across the street has a new wrapper in which she is even more cold and haughty than before. "I sing Tarrara boom deay and she keeps from liking me."

DICK.

PARIS, May 14th, 1893.

DEAR NORA:

Things are getting more interesting here and I shall probably have something to write about after all, although I shall not know the place as I did London. Will Rothenstein has drawn a picture of me that I like very much and if mother likes it *very, very* much she may have it as a loan but she may not like it. I did not like to take it so I bought another picture of him, one of Coquelin cadet and now I have two. Coquelin gave him his first commission when he was nineteen, two years ago, and then asked him to do two sketches. After these were done Coquelin told him by letter that he would give him half what they had agreed upon for the big picture for the two sketches

THE MEDITERRANEAN AND PARIS

and begged the big picture as a gift. So Rothenstein cut the head and shoulders out of the big one and sent him the arms and legs. It is the head he cut out that I have. When Rothenstein and I and Coquelin become famous, that will make a good story. I have also indulged myself in the purchase of several of Cherets works of art. They cost three francs apiece. We have had some delightful lunches at the Ambassadeurs with Cushing and other artists and last night I went out into the Grande Monde to a bal masque for charity at the palace of the Comtesse de la Ferrondeux. It was very stupid and the men outnumbered the women 30 to 1, which are interesting odds. To-day we went to Whistler's and sat out in a garden with high walls about it and drank tea and laughed at Rothenstein. The last thing he said was at the Ambassadeurs when one of the students picking up a fork said, "These are the same sort of forks I have." Rothenstein said "yes, I did not know you dined here that often." Some one asked him why he wore his hair long, "To test your manners" he answered. He is a disciple of Whistler's and Wilde's and said "yes, I defend them at the risk of their lives." Did I tell you of his saying "It is much easier to love one's family than to like them." And when some one said "Did you hear how Mrs. B. treated Mr. C., (a man he dislikes) he said, "no, but I'm glad she did." It was lovely at Whistler's and such a contrast to the other American salon I went to last Sunday. It was so quiet, and green and pretty and everybody was so unobtrusively polite.

Rothenstein wore my rosette and made a great sensation and I was congratulated by Whistler and Abbey and Pennell. Rothenstein said he was going to have a doublebreasted waistcoat made with rosettes of decorations for buttons. Tomorrow Lord Dufferin has asked me to breakfast at the Embassy. He was at the masked ball last night and was very nice. He reminds me exactly of Disraeli in appearance. It is awfully hot here and a Fair for charity has asked me to put my name in "Gallegher" to have it raffled for. "Dear" Bonsal arrives here next Sunday, so I am in great anticipation. I am very well, tell mother, and amused. Lots of love.

DICK.

PARIS, June 13, 1893.

DEAR MOTHER:

There is nothing much to say except that things still go on. I feel like one of those little India rubber balls in the jet of a fountain being turned and twisted and not allowed to rest. Today I have been to hear Yvette Guilbert rehearse and thought her all Chas thinks her only her songs this season are beneath the morals of a medical student. It is very hot and it is getting hotter. I had an amusing time at the Grand Prix where Tina won a lot of money on a tip I gave her which I did not back myself. In the evening Newton took me to dinner and to the Jardin de Paris where they had 10 franc admittance and where every thing went that wasn't nailed. The dudes put candles on their high hats and the girls snuffed them out with kicks and at one time the crowd mobbed the band stand and then the stage and played on all the instruments. The men were all swells in evening dress and the women in beautiful ball dresses and it was a wonderful sight. It only happens once a year like the Yale-Princeton night at Koster and Bials except that the women are all very fine indeed. They rode pig-a-back races and sang all the songs. I had dinner with John Drew last night. I occasionally sleep and if Nora doesn't come on time I shall be a skeleton and have no money left. As a matter of fact I am fatter than ever and can eat all sorts of impossible things here that I could never eat at home. I lunch every day with the Eustises and we dine out almost every night. I consort entirely with the poorest of art students or the noblest of princesses and so far have kept out of mischief, but you can never tell for this is a wicked city they say, or it strikes me as most amusing at present only I cannot see what Harper and Bros. are going to get out of it. I said that of London so I suppose it will all straighten out by the time I get back.

DICK.

CHAPTER VII

FIRST PLAYS

When the season in Paris had reached its end, Richard returned to London and later on to Marion, where he spent the late summer and early fall, working on his Mediterranean and Paris articles, and completing his novel "Soldiers of Fortune." In October he returned to New York and once more assumed his editorial duties and took his usual active interest in the winter's gayeties.

The first of these letters refers to a dinner of welcome given to Sir Henry Irving. The last two to books by my mother and Richard, and which were published simultaneously.

New York, November 27, 1893.

Dear Mother:

The dinner was very fine. I was very glad I went. Whitelaw Reid sat on one side of Sir Henry Irving and Horace Porter on the other. Howells and Warner came next. John Russell Young and Mark Twain, Millet, Palmer, Hutton, Gilder and a lot more were there. There were no newspaper men, not even critics nor actors there, which struck me as interesting. The men were very nice to me. Especially Young, Reid, Irving and Howells. Everybody said when I came in, "I used to know you when you were a little boy," so that some one said finally, "What a disagreeable little boy you *must* have been." I sat next a chap from Brazil who told me lots of amusing things. One story if it is good saves a whole day for me. One he told was of a German explorer to whom Don Pedro gave an audience. The Emperor asked him, with some touch of patronage, if he had ever met a king before. "Yes," the German said thoughtfully; "five, three wild and two tame."

Mark Twain told some very funny stories, and captured me because I never thought him funny before, and Irving told some about Stanley, and everybody talked interestingly. Irving said he was looking forward to seeing Dad when he reached Philadelphia. "It is nice to have seen you," he said, "but I have still to see your father," as though I was not enough.

DICK.

NEW YORK, 1893.
DEAREST MOTHER:

I cannot tell you how touched and moved I was by the three initials in the book. It was a genuine and complete surprise and when I came across it while I was examining the letterpress with critical approbation and with no idea of what was to come, it left me quite breathless— It was so sweet of you— You understand me and I understand you and you know how much that counts to me— I think the book is awfully pretty and in such good taste— It is quite a delight to the eye and I am much more keen about it than over any of my own— I have sent it to some of my friends but I have not read it yet myself, as I am waiting until I get on the boat where I shall not be disturbed— Then I shall write you again— It was awfully good of you, and I am so pleased to have it to give away. I never had anything to show people when they asked for one of your other books and this comes in such an unquestionable form— With lots of love.

DICK.

NEW YORK, 1893.

DEAR MOTHER:

I got your nice letter and one from Dad. Both calling me many adjectives pleasing to hear although they do not happen to fit. So you are in a third edition are you? These *young* writers are crowding me to the wall. I feel thrills of pride when I see us sitting cheek by jowl on the news-stands.

Lots of love. DICK.

In February, 1894, Richard was forced by a severe attack of sciatica to give up temporarily the gayeties of New York and for a cure he naturally chose our home in Philadelphia, where he remained for many weeks. Although unable to leave his bed, he continued to do a considerable amount of work, including the novelette "The Princess Aline," in the writing of which I believe my brother took more pleasure than in that of any story or novel he ever wrote. The future Empress of Russia was the heroine of the tale, and that she eventually read the story and was apparently delighted with it caused Richard much human happiness.

PHILADELPHIA.
March 5th.

DEAR CHAS:

I am getting rapidly better owing to regular hours and light literature and home comforts. I am not blue as I was and my morbidness has gone and I only get depressed at times. I am still however feeling tired and I think I will take quite a rest before I venture across the seas. But across them I will come no matter if all the nerves on earth jump and pull. Still, I think it wiser for all concerned that I get thoroughly well so that when I do come I won't have to be cutting back home again as I did last time. We are young yet and the world's wide and there's a new farce comedy written every minute and I have a great many things to do myself so I intend to get strong and then do them. I enclose two poems. I am going to have them printed for my particular pals later. I am writing one to all of you folks over there.

DICK.

TAKE ME BACK TO BROADWAY, WHERE THE ORCHIDS GROW

WITH APOLOGIES TO THE WESTERN DIALECT POETS

"I have wandered up and down somewhat in many different lands
I have been to Fort Worth, Texas, and I've tramped through Jersey sands,
I have seen Pike's Peak by Moonlight, and I've visited the Fair
And to save enumeration I've been nearly everywhere.
But no matter where I rested and no matter where I'd go,
I have longed to be on Broadway
    Where
      the
       Orchids
        Grow.

Some people love the lilies fair that hide in mossy dells
Some folks are fond of new mown hay, before the rainy spells
But give to me the orchids rare that hang in Thorley's store,
And in Fleischman's at the Hoffman, and in half a dozen more
And when I see them far from home they make my heart's blood glow

For they take me back to Broadway
   Where
     the
       Orchids
         Grow.

Let Paris boast of boulevards where one can sit and drink
There is no such chance on Broadway, at the Brower House,
 'I don't think.'
And where else are there fair soubrettes in pipe clayed tennis
 shoes,
And boys in silken sashes promenading by in twos
Oh you can boast of any street of which you're proud to know
But give me sleepy Broadway
   Where
     the
       Orchids
         Grow.

Let poets sing of chiming bells and gently lowing kine
I like the clanging cable cars like fire engines in line
And I never miss the sunset and for moonlight never sigh
When 'Swept by Ocean Breezes,' flashes out against the sky.
And when the Tenderloin awakes, and open theatres glow
I want to be on Broadway
   Where
     the
       Orchids
         Grow."

    . . . .

À VOUS, JOHN DREW

"John Drew, I am your debtor
For a very pleasant letter
And a lot of cabinet photos
Of the 'Butterflies' and you.
And I think it very kind
That you kept me so in mind
And pitied me in exile
So I do, John Drew.

With John Drew at Marion, 1909.

2

John Drew, 'twixt you and me
Precious little I can see
Of that good there is in Solitude
That poets say they view.
For *I* hate to be in bed
With a candle at my head
Sitting vis à vis with Conscience.
So would you, John Drew.

3

John Drew, then promise me
That as soon as I am free
I may sit in the first entrance
As Lamb always lets me do.
And watch you fume and fret
While the innocent soubrette
Takes the centre of the stage a—
Way from you, John Drew."

R. H. D.

In the summer of 1894 Richard went to London for a purely social visit, but while he was there President Carnot was assassinated, and he went to Paris to write the "story" of the funeral and of the election of the new President.

VERSAILLES, June 24, 1894.

I am out here to see the election of the new President. I jumped on the mail coach and came off in a hurry without any breakfast, but I had a pretty drive out, and the guard and I talked of London. The palace is closed and no one is admitted except by card, so I have seen only the outside of it. It is most interesting. There is not a ribbon or a badge; not a banner or a band. The town is as quiet as always, and there are not 200 people gathered at the gate through which the deputies pass. Compared to an election convention in Chicago, it is most interesting. How lively it is inside of the chamber where the thing is going on I cannot say. I shall not wait to hear the result, but will return on the coach.

Nothing could be more curious than the apparent indifference of the people of Paris to the assassination of the President. Two days after he died there was not a single flag at half mast among the private residences. The Government buildings, the hotels and the stores were all that advertised their grief. I shall have an interesting story to write of it for the Parisian series. Dana Gibson and I will wait until after the funeral and then go to Andorra. If he does not go, I may go alone, but perhaps I shall go back to London at once. This has been an interesting time here, but only because it is so different from what one would expect. It reads like a burlesque to note the expressions of condolence from all over the world, and to mark the self-satisfaction of the French at attracting so much sympathy, and their absolute indifference to the death of Carnot. It is most curious. We have an ideal time. Never before have I had such jolly dinners, with such good talk and such amusing companions.

DICK.

LONDON, July 15, 1894.
DEAR MOTHER:

Mr. Irving gave a supper last night to Mme. Bernhardt and Mme. Réjane. There were about twenty people, and we ate in the Beefsteak Room of the Lyceum Theater, which is so called after the old Beefsteak Club which formerly met there. I had a most

FIRST PLAYS

delightful time, and talked to all the French women and to Miss Terry, who sent her love to Dad. She said, "I did not see him this last visit; that is, I saw him but I did not *see* him." Her daughter is a very sweet girl, and the picture Miss Terry made on her knees looking up at Bernhardt and Réjane when they chattered in French was wonderful. Neither she nor Irving could speak a word of French, and whenever any one else tried, the crowd all stood in a circle and applauded and guyed them. After it was over, at about three in the morning, Miss Terry offered me a lift home in her open carriage, so she and her daughter and I rode through the empty streets in the gray light for miles and miles, as, of course, I did not get out of such company any sooner than I had to do. They had taken Irving's robe of cardinal red and made it into cloaks, and they looked very odd and eerie with their yellow hair and red capes, and talking as fast as they could.

DICK.

CHAPTER VIII

CENTRAL AND SOUTH AMERICA

About January 1, 1895, Richard accompanied by his friends Somers Somerset and Lloyd C. Griscom, afterward our minister to Tokio and ambassador to Brazil and Italy, started out on a leisurely trip of South and Central America. With no very definite itinerary, they sailed from New Orleans, bent on having a good time, and as many adventures as possible, which Richard was to describe in a series of articles. These appeared later on in a volume entitled "Three Gringos in Venezuela."

January, 1895.

Dear Fam:

On board *Breakwater* at anchor. You will be pleased to hear that I am writing this in a fine state of perspiration in spite of the fact that I have light weight flannels, no underclothes and all the windows open. It is going to storm and then it will be cooler. We have had a bully time so far although the tough time is still to come, that will be going from Puerto Cortez to Tegucigalpa. At Belize the Governor treated us charmingly and gave us orderlies and launches and lunches and advice and me a fine subject for a short story. For nothing has struck me as so sad lately as did Sir Anthony Moloney K. C. M. G. watching us go off laughing and joking in his gilded barge to wherever we pleased and leaving him standing alone on his lawn with some papers to sign and then a dinner tête-à-tête with his Secretary and so on to the end of his life. It was pathetic to hear him listen to all the gossip from the outside world and to see how we pleased him when we told him we were getting more bald than he was and that he would make a fine appearance in the Row at his present weight. He had not heard of Trilby!!

We struck a beautiful place today called Livingston where we went ashore and photographed the army in which there was no boy older than eighteen and most of them under ten. It was quite like Africa, the homes were all thatched and the children all naked and the women mostly so. We took lots of photographs and got on most excellently with the natives who thought we were as funny as we thought them. Almost every place we go word has been sent ahead and agents and consuls and custom house chaps come out to meet me and ask what they can do. This is very good and keeps Griscom and Somerset in a proper frame of awe. But seriously I could not ask for better companions, they are both enormously well informed and polite and full of fun. The night the Governor asked Somers to dinner and did not ask us we waited up for him and then hung him out over the side of the boat above the sharks until he swore he would never go away from us again. Griscom is more aggravatingly leisurely but he has a most audacious humor and talks to the natives in a way that fills them with pleasure but which nearly makes Somers and I expose the whole party by laughing. Today we lie here taking in banannas and tomorrow I will see Conrad, Conrad, Conrad!! Send this to the Consul. Lots of love.

DICK.

SAN PEDRO—SULA—February, 1895.

MY DEAR FAMILY:

The afternoon of the day we were in Puerto Cortez the man of war *Atlanta* steamed into the little harbor and we all cheered and the lottery people ran up the American flag. Then I and the others went out to her as fast as we could be rowed and I went over the side and the surprise of the officers was very great. They called Somers and Griscom to come up and we spent the day there. They were a much younger and more amusing lot of fellows than those on the *Minneapolis* and treated us most kindly. It was a beautiful boat and each of us confessed to feeling quite tempted to go back again to civilization after one day on her. Their boat had touched at Tangier and so they claimed that she was the one meant in the Exiles. They told me that the guide Isaac Cohen whom I mentioned in *Harper's Weekly* carries it around as an advertisement and wanted to ship with them as cabin boy. We left the next day on the railroad and the boys finding that two negroes sat on the cowcatcher to throw sand on the rails in slippery places bribed them for their places and I sat on the sand box. I never took a more beautiful drive. We did not go faster than an ordinary horse car but still it was exciting and the views and vistas wonderful. Sometimes we went for a half mile under arches of cocoanut palms and a straight broad leafed palm called the manaca that rises in separate leaves sixty feet from the ground. Imagine a palm such as we put in pots at weddings and teas as high as Holy Trinity Church and hundreds and hundreds of them. The country is very like Cuba but more luxuriant in every way. There are some trees with marble like trunks

Three Gringos in Venezuela.
Somers Somerset, R. H. D., and Lloyd C. Griscom.

and great branches covered with oriole nests and a hundred orioles flying in and out of them or else plastered with orchids. If Billy Furness were to see in what abundance they grew he would be quite mad. It is a great pity he did not come with us. This little town is the terminus of the railroad and we have been here four days while Jeffs the American Colonel in the Hondurean Army is getting our outfit. It has been very pleasant and we are in no hurry which is a good thing for us. It is a most exciting country and as despotic as all uncivilized and unstable governments must be. But we have called on the Governor of the district with Jeffs and he gave us a very fine letter to all civil and unmilitary authorities in the district calling on them to aid and protect us in every way. I am getting awfully good material for my novel and for half a dozen stories to boot only I am surprised to find how true my novel was to what really exists here. About ten years ago —— disappeared, having as I thought drunk himself to death. He came up to me here on my arrival with a lot of waybills in his hand and I learned that he had been employed in this hole in the ground by a railroad for two years. I remembered meeting him at Newport when I was still at Lehigh, and last night he asked me to dinner and told me what he had been doing which included everything from acting in South America to blacking boots in Australia. His boss was a Pittsburgh engineer who is apparently licking him into shape and who told me to tell his father that he had stopped drinking absolutely. His colored "missus" sat with us at the table and played with a beetle during the three hours I stayed there during which time he asked me about —— who he said had ruined him. He told me of how —— had done and said this, and the contrast to the thatched roof and the mud floor and the Scotch American engineer and the mulatto girl was rather striking. I never had more luck in any trip than I have had on this one and the luck of R. H. D. of which I was fond of boasting seems to hold good. That man of war, for instance, was the only American one that had touched at Puerto Cortez in *ten* years and it came the day we did and left the day we did. We saw a big lithograph of Eddie Sothern in a palm hut here so we went before a notary and swore to it and had three seals put on the paper and sent it him as a joke. We start tomorrow the 22nd so you see we are behind our schedule and I suppose you people are all worried to death about us. We will be much longer than six days on our way to Tegucigalpa as we are going shooting and also to pay our respects to Bogran the ex-president and the man who is getting up the next revolution. But we take care to tell everyone we are travelling for pleasure and are great admirers of Bonilla the present president. Somers and I are getting on famously. He is a very fine boy with a great sense of humor and apparently very fond of me. We had five men counting Jeffs who we call our military attache and Charwood and four drivers and eleven mules so it is quite an outfit. In Ecuador with one more man it would constitute a revolution.

DICK.

Dear Fam: Santa Barbara—January 25, 1895.

We are not at Tegucigalpa as you observe but travelling in this country. "As you see it on Broadway" and as you see it here are two different things. We have had five days of it so far and rested here today in order to pay our respects to General Bogran the ex-president of the Republic. It is still six days to Tegucigalpa. The trip across Central America will certainly be one of the most interesting experiences of my life. It is the most beautiful country I have seen and the most barbarous. It is also the hottest and the most insect-ious and the dirtiest. This latter seems a little view to take of it but it means a great deal as the insects prevent your doing anything in a natural way; as for instance sitting on the grass or sleeping on the ground or hunting through the bushes. It is pretty much as you imagine it is from what you have read, that covers it, and I have discovered nothing new by coming to see it. I only verify what others have seen. The people are most uninteresting chiefly because they are surly to Americans and do not make you feel welcome. I do not mean that I did not do well to come for I am more glad that I did than I can say only I have not, as I have been able to do before, found something that others have not seen. I never expect to see such a country again unless in Africa. If you leave the path for ten yards you would never get back to it except by accident and you could not get that far away unless you cut yourself a trail. In some places the mail route which we follow and over which the mail is carried on the backs of runners is cut in the rock and we go down steps as even as those of the City Hall and for hours we travel over rough rocks and stones and a path so narrow that your knees catch in the vines at the side. The mules are wonderfully sure footed and never slip although they are very little, and I am pretty heavy. The heat is something awful. It bakes you and will dry your pith helmet in ten minutes after you have soaked it in water. But the scenery is magnificent, sometimes we ride above the clouds and look down into valleys stretching fifty miles away and see the buzzards half a mile below us. Then we go through forests of manaca palms that spread out on a single stem sideways and form arches over our heads with the leaves hanging in front of us like portiers or we cross great plains of grass and cactus and rock. The best fun is the baths we take in the mountain streams. They are almost as cool as one could wish and we shoot the rapids and lie under the waterfalls and come out with all the soreness rubbed out of us as though we had been massaged. We went shooting for two days but as they had no dogs we did not do much. I got the best shot of the trip and *missed it.* It was a large wild cat and he turned his side full on but I fired over him. Somers and I spent most of the time firing chance shots at alligators, but they never gave us a good chance as the birds warn them when they are in danger. One old fellow fifteen feet long beat us for some time and then Somers and I started across the river to catch him asleep. It was like the taking of Lungtepen. We had our money belts around our necks and our shoes in one hand and rifles in the other. The rapids ran very fast and the last I saw of Somerset he was sitting on the bank he had started from counting out wet bank notes and blowing the water out of his gun barrel. I got across all right by sticking my feet between rocks and put on my shoes and crawled up on the old Johnnie. He smelt of musk so strong that you could have found him in the dark. I had a beautiful shot at him at fifty yards but I was too greedy and ran around some rocks to get nearer and he heard me and dived. I shot a macaw, one of those overgrown parrots with tail feathers three feet from tip to tip. I got him with a rifle and as Griscom had got his with a shotgun I came out all right as a marksman although I was very sore at missing the wild cat. We sleep in hats and we sleep precious little for the dogs and pigs and insects all help to keep us awake and I cannot get used to a hammock. The native beds are made of matting such as they put over tea chests, or bull's hide stretched. Last night I slept in a hut with a woman and her three daughters all over fifteen and they sat up and watched me prepare for bed with great interest. I would not have missed this trip for any other I know. I wanted to rough it and we've roughed it and we will have another week of it too. We have some remarkable photographs and the article ought to be most interesting. Bogran proved to be a very handsome and remarkable man and we had a very interesting talk with him. From Tegucigalpa we will probably go directly to Venezuela across the Isthmus of Panama and not visit another Republic. We have all travelled too much to care to duplicate, and that is what we would be doing by remaining longer in Central America. A month of it will be enough of it and we will not get away from Amapala before the first of February. We are all well and happy and dirty and sing and laugh and tell stories and listen to Griscom's anecdotes of the aristocracy as we pick our way along. So goodbye and God bless you all.

DICK.

TEGUCIGALPA, CENTRAL AMERICA.
February 1st, 1895.
and 4th, 1895.

DEAR FAMILY:—

Here we are at last, the trip from Santa Barbara where I last wrote you was made in six days. It was not so interesting as the first part because it was very high up and the tropical scenery gave way to immensely tall pines and other trees that might have been in California, or the Rockies. The Corderillas which is the name of the mountains we crossed are a continuation, by the way, of the Rockies, and the Andes but are not more than 4,000 feet high. We had two very hot days of it in the plains of Comgaqua where there was once a city of 60,000 founded by Cortez but where there are not now more than 6,000. The heat was awful. We peeled all over our faces and hands and dodged and ducked our heads as though some one were biting at us. My saddle and clothes were so hot that I could not place my hand on them. At one village we heard that a bull fight was to be given at the next fifteen miles away, so we rode on there and arrived in time to take part. They had enclosed the plaza with a barricade of logs seven feet high, bound together with vines. They roped a big bull and lassoed him all over and then a man got on his back with spurs on his bare feet and held on by the ropes around the bull's body and by his toes and threw a cloak over the bull's eyes when ever it got too near any one— They stuck it with spears until it was mad and then let the lassoes slip and the bull started off to tear out the torreadors. I thought it would be a great sporting act to kodak a bull while it was charging you and so we all volunteered to act as torreadors and it was most exciting and funny. It was rather late to get good results but I got some pretty good pictures of the bull coming at me with his head down and then I'd skip into a hole in the wall. The best pictures I got were of Somers and Griscom scrambling over the seven foot barriers with the bull in hot chase. We all looked so funny in our high boots and helmets and so much alike that the savages yelled with delight and thought we had been engaged especially for their pleasure. Our "mosers," or mule drivers treated us most insolently but we could not do anything because Jeffs. had engaged them and we did not want to interfere with his authority but at a place the last day out one of them told Jeffs he lied and that we all lied. He had lost or stolen a canteen of Griscom's and they had said we had not given it to him. Jeffs. went at him right and left and knocked him all over the shop. There were half a dozen drunken mule drivers at the place and we thought they would take a hand but they did not. That night Jeffs. thought to try us to see what we would have done and left us bathing in a mountain stream and rode on ahead and hid himself behind a rock in a cañon and lay in ambush for us. We were jogging along in the moonlight and Somerset was reciting the "Walrus and the Carpenter," when suddenly Jeffs. let out a series of yells in Spanish and opened fire on us over our heads. Somerset was riding my mule and I had no weapons, so I yelled at him to shoot and he fell off his mule and ran to mine and let go at the rock behind which Jeffs. was with the carbines. So that in about five seconds Jeffs.' curiosity was perfectly satisfied as to what we would do, and he shouted for mercy. We thought it was a sentry or brigands and were greatly disappointed when it turned out to be Jeffs. We got here last night and a dirtier or more dismal place you never saw. We had telegraphed ahead for rooms but nothing was in order and we were lodged much worse than we had been several times in the interior where there was occasionally a clean floor. This morning we wrote direct to the President, asking for an interview or audience and did not ask our Consul to help us because Jeffs. had asked him in our presence to come meet us and he said he would after he had done talking to some other men, but he never came. Before we heard from Bonilla however, we learned that the Vice-president who has the same name was to be sworn in so we went to the palace along with the populace in their bare feet. We sat out of sight but the English Consul who was the finest looking person in the chamber—all over gold lace—saw us and asked that we be given places in front, which the minister of something asked us to take but we objected on account of our clothes. Somers had on a flannel suit that looked exactly like pajamas and lawn tennis shoes. But as soon as the ceremony was over they insisted on our going in to the banquet hall and in spite of our objections we were there conveyed and presented to Bonilla who behaved very well and after saying he had received our letters but had not had time to read them left us and avoided us, which was what we wanted for we looked like the devil. We met everybody else though and took the English and Guatemalian Consuls back to our rooms and gave them drinks and then we went to their rooms, so the day went very pleasantly. The President sent us a funny printed card appointing an audience at eleven to-morrow. It is exactly what you would imagine it would be, the soldiers are barefooted except about fifty and the President leaned out of the window in his shirt sleeves after the review and they have not plastered up the holes in his palace that his cannon made in it just a year ago to-day, when he was fighting Vasquez, and Vasquez was then on the inside and Bonilla on the hills. I forgot to tell you that this morning a boy about sixteen years old, with a policeman's badge and club came to our window and talked pleasantly with us or at us rather, while we shaved and guyed him in English. Finally we found that he had come to arrest Jeffs. so we told him where Jeffs. was but he preferred to watch us shave and we finished it under his custody. Then we went to the Commandante and found that the mosers had had Jeffs. arrested for not paying them on their arrival at Tegucigalpa, as we had distinctly told them we would not do but at San Pedro from where we took them, on their return. It was only a spite case suggested by Jeffs. thrashing their leader. The Commandante gave them a scolding and we went out in triumph.

February 4th—
Your cable received all right. We were very glad to hear. We have decided to go on by mules to Manaqua, the Capital of Nicaragua, and from there either to Corinto or to Lemon on the Atlantic side. We had to do this or wait here ten days for the boat going south at Amapala. It is moonlight now so that we can avoid the heat of the day. Yesterday we went out riding with the President, who put a gold revolver in his hip pocket before he started and made us feel that uneasy lies the head that rules in this country. He had two horses that had never been ridden before, as a compliment to our powers, the result was that the Vice-president's horse almost killed him, which I guess the President intended it should and the horse Griscom rode backed all over the town. He was a stallion and had never been ridden before that day. Mine was a gentle old gee-gee and yet I felt good when

we were all on the ground again. The British consul gave Somers a fine reception and raised the flag for him and had the band there to play "God Save the Queen," which he had spent the whole morning in teaching them. Griscom and I called on our Consul and played his guitar. We bought one for ourselves for the rest of the trip.

I want you to do something for me: keep all the unfavorable notices you get. I know Mother won't do it, so I shall expect Nora to make a point of saving them from the waste-paper basket. If there is not a lot of them when I get back, I will raise a row.

DICK.

MANAQUA—NICARAGUA—February 13, 1895.

DEAR FAM:

I had a great deal to tell you, but we have just received copies of the Panama *Star* and have read of the trolley riots in Brooklyn, a crisis in France, War in the Balkans, a revolution in Honolulu and another in Colombia. The result is that we feel we are not in it and we are all kicking and growling and abusing our luck. How Claiborne and Russell will delight over us and in telling how the militia fired on the strikers and how Troop A fought nobly. Never mind our turn will come someday and we may see something yet. We have had the deuce of a time since we left Tegucigalpa. Now we are in a land where there are bull hide beds and canvas cots instead of hammocks and ice and railroads and direct communication with steamship lines. Hereafter all will be merely a matter of waiting until the boat sails or the train starts and the uncertainties of mules and cat boats are at an end. It is hard to explain about our difficulties after we left Tegucigalpa but they were many. We gave up our idea of riding here direct because they assured us we could get a steam launch from Amapala to Corinto so we rode three days to San Lorenzo on the Pacific side and took an open boat from there to Amapala. It was rowed by four men who walked up a notched log and then fell back dragging the sweeps back, with the weight of their bodies.

It was a moonlight night and they looked very picturesque rising and sinking back and outlined against the sky. They were naked to the waist and rowed all night and I had a good chance to see them as I had to lie on the bottom of the boat on three mahogany logs. By ten the next day we were too cramped to stand it, so we put ashore on a deserted island and played Robinson Crusoe. We had two biscuits and a box of sardines among five of us but we found oysters on the rocks and knocked a lot off with clubs and stones and the butts of our guns. They were very good. We also had a bath until a fish ran into me about three feet long and cut two gashes in my leg. We reached Amapala about four in the afternoon. It was an awful place; dirt and filth and no room to move about, so we chartered an open boat to sail or row to Corinto sixty miles distant. You see, we could not go back to Tegucigalpa until the steamer arrived which is to take us South of Panama and we could not go to Manaqua either and for the same reason that we had sent back our mule train and we would not wait in Amapala partly because of fever which had been there and partly because we wanted to get to Corinto where they have ice and to see Manaqua. The boat was about as long as the *Vagabond* and twice as deep and a foot or two more across her beam. There were four of us, five of the crew and two natives who wanted to make the trip and who we took with us. It was pretty awful. The old tub rocked like a milk shake and I was never so ill in my life, we all lay packed together on the ribs of the boat and could not move and the waves splashed over us but we were too ill to care. The next day the sun beat in on us and roasted us like an open furnace. The boat was a pit of heat and outside the swell of the Pacific rose and fell and reflected the sun like copper. We reached Corinto in about twenty four hours and I was never so glad to get any place before. The town turned out to greet us and some Englishmen ran to ask from what boat we had been ship wrecked. They would not believe we had taken the trip for any other reason. They helped us very kindly and would not let us drink all the iced water we wanted and sent us in to bathe in a place surrounded by piles to keep out the sharks and by a roof to shelter one from the sun. Corinto proved to be all that Amapala was not; clean, cool with very excellent food and broad beds of matting. I liked it better than any place at which we have been, we came on here the next day to see the President and found the city hot, dusty and of no interest. There is an excellent hotel however and we had a talk with the President who was a much better chap than Bonilla being older and more civilized. Of course there is absolutely no reason or excuse for us if we do not get control of this canal. If only that it would allow our ships of war to pass from Ocean to Ocean instead of going around the horn. The women are really beautiful but that has nothing to do with the canal. Tomorrow morning we return to Corinto as Somers and

I like it best. Griscom would like to go on across by the route of the canal which would be a good thing were we certain of meeting a steamer at Simon or Greytown, but the Minister who went last month that way had to wait there sixteen days. So, we will probably leave Corinto on the 17th or 20th, there are two steamers, one that stops at ports and one that does not. They both arrive together. I do not know which we will take but—this letter will go with me. Up to date I think the trip will make a good story but it will have to be a personal one about the three of us for the country as it stands is uninteresting to the general reader for the reason that it *duplicates* itself in everything. But with our photographs and a humorous story, it ought to be worth reading and I have picked enough curious things to make it of some value.

February 15,—Corinto.

We are back here now and rid of that dusty, dirty city. You would be amused if you saw this place and tried to understand why we prefer it to any place we have seen. There is surf bathing at a half mile distant and a good hotel with a great bar where a Frenchman gives us ice and the sea captains and agents for mines and plantations in the interior gather to play billiards. Outside there are rows of handsome women with decollete gowns and shining black hair and colored silk scarfs selling fruit and down the one street which faces the bay are a double row of palms and the store where two American boys have a phonograph. They are the only Americans I have met who have or are taking a dollar out of this country. They play the guitar and banjo very well. One of them was on the

Princeton glee club and their stories of how they have toured Central America are very amusing. Lots of Love.

DICK.

S. S. *Barracouta*—Off San Juan
February 21, 1895.

DEAR MOTHER:

Today I believe is the 21st. We are out two days from Corinto off San Juan on the boundary of Costa Rica and lie here some hours. Then we go on without stopping to Panama arriving there about the 25th. On the 28th we take the steamer to Caracas. We will be at Caracas a week and then go straight home. But in the meanwhile we will have got one mail at Colon when we go there to take the boat for Caracas and glad I will be to get it. We have had a summary of the news in the Panama *Star* and a bundle of *Worlds* telling all about the trolley strike and that is all except Dad's cable at Tegucigalpa that we have heard in nearly two months. I am very sorry that the distances have turned out so much longer than we expected and that we had that unfortunate ten days wait for the steamer. I know you want me home and I would like to be there but I do not think I ought to go without seeing Caracas. It helps the book so much too if one runs it into South America for no one in the States thinks much of Central and does not want to read about it. At least I know I never did. We have had a most amusing time with the two phonograph chaps. One of them has been an advertising agent and a deputy sheriff and chased stage coach robbers and kept a hard ware store and is only twenty-five and the other has not had quite as much experience but has been to Princeton, he is

23. The mixture of narratives which change from tricks of the hard-ware trade to dances at Buckingham Palace and anecdotes of Cliff House supper parties at San Francisco are very interesting. I am going to write a book for them and call it "Through Central America with a Phonograph" or "Who We Did, and How We Done Them." We sing the most beautiful medleys and contribute to the phonograph. I had to protest against them announcing "Her Golden Hair was Hanging Down her Back" by Richard Harding Davis and Somerset kicked at their introducing "God Save the Queen" as sung by "His Grace the Duke of Bedford" which they insist in thinking his real title and his name; if he would only confess the truth. You cannot have any idea of how glad I am that I took this trip, just this particular trip, not for any interest it will be to the gentle reader but for the benefit it has been to me. All the things I was nervous about have been done and should I get nerves again as I suppose I always will in one form or another I can get rid of them by remembering how I got rid of them before during this most peculiar excursion. For though I and we all told the truth about being well, we were in a most trying place at times and the ride we took and the sail to get away from possible fever was very much of a strain. I do not see how Griscom kept up as he did for he was an invalid and very nervous when he started. But he showed great sporting blood. It was much better having three than two and he furnished us with much amusement at which he never complains. His artlessness and his bad breaks which keep us filled with terror make the most entertaining narratives and he tells them on himself and then keeps on making new ones. One night Jeffs came down with

fever through bathing in the mountain streams, a practice which did not hurt us but which natives of the country cannot do in safety, and I confess I was scared. Jeffs pulled through in a few days. It was odd that the man who had lived here eleven years should have been the only one to give up throughout the whole trip and he was a good sport, too.

I will have the Central American stories all done or nearly so by the time we reach New York which is one of the comforts of this over abundance of sea voyages. I have the lottery story nearly written and am wondering now if Bissell will let me publish it. Would it not be a good idea to have Dad, if he knows him, explain about how I went South to write it and just what it is and get his official sanction or shall I write or get the Harper's to write when I get back. The lottery people in joke offered $10,000 if they could write the story themselves. And sometimes I wish they would for it is the hardest kind of work. I do not want to advertise their old game and yet I cannot help doing it, in a way. We put in at Punta Arenas and I found a woman looking at us with an opera glass and shortly after she sent out to say she knew me and that she wanted me to come up. It seemed I met her in Elizabeth, New Jersey with Eddie Coward where she was playing in private theatricals. Since then as a punishment no doubt she has lived here and her husband is Minister of the Navy with one gun boat. This trip is very hot and I sleep on deck and look up at the stars and the light on the jib and the smoke spoiling the firmament. It makes you feel terribly far away from the centre of civilization in front of the fire and you all trying to make out where we are at. I hope you know more about it than we do.

CENTRAL AND SOUTH AMERICA 159

It is the worst country for getting about that I ever heard of. It has revived my interest and belief in all such beautiful things as buried treasures and hidden cities and shooting men against stone walls and filibusters. There are not many of these stories but every man tells them differently so they have all the freshness of a new tale. There is no ice on this boat or lemons or segars. It is the first time so they say that it has happened in twelve months, but after this it must be better. At Panama they fine the ice man $1000 every day his machine breaks and so we have hopes. I feel so very, very selfish off down here and leaving you all alone and it makes me lose my temper more than usual when all these delays occur but I promise to be good hereafter and we will be together soon now by the end of March sure and I hope you will not miss me too much, as much as I miss all of you. Sometimes I wish you could see some of these islands and the long shadowy sharks and the turtles, there are thousands of turtles as big as tubs just floating around like empty bottles, but I have never on the whole taken a trip when I so seldom wished that the family were around to enjoy it. It used to hurt me during the Mediterranean trip but there is not much that would please you in this outfit. I like it because I am satisfied to go dirty for weeks at a time and to talk to the engineer or the queer passengers and to pick up stories and improve my geography but I do not think the scenery would compensate either Nora or you or Dad for the lack of necessities and *cleanth*. When we were crossing the continent I don't believe I had a spot on me as big as a nickel without three bites on it, all sorts of bites, they just swarmed over you all sizes, colors and varieties. They came from dogs, from the sand, from trees, from the grass, from the air. The worst were little red bugs that lay under the leaves called carrapati's and that came off on you in a hundred at a time. And there were also "jiggers" that get under your nails and leave eggs there. Some times we could not sleep at all for the bites and you had to carry a brush to brush the carripats off every time you passed through bushes. It's the damnedest country I was ever in now that I have time to think of it. The other day I was going in to bathe and the sand was so hot that I could not get to the breakers and so I went yelling and jumping back to the grass and the grass was just one mass of burrs, so I gave another yell and leaped on to a big log and the log was full of thorns. That's the sort of country it is. And then after you do make a dash for the surf a shark makes a dash for you and you don't know what you are here for anyway. It had its humorous side and it was very funny, especially as it never turned out otherwise, to see the men scamper when the sharks came in. They never scented us for ten minutes or so and then they would swim up and we would give a yell and all make for the shore head over heels and splashing and shrieking and scared and excited. There would always be one man who was further out than the rest and he could not hear on account of the waves and we would all line up on the beach and yell and dance up and down and try to attract his attention. But you would see him go on diving and playing along in horrible loneliness until he turned to speak to some one and found the man gone and then he would look for the others and when he saw us all on the shore he would give one wild whoop out of him and go falling over himself with his hair on end and his eyes and mouth wide open. I saw one shark ten feet long but we would have died of the heat if we had not bathed so we thought it was worth it. That's over now because we cannot get any more sea bathing. Just around Panama. Finest place seen yet.

RICHARD.

PANAMA, February 28th, 1895.

DEAR MOTHER:

Griscom has awakened to the fact that he is a Press correspondent and is interviewing rebels who come stealthily by night followed by spies of the government and sit in Griscom's room with the son of the Consul General, as interpreter. Somerset and I refuse to be implicated and sit in the plaza waiting for a file of soldiers to carry Griscom off which is our cue for action. There is a man-of-war, the *Atlanta*, the one we made friends with at Puerto Cortez, lying at Colon and so we feel safe. We may now be said to be absorbing local color. That is about all we have done since we left Amapala. And if it were not that you are all alone up there, I would not mind it. I would probably continue on. We know it now as we do London or Paris. We can distinguish sea captains, lawyers in politics, commandantes, oldest residents, gentlemenly good for nothings, shipping agents and commission dealers, coffee planters and men who are "on the beach" with unerring eye. We know the story of each before he tells it, or it is told by some one else. The Commandante shot a lot of men by the side of a road during the last revolution, first allowing them to dig their own graves and is here now so that he can pay himself by stealing the custom dues, the lawyer politician has been to Cornell and taken a medical degree in Paris and aspires to be a deputy and only remembers New York as the home of Lillian Russell. The commission merchants are all Germans and the coffee planters are all French. They point with pride to little bare-foot boys selling sea shells and cocoanuts as their offspring, although they cannot remember their names. The sea captains you can tell by their ready made clothes of a material that would be warm in Alaska and by them wearing Spanish dollars for watch guards and by the walk which is rolling easily when sober and pitching heavily toward the night. The oldest resident always sits in front of the hotel and in the same seat, with a tortoise shell cane and remembers when Vasquez or Mendoza or Barrios, or Bonilla occupied the Cathedral and fired hot shot into the Palace and everybody took refuge in the English Consulate and he helped guard the bank all night with a Springfield rifle. The men who are on the beach have just come out of the hospital where they have had yellow fever and they want food. This story is intended to induce you to get rid of them hurriedly by a small token. Sometimes out of this queer combination you will get a good story but generally they want to show you a ruined abbey or a document as old as the Spanish occupation or to make you acquainted with a man who has pearls to sell, or a coffee plantation or a collection of unused stamps which he stole while a post-office employee. Our chief sport now is to go throw money at the prisoners who are locked up in a row of dungeons underneath the sea wall. The people walk and flirt and enjoy the sea breeze above them and the convicts by holding a mirror between the bars of the dungeons can see who is leaning over the parapet above them. Then they hold out their hands and you drop nickels and they fail to catch them and the sentry comes up and teases them by holding the money a few inches beyond their reach. They climb all over the crossbars in their anxiety to get the money and look like great monkeys. At night it is perfectly tremendous for their is only a light over their heads and they crawl all over the bars beneath this, standing on each other's shoulders and pushing and fighting and yelling half naked and wholey black and covered with sweat. As a matter of fact they are better content to stay in jail than out and when the British Consul offered to send eight of them back to Jamaica they refused to go and said they would rather serve out their sentence of eight years. This is the way the place looks and I am going to introduce it in a melodrama and have some one lower files down to the prisoners.

DICK.

After some not very eventful or pleasant days at Caracas, Richard sailed for home and from the steamer wrote the following letter:

March 26th—On board S. S. Caracas.

DEAR CHAS:

Off the coast of God's country. Hurrah! H—— did not come near us until the morning of our departure when he arrived at the Station trembling all over and in need of a shave. But in the meanwhile the consul at Caracas picked Griscom and myself up in the street and took us in to see Crespo who received us with much dignity and politeness. So we met him after all and helped the story out that much.

There is not much more to tell except that I was never so glad to set my face home as I am now and even the roughness of this trip cannot squelch my joy. It seems to me as if years had passed since we left and to think we are only three days off from Sandy Hook seems much too wonderfully good to be possible. Some day when we have dined alone together at Laurent's I will tell you the long story of how Somers and Gris came to be decorated with the Order of the Bust of Bolivar the Liberator of Venezuela of the 4th class but at present I will only say that there is a third class of the order still coming to me in Caracas, as there is 20 minutes still coming to Kelly in Brooklyn. It was a matter of either my getting the third class, which I ought to have had anyway having the third class of another order already, and *their getting nothing*, or our all getting the 4th or 5th class and of course I choose that they should get something and so they did and for my aimable unselfishness in the matter they have frequently drunken my health. I was delighted when Somers got his for he was happier over it than I have ever seen him over anything and kept me awake nights talking about it. I consider it the handsomest order there is after the Legion of Honor and I have become so crazy about Bolivar who was a second Washington and Napoleon that I am very glad to have it, although I still sigh for the third class with its star and collar.

The boys are especially glad because we have organized a Traveller's Club of New York of which we expect great things and they consider that it starts off well in having three of the members possessors of a foreign order. We formed the club while crossing Honduras in sight of the Pacific Ocean and its object is to give each other dinners and to present a club medal to people who have been nice to and who have

CENTRAL AND SOUTH AMERICA 165

helped members of the club while they were in foreign parts. It is my idea and I think a good one as there are lots of things one wants to do for people who help you and this will be as good as any. Members of the club are the only persons not eligible to any medal bestowed by the club and the eligibility for membership is determined by certain distances which a man must have travelled. Although the idea really is to keep it right down to our own crowd and make each man justify the smallness of the club's membership by doing something worth while. I am President. Bonsal is vice president. Russell treasurer and Griscom Secretary. Somerset is the solitary member. You and Sam and Helen and Elizabeth Bisland are at present the only honorary members. We are also giving gold medals to the two chaps who crossed Asia on bicycles, to Willie Chanler and James Creelman, but that does not make them members. It only shows we as a club think they have done a sporting act. I hope you like the idea. We have gone over it for a month and considered it in every way and I think we are all well enough known to make anybody pleased to have us recognize what they did whether it was for any of us personally or for the public as explorers. On this trip for instance we would probably send the club medals in silver to Admiral Meade, to Kelly, to Royas the Venezuelan Minister for the orders to the Governor of Belize, to the consul at La Guayra and to one of the phonograph chaps. In the same way if you would want to send a medal to any man or woman prince or doctor who had been kind, courteous, hospitable or of official service to you you would just send in a request to the committee. Write me soon and with lots of love

DICK.

In April, 1895, Richard was back in New York, at work on his South and Central American articles, and according to the following letters, having a good time with his old friends.

NEW YORK, April 27, 1895.
DEAR CHAS:

I read in the paper the other morning that John Drew was in Harlem, so I sent him a telegram saying that I was organizing a relief expedition, and would bring him out of the wilderness in safety. At twelve I sent another reading, "Natives from interior of Harlem report having seen Davis Relief Expeditionary Force crossing Central Park, all well. Robert Howard Russell." At two I got hold of Russell, and we telegraphed "Relief reached Eighty-fifth street; natives peacefully inclined, awaiting rear column, led by Griscom; save your ammunition and provisions." Just before the curtain fell we sent another, reading: "If you can hold the audience at bay for another hour, we guarantee to rescue yourself and company and bring you all back to the coast in safety. Do not become disheartened." Then we started for Harlem in a cab with George and another colored man dressed as African warriors, with assegai daggers and robes of gold and high turbans and sashes stuck full of swords. I wore my sombrero and riding breeches, gauntlets and riding boots, with cartridge belts full of bum cartridges over my shoulder and around the waist. Russell had my pith helmet and a suit of khaki and leggins. Griscom was in one of my coats of many pockets, a helmet and boots. We all carried revolvers, canteens and rifles. We sent George in with a note saying we were outside the zareba and could not rescue him because the man on watch objected to our guns. As soon as they saw George they rushed out and brought us all in. Drew was on the stage, so we tramped into the first entrance, followed by all the grips, stage hands and members of the company. The old man heard his cue just as I embraced him, and was so rattled that when he got on the stage he could not say anything, and the curtain went down without any one knowing what the plot was about. When John came off, I walked up to him, followed by the other four and the entire company, and said: "Mr. Drew, I presume," and he said: "Mr. Davis, I believe. I am saved!" Helen Benedict happened to be in Maude Adams' dressing-room, and went off into a fit, and the company was delighted as John would have been had he been quite sure we were not going on the stage or into a box. We left them after we had had a drink, although the company besought us to stay and protect them, and got a supper ready in Russell's rooms, at which Helen, Ethel Barrymore, John and Mrs. Drew, Maude Adams and Griscom were present.

DICK.

NEW YORK, November, 1895.
DEAR MOTHER:—

The china cups have arrived all right and are a beautiful addition to my collection and to my room, in which Daphne still holds first place.

What do you think Sir Henry sent me? The medal and his little black pipe in a green velvet box about as big as two bricks laid side by side with a heavy glass top with bevelled edges and the medal and pipe lying on a white satin bed, bound down with silver—and a large gold plate with the inscription "To Richard Harding Davis with the warmest greetings from Gregory Brewster—1895"— You have no idea how pretty it is, Bailey, Banks and Biddle made it— It is just like him to do anything so sweet and thoughtful and it has attracted so many people that I have had it locked up— No Burden jewel robbers here— My friend, the Russian O—— lady still pursues me and as she has no sense of humor and takes everything seriously, she frightens me— I am afraid she will move in at any moment— She has asked me to spend the summer with her at Paris and Monte Carlo, and at her country place in Norfolk and bombards me with invitations to suppers and things in the meantime. She has just sent me a picture of herself two feet by three, with writing all over it and at any moment, I expect her to ring the bell and order her trunks taken up stairs— I am too attractive— Last night I dined with Helen and Maude Adams, who is staying with her. I want them to board me too. Maude sang for us after dinner and then went off to see Yvette Guilbert at a "sacred concert" to study her methods. I went to N——'s box to hear Melba and we chatted to the accompaniment of Melba, Nordica and Plancon in a trio—the Ogre, wore fur, pearls, white satin and violets. It was a pink silk box. Then I went down to a reception at Mrs. De Koven's and found it was a play. Everybody was seated already so I squatted down on the floor in front of Mrs. De Koven and a tall woman in a brocade gown cut like a Japanese woman's— It was very dark where the audience was, so I could not see her face but when the pantomime was over I looked up and saw it was Yvette Guilbert. So I grabbed Mrs. De Koven and told her to present me and Guilbert said in English— "It is not comfortable on the floor is it?" and I said, "I have been at your feet for three years now, so I am quite used to it"—for which I was much applauded— Afterwards I told some one to tell her in French that I had written a book about Paris and about her and that I was going to mark it and send it and before the woman could translate, Guilbert said, "No, send me the Van Bippere book"—So we asked her what she meant and she said, "M. Bourget told me to meet you and to read your Van Bippere Book, you are Mr. Davis, are you not?"—So after that I owned the place and refused to meet Mrs. Vanderbilt.

Yvette has offered to teach me French, so I guess I won't go to Somerset's wedding, unless O—— scares me out of the country. I got my $2,000 check and have paid all my debts. They were not a third as much as I thought they were, so that's all right.

Do come over mother, as soon as you can and we will meet at Jersey City, and have a nice lunch and a good talk. Give my bestest love to Dad and Nora. How would she like Yvette for a sister-in-law? John Hare has sent me seats for to night— He is very nice— I have begun the story of the "Servants' Ball" and got well into it.

Lots and lots of love.

DICK.

The following letter was written to me at Florence. The novel referred to was "Soldiers of Fortune," which eventually proved the most successful book, commercially, my brother ever wrote. Mrs. Hicks, to whom Richard frequently refers, is the well-known English actress Ellaline Terriss, the wife of Seymour Hicks. Somerset is Somers Somerset, the son of Lady Henry Somerset, and the Frohman referred to is Daniel Frohman, who was the manager of the old Lyceum Theatre.

Early in November, William R. Hearst asked my brother to write a description of the Yale-Princeton football game for *The Journal*. Richard did not want to write the "story" and by way of a polite refusal said he could not undertake it for less than $500.00. Greatly to his surprise Hearst promptly accepted the offer. At the time, I imagine this was by far the largest sum ever paid a writer for reporting a single event.

December 31st, 1895.
New York.
The Players.
New Year's Eve.

DEAR CHAS:

I am not much of a letter writer these days, but I have finished the novel and that must make up for it. It goes to the Scribners for $5,000 which is not as much as I think I should have got for it. I am now lying around here until the first of February, when I expect to sail to Somerset's wedding, reaching you in little old Firenzi in March. We will then paint it. After that I do not know what I shall do. *The Journal* is after me to do almost anything I want at my own figure, as a correspondent. They have made Ralph London correspondent and their paper is the only one now to stick to. They are trying to get all the well known men at big prices.

I have had such a good time helping Mrs. Hicks in Seymour's absence. She had about everything happen to her that is possible and she is just the sort of little person you love to do things for. She finally sailed and I am now able to attend to my own family.

The Central American and Venezuelan book comes out on February 1st. Several of the papers here jokingly alluded to the fact that my article on the Venezuelan boundary had inspired the President's message. Of course you get garbled ideas of things over there and exaggerated ones, as for instance, on the Coxey army. But you never saw anything like the country after that war message. It was like living with a British fleet off Sandy Hook. Everybody talked of it and of nothing else. I went to a dinner of 300 men all of different callings and I do not believe one of them spoke of anything else. Cabmen, car conductors, barkeepers, beggars and policemen. All talked war and Venezuela and the Doctrine of Mr. Monroe. In three days the country lost one thousand of millions of dollars in values, which gives you an idea how expensive war is. It is worse than running a newspaper. Now, almost everyone is for peace, peace at any price. I do not know of but one jingo paper, *The Sun*, and war talk is greeted with jeers. It was as if the people had suddenly had their eyes opened to what it really meant and having seen were wiser and wanted no more of it. Your brother, personally, looks at it like this. Salisbury was to blame in the first place for being rude and not offering to arbitrate as he had been asked to do. When he said to Cleveland, "It's none of your business" the only answer was "Well, I'll make it my business" but instead of stopping there, Cleveland uttered a cast iron ultimatum instead of leaving a loophole for diplomacy and a chance for either or both to back out. That's where I blame him as does every one else.

Sam Sothern is in Chicago and we all wrote him guying letters about the war. Helen said she was going to engage "The Heart of Maryland" company to protect her front yard, while Russell and I have engaged "The Girl I Left Behind Me" company with Blanch Walsh and the original cast.

We sent Somerset a picture of himself riddled with bullets. And Mrs. Hicks made herself famous by asking if it was that odious Dunraven they were going to war about.

My article was a very lucky thing and is greatly quoted and in social gatherings I am appealed to as a final authority.

The football story, by the way, did me a heap of good with the newspapers and the price was quoted as the highest ever paid for a piece of reporting. People sent for it so that the edition was exhausted. *The Journal* people were greatly pleased.

Yvette Guilbert is at Hammerstein's and crowds the new music hall nightly, at two dollars a seat. Irving and Miss Terry have been most friendly to me and to the family. Frohman is going to put "Zenda" on in New York because he has played a failure, which will of course kill it for next year for Eddie, when he comes out as a star. I have never seen such general indignation over a private affair. Barrymore called it a case of Ollaga Zenda. They even went to Brooklyn when Eddie was playing there and asked him to stage the play for them and how he made his changes and put on his whiskers. Poor Eddie, he lacks a business head and a business manager—and Sam talks and shakes his head but is little better. Lots of love and best wishes for the New Year.

Dick.

CHAPTER IX

MOSCOW, BUDAPEST, LONDON

The years 1896–1897 were probably the most active of Richard's very active life. In the space of twelve months he reported the Coronation at Moscow, the Millennial Celebration at Budapest, the Spanish-Cuban War, the McKinley Inauguration, the Greek-Turkish War and the Queen's Jubilee. Although this required a great deal of time spent in travelling, Richard still found opportunity to do considerable work on his novel "Captain Macklin," to which he refers in one of his letters from London.

As correspondent of the New York *American*, then *The Journal*, Richard went from Florence, where he was visiting me, to Moscow. He was accompanied by Augustus Trowbridge, an old friend of my brother's and a rarely good linguist. The latter qualification proved of the greatest possible assistance to Richard in his efforts to witness the actual coronation ceremony. To have finally been admitted to the Kremlin my brother always regarded as one of his greatest successes as a correspondent.

En route—May 1896.
Dear Chas:
The night is passed and with the day comes "a hope" but during the blackness I had "a suffer"— I read until two—five hours—and then slept until five when the middle man who had slept on my shoulder all

night left the train and the second one to whom Bernardi was so polite left me alone and had the porter fit me up a bed so that I slept until seven again— Then the Guardian Angel returned for his traps and I bade him a sleepy adieu and was startled to see two soldiers standing shading their eyes in salute in the doorway and two gentlemen bowing to my kind protector with the obsequiousness of servants— He sort of smiled back at me and walked away with the soldiers and 13 porters carrying his traps. So I rung up the conductor and he said it was the King's Minister with his eyes sticking out of his head—the conductor's eyes —not the Minister's. I don't know what a King's Minister is but he liked your whiskey— I am now passing through the Austrian Tyrol which pleases me so much that I am chortling with joy— None of the places for which my ticket call are on any map—but don't you care, I don't care— I wish I could adequately describe last night with nothing but tunnels hours in length so that you had to have all the windows down and the room looked like a safe and full of tobacco smoke and damp spongey smoke from the engine, and bad air. That first compartment I went in was filled later with German women who took off their skirts and the men took off their shoes. Everybody in the rear of the car is filthy dirty but I had a wash at the Custom house and now I am almost clean and quite happy. The day is beautiful and the compartment is all my own— I am absolutely enchanted with the Tyrol— I have never seen such quaint picture book houses and mills with wheels like that in the Good for Nothing and crucifixes wonderfully carved and snow mountains and dark green forests— The sky is perfect and the air is filled with the sun and the train moves so smoothly that I can see little blue flowers, baby blue, Bavarian blue flowers, in the Spring grass. Such dear old castles like birds nests and such homelike old mills and red-faced millers with feathers in their caps you never saw out of a comic opera— The man in here with me now is a Russian, of course, and saw the last Coronation and knows that my suite is on the principal Street and attends to my changing money and getting an omelette— I can survive another night now having had an omelette not so good as Madam Masi's but still an omelette— I have now left Munich and the Russian and a conductor whom I mistook for a hereditary prince of Bavaria, with tassels down his back, has assured me he is going to Berlin, and that I am going to Berlin and much else to which I smile knowingly and say mucho gracia, wee wee, ya ya, ich slemmer, ich limmer and other long speeches ending with "an er—"

DICK.

May 15th, 1896. Moscow.
DEAR CHAS:

We left Berlin Monday night at eleven and slept well in a wagon-lit. That was the only night out of the five that I spent in the cars that I had my clothes off, although I was able to stretch out on the seats, so I am cramped and tired now. At seven Monday morning the guard woke us and told us to get ready for the Custom House and I looked out and saw a melancholy country of green hills and black pines and with no sign of human life. It was raining and dreary looking and then I saw as we passed them a line of posts painted in black and white stripes a half mile apart on each side of the train and I knew we had crossed the boundary and that the line of posts stretched from the Arctic

Ocean to the Black Sea and from the Pacific to the Caucasus Mountains and the Pamirs. It gave me a great thrill but I have had so many to-day, that I had almost forgotten that one. For two days we jogged along through a level country with mean thatched huts and black crows flying continually and peasants in sheepskin coats, full in the skirt and tight at the waist, with boots or thongs of leather around their feet. The women wore boots too and all the men who were not soldiers had their hair cropped short like mops. We could not find any one who understood any language, so as we never knew when we would stop for food, we ate at every station and I am of the opinion that for months I have been living on hot tea and caviar and hash sandwiches. The snow fell an inch deep on Wednesday and dried up again in an hour and the sun shone through it all. So on the whole it was a good trip and most interesting. But here we are now in a perfect pandemonium and the Czar has not yet come nor one-fifth even of the notables. It is a great city, immense and overpowering in its extent. The houses are ugly low storied and in hideous colors except the churches which are like mosques and painted every color. I confess I feel beaten to night by the noise and rush and roar and by so many strange figures and marvellous costumes. Our rooms are perfect that is one thing and the situation is the very best. If the main street were Fifth Avenue and Madison Square the Governor's Square, his palace would be Delmonico's and our rooms would be the corner rooms of the Brunswick, so you can see how well we are placed. We can sit in our windows and look down and up the main street and see every one who leaves or calls upon the Governor. We are now going out for a dinner and to one of many café-chantants and I will tell you the rest to-morrow, when I get sleep, for after five nights of it I feel done up, but I feel equally sure it is going to be a great experience and I cannot tell you how glad I am that I came. Love to you all and to dear Florence in which Trowbridge, who is a brick, joins me.

DICK.

Moscow—May 1896.

DEAR CHAS:

There was a great deal to tell when I shut down last night, but I thought I would have had things settled by this time and waited, but it looks now as though there was to be no rest for the weary until the Czar has put his crown on his head. The situation is this: there are ninety correspondents, and twelve are to get into the coronation, two of these will be Americans. There are five trying for it.

Count Daschoff, the Minister of the Court, has the say as to who gets in of those five. T. and I called on him with my credentials just as he was going out. Never have I seen such a swell. He made us feel like dudes from Paterson, New Jersey. He had three diamond eagles in an astrakan cap, a white cloak, a gray uniform, top boots and three rows of medals. He spoke English perfectly, with the most politely insolent manner that I have ever had to listen to; and eight servants, each of whom we had, in turn, mistaken for a prince royal, bowed at him all the brief time he talked over our heads. He sent us to the bureau for correspondents, where they gave me a badge and a pocketbook, with my photo in it. They are good for nothing, except to get through the police lines. No one at the bureau gave us the least encouragement as to my getting in at the coronation. We were frantic, and I went back to Breckenridge, our Minister, and wrote him a long letter explaining what had happened, and that what I wrote would "live," that I was advertised and had been advertised to write this story for months. I dropped *The Journal* altogether, and begged him to represent me as a literary light of the finest color. This he did in a very strong letter to Daschoff, and I presented it this morning, but the Minister, like Edison, said he would let me know when he could see me. Then I wrote Breck a letter of thanks so elegant and complimentary that he answered with another, saying if his first failed he would try again. That means he is for me, and at the bureau they say whichever one he insists on will get in, but they also say he is so good-natured that he helps every one who comes. I told him this, and he has promised to continue in my behalf as soon as we hear from Daschoff.

The second thing of importance is the getting the story, *if we get it*, on the wire. That, I am happy to say, we are as assured of as I could hope to be. I own the head of the Telegraph Bureau soul, body and mind. He loves the ground T. and I spurn, and he sent out my first cable today, one of interrogation merely, ahead of twelve others; he has also given us the entrée to a private door to his office, all the other correspondents having to go to the press-rooms and undergo a sort of press censorship, which entails on each man the cutting up of his story into three parts, so as to give all a chance. I gave T. three dictums to guide him; the first was that we did not want a fair chance—we wanted an unfair advantage over every one else. Second, to never accept a "No" or a "Yes" from a subordinate, but to take everything from headquarters. Third, to use every mouse, and not to trust to the lions. He had practise on the train. When he told me we would be in Moscow in ten hours, I would say, "Who told you that," and back he would go to the Herr Station Director in a red gown, and return to say that we would get there in twenty hours. By this time I will match him against any newspaper correspondent on earth. He flatters, lies, threatens and bribes with a skill and assurance that is simply beautiful, and his languages and his manners pull me out of holes from which I could never have risen. With it all he is as modest as can be, and says I am the greatest diplomat out of office, which I really think he believes, but I am only using old reporters' ways and applying the things other men did first.

My best stroke was to add to my cable to *The Journal*, "Recommend ample recognition of special facilities afforded by telegraph official"—and then get him to read it himself under the pretext of wishing to learn if my writing was legible. He grinned all over himself, and said it was. After my first story is gone I will give him 200 roubles for himself in an envelope and say *Journal* wired me to do it. That will fix him for the coronation story, as it amounts to six months' wages about. But, my dear brother, in your sweet and lovely home, where the sun shines on the Cascine and the workmen sleep on the bridges, and dear old ladies knit in the streets, that is only one of the thousand things we have had to do. It would take years to give you an account of what we have done and *why* we do it. It is like a game of whist and poker combined and we bluff on two flimsy fours, and crawl the next minute to a man that holds a measly two-spot. There is not a wire we have not pulled, or a leg, either, and we go dashing about all day in a bath-chair, with a driver in a bell hat and a blue nightgown, leaving cards and writing notes and giving drinks and having secretaries to lunch and buying flowers for wives and cigar boxes for husbands, and threatening the Minister with Cleveland's name.

John A. Logan, Jr., is coming dressed in a *Russian Uniform*, and he wore it on the steamer, and says he is the special guest of the Czar and the Secretary of the visiting mission. Mrs. P. P. is paying $10,000 for a hotel for one week. That is all the gossip there is. We lunched with the McCooks today and enjoyed hearing American spoken, and they were apparently very glad to have us, and made much of T. and of me. We only hope they can help us; and I am telling the General the only man to meet is Daschoff, and when he does I will tell him to tell Daschoff I am the only man to be allowed in the coronation. I wish I could tell you about the city, but we see it only out of the corner of our eyes as we dash to bureau after bureau and "excellency" and "royal highness" people, and then dash off to strengthen other bridges and make new friends. It is great fun, and I am very happy and T. is having the time of his life. He told me he would rather be with me on this trip than travel with the German Emperor, and you will enjoy to hear that he wrote Sarah I was the most "good-natured" man he ever met. God bless you all, and dear, dear Florence. Lots of love.

DICK.

Moscow—May, 1896.

DEAR CHAS.:

I have just sent off my coronation story, and the strain of this thing, which has really been on me for

MOSCOW, BUDAPEST, LONDON 181

six months, is off. You can imagine what a relief it is, or, rather, you cannot, for no one who has not been with us these last ten days can know what we have had to do. The story I sent is not a good one. It was impossible to tell it by cable, and the first one on the entry was a much better one. I do not care much, though; of course, I do care, as I ought to have made a great hit with it, but there was no time, and there was so much detail and minutia that I could not treat it right. However, after the awful possibility, or rather certainty, that we have had to face of not getting any story at all, I am only too thankful. I would not do it again for ten thousand dollars. Edwin Arnold, who did it for *The Telegraph*, had $25,000, and if I told you of the way Hearst acted and Ralph interfered with impertinent cables, you would wonder I am sane. They never sent me a cent for the cables until it was so late that I could not get it out of the bank, and we have spent and borrowed every penny we have. Imagine having to write a story and to fight to be allowed a chance to write it, and at the same time to be pressed for money for expenses and tolls so that you were worn out by that alone. The brightest side of the whole thing was the way everybody in this town was fighting for me. The entire town took sides, and even men who disliked me, and who I certainly dislike, like C. W. and R—— of the Paris Embassy, turned in and fought for my getting in like relations. And the women—I had grand dukes and ambassadors and princes, whom I do not know by sight, moving every lever, and as Stanhope of *The Herald*, testified "every man, woman and child in the visiting and resident legation is crazy on the subject of getting Davis into the coronation." They made it a personal matter, and when I got my little blue badge, the women kissed me and each other, and cheered, and the men came to congratulate me, and acted exactly as though they had got it themselves.

It was a beautiful sight; the Czarina much more beautiful and more sad-looking than ever before. But it was not solemn enough, and the priests groaned and wailed and chanted and sang, and every one stood still and listened. All that the Czar and Czarina did was over ten minutes after they entered the chapel, and then for three hours the priests took the center of the stage and groaned. I was there from seven until one. Six solid hours standing and writing on my hat. It was a fine hat, for we were in court costume, I being a distinguished visitor, as well as a correspondent. That was another thing that annoyed me, because Breckinridge, who has acted like a brick, did not think he could put me on both lists, so I chose the correspondents' list, of course, in hopes of seeing the ceremony, but knowing all the time that that meant no balls or functions, so that had I lost the ceremony I would have had nothing; but he arranged it so that I am on both lists. Not that I care now. For I am tired to death; and Trowbridge did not get on either list, thanks to the damned *Journal* and to his using all his friends to help me, so that I guess I will get out and go to Buda Pest and meet you in Paris. Do not consider this too seriously, for I am writing it just after finishing my cable and having spent the morning on my toes in the chapel. I will feel better tomorrow. Anyway, it is done and I am glad, as it was the sight of the century, and I was in it, and now I can spend my good time and money in gay Paree. Love to all.

DICK.

From Moscow Richard went direct to Buda Pest, where he wrote an article on the Hungarian Millennial.

BUDA PEST
May 8th, 1896.
DEAR CHAS:

I have just returned from the procession of the Hungarian Nobles. It was even more beautiful and more interesting than the Czar's entry than which I would not have believed anything could have been more impressive— But the first was military, except for the carriages, which were like something out of fairyland—to-day, the costumes were all different and mediæval, some nine hundred years old and none nearer than the 15th Century. The mis en scene was also much better. Buda is a clean, old burgh, with yellow houses rising on a steep green hill, red roofs and towers and domes, showing out of the trees— It is very high but very steep and the procession wound in and out like a fairy picture— I sat on the top of the hill, looking down it to the Danube, which separates Buda from Pest— The Emperor sat across the square about 75 yards from our tribune in the balcony of his palace. We sat in the Palace yard and the procession passed and turned in front of us— There were about 1,500 nobles, each dressed to suit himself, in costumes that had descended for generations—of brocade, silk, fur, and gold and silver cloth— Each costume averaged, with the trappings of the horse, 5,000 dollars. Some cost $1,000, some $15,000. Some wore complete suits of chain armor, with bearskins and great black eagle feathers on their spears just as they were when they invaded Rome— Others wore gold chain armor and leopard or wolf skins and their horses were studded with turquoises and trappings of gold and silver and smothered in silver coins— It would have been ridiculous if they had not been the real thing in every detail and if you had not known how terribly in earnest the men were. There is no other country in the world where men change from the most blase and correct of beings, to fairy princes in tights and feathers and jewelled belts and satin coats— They were an hour in passing and each one seemed more beautiful than the others— I am very glad I came although I was disappointed at missing the accident at Moscow. It must have been more terrible than Johnstown. I found the ——s quite converted into the most awful snobs but the people they worship are as simple and well bred as all gentle people are and I have had the most delightful time with them. It is so small and quiet after Moscow, and instead of being lost in an avalanche of embassies and suites and missions, I have a distinct personality, as "the American," which I share with "the" Frenchman and four Englishmen. We are the only six strangers and they give us the run of all that is going on— At night we dine at the most remarkable club in the world, on the border of the Park, where the best of all the Gypsey musicians plays for us— The music is alone worth having come to hear, and the dear souls who play it, having been told that I like it follow me all around the terrace and sit down three feet away and fix their eyes on you, and then proceed to pull your nerves and heart out of you for an hour at a time— One night a man here dipped a ten thousand franc note in his champagne and pasted it on the leader's violin and bowed his thanks, and the leader bowed in return and the next morning sent him the note back in an envelope, saying that the compliment was worth more than the money— The leader's name is Berchey and the Hungarians have never allowed him to leave the country for fear he would not be allowed to come back— He is a fat, half drunken looking man, with his eyes full of tears half the time he plays. He looks just like a setter dog and he is so terribly in earnest that when he fixes me with his eyes and plays at me, the court ladies all get up and move their chairs out of his way just as though he were a somnambulist—

I leave here Wednesday and reach Paris Friday *morning* the eleventh— You must try to meet me at the Café de la Paix at half past nine— Wait in the corner room if you don't wish to sit outside and as soon as I get washed I will join you for coffee. It will be fine to see you again and to be done with jumping about from hotel to hotel and to be able to read the signs and to know how to ask for food. Russian, German and Hungarian have made French seem like my mother tongue—

DICK.

CHAPTER X

CAMPAIGNING IN CUBA AND GREECE

In December, 1896, Richard and Frederic Remington, the artist, were commissioned by the New York *Journal* to visit Cuba which was then at war with Spain. It was their intention to go from Key West in the *Vamoose*, a very fast but frail steam-launch, and to make a landing at some uninhabited point on the Cuban coast. After this their plans seem to have been to trust to luck and the kindliness of the revolutionists. After waiting for some time at Key West for favorable weather, they at last started out on a dark night to make the crossing. A few hours after the *Vamoose* had left Key West a heavy storm arose—apparently much too violent for the slightly built launch. The crew struck and the captain finally refused to go on to Cuba and put back to Key West. Shortly after this Remington and my brother reached Havana by a more simple and ostentatious route. This was my brother's first effort as a war correspondent, and I presume it was this fact and the very indefiniteness of the original plan that caused his mother and father so much uneasiness. And, indeed, it did prove eventually a hazardous exploit.

On way to Key West.
December 19, 1896.

Dear Mother:

I hope you won't be cross with me for going off and not letting you know, but I thought it was better to do it that way as there was such delay in our getting started. I am going to Cuba by way of Key West with Frederic Remington and Michaelson, a correspondent who has been there for six months. We are to be taken by the *Vamoose* the fastest steam yacht made to Santa Clara province where the Cubans will meet us and take us to Gomez. We will stay a month with him, the yacht calling for copy and sketches once a week, and finally for us in a month. I get all my expenses and *The Journal* pays me $3,000 for the month's work. The *Harper's Magazine* also takes a story at six hundred dollars and Russell will reprint Remington's sketches and my story in book form, so I shall probably clear $4,000 in the next month or six weeks. I was a week in getting information on the subject so I know all about it from the men who have just been there and I want you to pay attention to what I tell you they told me and not to listen to any stray visitor who comes in for tea and talks without any tact or knowledge. There is no danger in the trip except the problem of getting there and getting away again, and that is now removed by *The Journal's* yacht. I would have gone earlier had any of the periodicals that asked me to go shown me any way to get there— *There is no fever this time of year* and as you know fever never touches me. It got all the others in Central America and never worried me at all. There is no danger of getting shot, as the province into which we go, the Santa Clara province, is owned and populated and patrolled by the Cubans. It is no more Spanish than New Jersey and the Spaniards cannot get in there. We have the strongest possible letters from the Junta, and I have from Lamont, Bayard and Olney and credentials in every language. We will sit around the Gomez camp and send messengers back to the coast. It is a three days trip and as Gomez may be moving from place to place you may not hear from us for a month and we may not hear from you but remember it was a much longer time than that before you heard from me when I went to Honduras. Also keep in mind that I am going as a correspondent only and must keep out of the way of fighting and that I mean to do so, as Chamberlain says we want descriptive stories not brave deeds— Major Flint who has arranged the trip for us was down there with Maceo as a correspondent. He saw six fights and never shot off his gun once because as he said it was not his business to kill people and he has persuaded me that he is right, so I won't do anything but look on— I have bought at *The Journal's* expense a fifty dollar field glass which is a new invention and the best made. I have marked it so that you can see a man five miles off and as soon as I see him I mean to begin to ride or run the other way—no one loves himself more than I do so you leave me to take care of myself. I wish I could give you any idea of the contempt the four returned correspondents who talked to me, have for the Spaniards. They have seen them shoot 2,500 rounds without hitting men at 200 yards and they run away if the enemy begins on them first. However, you trust to Richard— We have a fine escort arranged for us and Michaelson speaks Spanish perfectly and has been six months scouting over the country.

DICK.

KEY West, December 26, 1896.

DEAR FAMILY:

I got your letters late last night and they made me pretty solemn. It is an awfully solemn thing to have people care for you like that and to care for them as I do. I can't tell you how much I love you. You don't know how much the pain of worrying you for a month has meant to me, but I have talked it all out with myself, and left it to God and I am sure I am doing right. As Mrs. Crown said, "There's a whole churchful up here praying for you," and I guess that will pull me through. Of course, dear, dear Mother thought she was cross with me. She could not be cross with me, and her letter told me how much she cared, that was all, and made me be extra careful. But I need not promise you to be careful. You have an idea I am a wild, filibustering, hot-headed young man. I am not. I gave the guides to understand their duty was to keep us out of danger if we had to walk miles to avoid it. We are men of peace, going in, as real estate agents and coffee-planters and drummers are going in on every steamer, to attend to our especial work and get out again quick. I have just as strong a prejudice against killing a man as I have against his killing me.

Lots and lots of love. Don't get scared if you don't hear for a month, although we will try to get our stories back once a week, but you know we are at the convenience of the Cubans who will pocket our despatches and money and not take the long trip back. Thank dear Dad for his letter full of good advice. It was excellent. Remington and Michelson are good men and I like them immensely. Already we are firm friends.

Love, DICK.

KEY WEST—January 1, 1897.

DEAR MOTHER:

As you will know by my telegram we are either off on a safe sea going boat or waiting for one. There is no turning back from here and the only reason I thought of doing so was the knowledge of the way you would suffer and worry. I argued it out that it was selfish in me to weigh my getting laughed at and paragraphed as the war correspondent that always Turned Back against a month of uneasiness for you, but later I saw I could not do it much as I love you for the element of danger to me is non-existent; it is merely an exciting adventure and you will have to believe me and not worry but be a Spartan mother. I would not count being laughed at and the loss of my own self respect if I really thought there was great danger, but I do not. You will not lose me and if I go now I can sit still next time and say "I have done better things than that." If I had not gone it would have meant that I would have had to have done just that much harder a stunt next time to make people forget that I had failed in this one. Now do cheer up and believe in the luck of Richard Harding Davis and the British Army. We have carte blanche from *The Journal* to buy or lease any boat on the coast and I rocked them for $1000 in advance payment because of the delay over the *Vamoose*.

I am so happy at thinking I am going, I could not have faced anyone had I not, although we had nothing to do with the failure, we tried to cross fairly in the damn tub and it was her captain who put back. I lay out on the deck and cried when he refused to go ahead, we had waited so long. The Cubans and Remington and Michelson had put on all their riding things but fortunately I had not and so was spared that humiliation. What I don't know about the Fine Art of Filibustering now is unnecessary. I find many friends of my Captain Boynton or "Capt. Burke." Tonight the officers of the *Raleigh* give me a grand dinner at which I wear a dress suit and make speeches —they are the best chaps I ever met in the Navy. Lots of love and best wishes to Dad and to Nora for a happy, happy New Year. You know me and you know my conscience but it would not let me go back in order to save you anxiety so you wont think me selfish. God bless you.

DICK.

KEY WEST, January 2nd, 1897.
DEAR FAMILY:

I have learned here that the first quality needed to make a great filibuster is Patience, it is not courage, or resources or a knowledge of the Cuban Coast line, it is patience. Anybody can run a boat into a dark bayou and dump rifles on the beach and scurry away to sea again but only heroes can sit for a month on a hotel porch or at the end of a wharf, and wait. That is all we do and that is my life at Key West. I get up and half dress and take a plunge in the bay and then dress fully and have a greasy breakfast and then light a huge Key West cigar, price three cents and sit on the hotel porch with my feet on a rail— Nothing happens after that except getting one's boots polished as the two industries of this place are blacking boots and driving cabs. I have two boys to black mine at the same time every morning and pay the one who does his the better of the two— It generally ends in a fight so that affords diversion— Then a man comes along, any man, and says, "Remington's looking for you" and I get up and look for Remington. There is only a triangle of streets where one can find him and I call at "Josh" Curry's first and then at Pendleton's News Store and read all the back numbers of the *Police Gazette* for the hundredth time and then call here at the Custom House and then look in at the Cable office, where Michaelson lives sending telegrams about anything or nothing and that brings me back to the hotel porch again, where I have my boots shined once more and then go into mid-day dinner. In the meanwhile Remington is looking for me a hundred yards in the rear. He generally gets to "Josh's" as I leave the Custom House— In the afternoon I study Spanish out of a text book and at three take a bicycle ride, at five I call at the garrison to take tea with the doctor and his wife, who is sweeter than angel's ever get to be with a miniature angel of a baby called Martha. I wait until retreat is sounded and the gun is fired at sunset and having commented unfavorably on the way the soldiers let the flag drop on the grass instead of catching it on the arms as a bluejacket does, I ride off to the bay for another bath— Then I take the launch to the *Raleigh* and dine with the officers and rejoice in the clean fresh paint and brass and decks and the lights and black places of a great ship of war, than which nothing is more splendid. We sit on the quarter-deck and smoke and play the guitar and I go home again, in time for bed. I vary this programme occasionally by spending the morning on the end of a wharf watching another man fish and reading old novels and the "Lives of Captain Walker" and "Captain Fry of the Virginius," two great books from each of which I am going to write a short story like the one of the Alamo or of the Jameson Raid— The life of Walker I found on the *Raleigh* and the life of Captain Fry with all the old wood cuts and the newspaper comments of the time at a book store here. I don't know when we shall get away but it is no use kicking about it, Michaelson is doing all he can and the new tug will be along in a week anyway. I shall be so glad to get to Cuba that I will dance with glee.

DICK.

MATANZAS, January 15th, 1897.
DEAR MOTHER:

I sent you a note by Remington which he will mail in the States— From here I go to Sagua La Grande. It is on the northern coast. I think from there I shall cross over to Cienfuegos on the Southern coast and then if I can catch a steamer go to Santiago to see my old friends, at the Juraqua mines and MacWilliams' ore road and "the Palms"— Everywhere I am treated well on account of Weyler's order and I am learning a great deal and talking very little, my Spanish being bad. There is war here and no mistake and all the people in the fields have been ordered in to the fortified towns where they are starving and dying of disease. Yesterday I saw the houses of these people burning on both sides of the track— They gave shelter to the insurgents and so very soon they found their houses gone. I am so relieved at getting old Remington to go as though I had won $5000. He was a splendid fellow but a perfect kid and had to be humored and petted all the time. I shall if I have luck be through with this in a few weeks but it has had such a set back at the start that I am afraid it can never make a book and I doubt if I can write a decent article even. I am so anxious not to keep you worrying any longer than is necessary and so I am hurrying along taking only a car window view of things. Address me care of Consul General Lee, Havana and confine your remarks to what is going on at home. I know what is going on here. I don't believe half I hear but I am being slowly converted. Remington is more excitable than I am, so don't misunderstand if he starts in violently. I am getting details and verifying things. He is right on a big scale but every one has lied so about this island that I do not want to say anything I do not believe is true. This is a beautiful little city and after Jaruco, where we slept two days ago, it is Paris. There we slept off the barnyard and cows and chickens walked all over the floor and fleas all over us. It was like Honduras only filthier. Speaking of Paris, tell the Kid I expect to go over to him soon after I return to New York.

Lots of love. DICK.

CARDENAS—North Coast of Cuba.
January 16th, 1897.

DEAR MOTHER:

It is very funny not knowing what sort of a place you are to sleep in next and taking things out of a grab bag, as it were— In Europe you can always guess what the well known towns will give you for you have a guide book, but here it is all luck. Matanzas was a pretty city but the people were awful, the hotel was Spanish and the proprietor insolent, though I was spending more of Willie Hearst's money than all of the officers spend in a week, the Consul could not talk English or Spanish, he said he hadn't come there "to go to school to no Spaniard" and he gloried in the fact he had been there three years without knowing a word of the language. His vice-Consul was worse and everything went wrong generally. Every one I met was an Alarmist and that is polite for liar. They asked Remington if he was the man who manufactured the rifles and gave us the *Iowa Democrat* to read. To night I reached here after a six hours ride through blazing fields of sugar cane and stopped on my way to the hotel to ask the Consul when the next boat went to Saqua la Grande— I had no letter of introduction to him as I had to the Matanzas consul, but as soon as he saw my card he got out of his chair and shook hands again and was as hearty and well bred and delightful as Charley himself and unlike Chas he did not ask me 14 francs for looking on him. He is out now chasing around to get me a train for to-morrow. But I won't go to-morrow. My hotel looks on the plaza and the proprietor and the whole suite of attendants are my slaves. It is just as different as can be. My interpreter does it, he calls himself *my valet*, although I point out to him that two shirts and twelve collars do not constitute a wardrobe even with a rubber coat thrown in. But he likes to play at my being a distinguished stranger and I can't say I object. Only when you remember the way I was invited to see Cuba and expected to see it, and now the way I am seeing it from car windows with *a valet*. What would the new school of yellow kid journalists say if they knew that. For the first time on this trip I have wished you were both with me, that was to night. I never see anything really beautiful but that it instantly makes me feel selfish and wish you could see it too. It has happened again and again and to night I wish you could be here with me on this balcony. The town runs down a slope to the bay and in the middle of it is the Plaza with me on the balcony which lets out of my sleeping room— "the room" so the proprietor tells me, "reserved only for the Capitain General." It is just like the description in that remarkable novel of mine where Clay and Alice sit on the balcony of the restaurant. I have the moonlight and the Cathedral with the open doors and the bronze statue in the middle and the royal palms moving in the breeze straight from the sea and the people walking around the plaza below. If it was in any way as beautiful as this Clay and Alice would have ended the novel that night.

I got a grand lot of letters to-day which Otto, my interpreter brought back from Havana after having conducted Remington there in safety. I must say you are writing very cheerfully now, but I don't wonder you worried at first but now that I am a commercial traveller with an order from Weyler which does everything when I find it necessary, you really must not worry any more but just let me continue on my uneventful journey and then come home. I shall have been gone so long and my friends, judging from Russell and Dana and Irene's letters, will be so glad to see me, that they will have forgotten I went out to do other things than coast around in trains. As a matter of fact this is a terribly big problem and most difficult to get the truth of, I find myself growing to be the opposite of the alarmist, whatever that is, although you would think the picturesque and dramatic and exciting thing would be the one I would rather believe because I want to believe it, but I find that that is not so, I see a great deal on both sides and I do not believe half I am told. As we used to say at college, "it is against history," and it is against history for men to act as I am told they are acting here— They show me the pueblo huddled together around the fortified towns, living in palm huts but I know that they have always lived in palm huts, the yellow kid reporters don't know that or consider it, but send off word that the condition of the people is terrible, that they have only leaves to cover them, and it sounds very badly. That is an instance of what I mean. In a big way there is no doubt that the process going on here is one of extermination and ruin. Two years ago the amount of sugar shipped from the port of Matanzas to the U. S. was valued at 11 millions a year. This last year just over shows that sugar to the amount of $800,000 was sent out. In '94, 154 vessels touched at Matanzas on their way to America. In '95 there were 80 and in '96 there are 16. I always imagined that houses were destroyed during a war because they got in the way of cannon balls or they were burned because they might offer shelter to the enemy, but here they are destroyed, with the purpose of making the war horrible and hurrying up the end. The insurgents began first by destroying the sugar mills, some of which were worth millions of dollars in machinery, and now the Spaniards are burning the homes of the people and herding them in around the towns to starve out the insurgents and to leave them without shelter or places to go for food or to hide the wounded. So all day long where ever you look you see great heavy columns of smoke rising into this beautiful sky above the magnificent palms the most noble of all palms, almost of all trees— It is the most beautiful country I have ever visited. I had no recollection of how beautiful it was or else I had not the knowledge of other places with which to compare it. Nothing out of the imagination can approach it in its great waterfalls and mossy rocks and grand plains and forests of white pillars with plumes waving above them. Only man is vile here and it is cruel to see the walls of the houses with blind eyes, with roofs gone and gardens burned, every church but one that I have seen was a fortress with hammocks swung from the altars and rude barricades thrown up around the doorways— If this is war I am of the opinion that it is a senseless wicked institution made for soldiers, lovers and correspondents for different reasons, and for no one else in the world and it is too expensive for the others to keep it going to entertain these few gentlemen— I have seen very little of it yet and I probably won't see much more, but I have seen all I want. Remington had his mind satisfied even sooner—but then he is an alarmist and exaggerates things— The men who wear the red badge of courage, I don't feel sorry for, they have their reward in their bloody bandages and the little cross on their tunic but those you meet coming back sick and dying with fever are the ones that make fighting contemptible—poor little farmers, poor little children with no interest in Cuba or Spain's right to hold it, who have been sent out to die like ants before they have learned to hold a mauser, and who are going back again with the beards that have grown in the field hospitals on their cheeks and their eyes hollow, and too weak to move or speak. Six of them died while I was in Jaroco, a town as big as Marion and that had been the average for two months, think of that, six people dying in Marion every day through July and August— I didn't stay in that town any longer than the train did— Well I have been writing editorials here instead of cheering you up but I guess I'm about right and when I see a little more I'll tell it over again to *The Journal*— It is not as exciting reading as deeds of daring by our special correspondent and I haven't changed my name or shaved my eyebrows or done anything the other men have done but I believe I am getting near the truth. They have shut off provisions going or coming from the towns, they have huddled hundreds of people who do not know what a bath means around these towns, and this is going to happen— As soon as the rains begin the yellow fever and smallpox will set in and all vessels leaving Cuban ports will be quarantined and the island will be one great plague spot. The insurgents who are in the open fields will live and the soldiers will die for their officers know nothing of sanitation or care nothing. The little Consul has just been here to see me and we have had a long talk and I got back at him. He told me he had seen the Franco-German war as a correspondent of *The Tribune* and I asked him if he had ever met another correspondent of *The Tribune* at that time a German student named Hans who cabled the story of the battle of Gravellote and who Archibald Forbes says was the first correspondent to use the cable. The Consul who looks like William D. Howells wriggled around in his chair and said "I guess you mean me but I was not a German student, I was born and raised in Philadelphia and Forbes got my name wrong, it is Hance." So then I got up and shook hands with him in my turn and told him I had always wanted to meet that correspondent and did not expect to do so in Cardenas, on the coast of Cuba.

Thank you all for your letters. I am glad you liked the Jameson book. I thought you knew I was a F. R. G. S. It was George Curzon proposed me and as he is a gold medallist of the Society it was easy getting in. Lots of love.

DICK.

Richard returned to New York from Cuba in February, 1897, but the following month started for Florence to pay me a long-promised visit. On his way he stopped for a few days in London and Paris.

>AMBASSADE DES ETATS-UNIS
>59 Rue Galilée,
>Paris, April 1st, 1897.

DEAR FAMILY:

I got over here to-day after the heaviest weather I ever tackled on this channel. Stephen Crane came with me. I gave him a lunch on Wednesday. Anthony Hope, McCarthy, Harold Frederic and Barrie came. Sir Evelyn Wood instead of coming was detained at the war office and sent instead a lance Sergeant on horseback with a huge envelope marked "On Her Majesty's Service," which was to be delivered into my hands— The entire Savoy was upset and it was generally supposed that war had been declared and that I was being ordered to the front— The whole hotel hung over us until I had receipted for the package and the soldier had saluted and clanked away. I gave Crane the letter as a souvenir. I also saw Seymour Hicks' first night and recognized 15 American songs in it.

The London *Times* offered me the position of correspondent on the Greek frontier. Every one in London thought it an enormous compliment and Harold Frederic, Ralph, Ballard Smith and the rest were very envious. I told them I could not go, but I was glad to have had the compliment paid me. Barrie has made out a scenario of the "Soldiers" for dramatic purposes and has asked the Haymarket management to consider it. So, that I guess that it must be good—

So, I also guess I had better finish it— I leave for Florence to night. I am having a fine, fine time and I am so glad you are all well.

Lots of love,

Dick.

Of the many happy days we have spent together, I do not believe there were any much more happy than the three weeks Richard remained with me. It was his first long visit to Italy and from the day of his arrival he loved the old town and its people who gave him a most friendly welcome. He had come at a time when Florence was at its best, its narrow quaint streets filled with sunshine and thronged with idling natives and the scurrying tourists that always came with the first days of spring. The Cascine and the pink-walled roads of the environs were ablaze with wild roses and here, after his rather strenuous experience in Cuba, Richard gave himself up to long days of happy idleness. Together we took voyages of discovery to many of the little walled and forgotten towns where the tourists seldom set foot. Once we even wandered so far as Monte Carlo, where my brother tried very hard to break the bank and did not succeed. But the Richard Harding Davis luck did not fail him completely and I remember I greatly envied him the huge pile of gold and notes that represented his winnings and which we did our very best to spend before we left the land of the Prince of Monaco. However, having had his first taste of war, Richard felt that he must leave the peace and content of Florence to see how the Greeks, with whom he had much sympathy, were faring with their enemies the Turks. As it happened, this expedition proved but a short interruption, and in less than a month he was once more back with his new-found friends in Florence.

April 28, 1897
On the Way to Patras on a Steamer.

DEAR FAMILY:

It has been a week since I wrote you last, when I sent you the Inauguration article. Since then I have been having the best time I ever had any place *alone*. I have had more fun with a crowd, but never have been so happy by myself. What I would have been had I taken some other chap with me I cannot imagine. But the people of this part of Greece have been so kind that I cannot say I have been alone. I never met with strangers anywhere who were so hospitable, so confiding and polite. After that slaughter-yard and pest place of Cuba, which is much more terrible to me now than it was when I was there, or before I had seen that war can be conducted like any other evil of civilization, this opera bouffe warfare is like a duel between two gentlemen in the Bois. Cuba is like a slave-holder beating a slave's head in with a whip. I am a war correspondent only by a great stretch of the imagination; I am a peace correspondent really, and all the fighting I have seen was by cannon at long range. (I was at long range, not the cannon.) I am doing this campaign in a personally conducted sense with no regard to the Powers or to the London *Times*. I did send them an article called "The Piping Times of War." If they do not use it I shall illustrate it with the photos I have taken and sell it, for five times the sum they would give, to the Harpers who are ever with us. As I once said in a noted work, "Greece, Mrs. Morris, restores all your lost illusions." For the last week I have been back in the days of Conrad, the Corsair, and "Oh, Maid of Athens, ere We Part." I have been riding over wind-swept hills and mountains topped with snow, and with sheep and goats and wild flowers of every color spreading for acres, and in a land where every man dresses by choice like a grand opera brigand, and not only for photographic purposes. I have been on the move all the time, chasing in the rear of armies that turn back as soon as I approach and apologize for disappointing me of a battle, or riding to the scene of a battle that never comes off, or hastening to a bombardment that turns out to be an attack on an empty fort.

I live on brown bread and cheese and goat's milk and sleep like a log in shepherds' huts. It is so beautiful that I almost grudge the night. Nora and Mother could take this trip as safely as a regiment and would see things out of fairyland. And such adventures! Late in life I am at last having adventures and honors heaped upon me. I was elected a captain of a band of brigands who had been watching a mountain pass for a month, and as it showed no signs of running away had taken to dancing on the green. I caught them at this innocent pastime and they allowed me to photograph them and give them wine at eight cents a quart which we drank out of a tin stovepipe. They drank about four feet of stovepipe or thirty-six cents' worth, then they danced and sang for me in a circle, old men and boys, then drilled with their carbines, and I showed them my revolver and field-glasses and themselves in the finder of the camera; and when I had to go they took me on their shoulders and marched me around waving their rifles. Then the old men kissed me on the cheek and we all embraced and they wept, and I felt as badly as though I were parting from fifty friends. They told my guide that if I would come back they would get fifty more "as brave as they" and I could be captain. I could not begin to tell you all the amusing things that have happened in this one week. I did not want to come at all, only a stern sense of duty made me. For I wanted to write the play in Charley's gilded halls and get to Paris and London. But I can never cease rejoicing that I took this trip. And it will make the book, "A Year from a Reporter's Diary," as complete as it can be. That was why I came. Now I have the Coronation of the Czar, the Millennial at Hungary, the Inauguration at Washington, the Queen's Jubilee, the War in Cuba, and the Greco-Turkish War. That is a good year's work and I mean to loaf after it. You will laugh and say that that is what I always say, but if you knew how I had to kick myself out of Florence and the Cascine to come here you would believe me. I want a rest and I am cutting this very short.

Don't fail to cut anything Dad and Mother don't like out of the Inauguration article. You will have me with you this winter on my little bicycle and going to dances and not paying board to anyone. Remember how I used to threaten to go to Greece when the coffee was not good. It seems too funny now, for I never was in a better place, or had more fun or saw less of war or the signs of war.

DICK.

May 7, 1897.
10 East Twenty-Eighth Street—NIT
Sponitza.

DEAR CHAS.

This is one of the places out of Phroso, but as you never read Phroso I will cut all that— I hate to say

In the Greco-Turkish War, 1897.

it so soon again but this is the most beautiful country to travel over I have seen— It is a fairy theatrical grand opera country where everybody dresses in petticoats and gold braided vests and carry carbines to tend sheep with— I rode from Santa Maura (see map) to a spot opposite Prevesa where they said there was going to be bombarding— There was not of course but I had I think the most beautiful ride of my life. I was absolutely happy—little lambs bleated and kids butted each other and peasants in fur cloaks without sleeves and in tights like princes sat on rocks and played pipes and the sky was blue, the mountains covered with snow and the fields and hills full of purple bushes and yellow and blue flowers and sheep— There was a cable station of yellow adobe. It was the only building and it looked across at Prevesa but nobody bombarded. The general gave me cognac and the cable operator played a guitar for me and the preyor sang a fine bass, the corporal not to be out done gave me chocolate and the army stood around in the sun and joined in the conversation correcting the general and each other and taking off their hats to all the noble sentiments we toasted. It was just like a comic opera. After a while when I had finished a fine hunck of cheese and hard eggs and brown bread I took a photograph of the General and the cable operator and the officer with the bass voice and half of the army— The other half was then sent to escort me to this place. It walked and I rode and there were many halts for drinks and cigarettes. They all ran after a stray colt and were lost for some time but we re-mobilized and advanced with great effect into this town. I was here taken in charge by at least fifty sailors and as many soldiers and comic opera brigands in drawers and white petticoats, who conducted me to a house on the hill where the innkeeper brought me a live chicken to approve of for dinner. Then the mayor of the town turned up in gold clothes and Barrison Sister skirts and said the General had telegraphed about me and that I was his— The innkeeper wept and said he had seen me first and the chorus of soldiers, sailors and brigands all joined in. I kept out of it but I knew the Mayor would win and he did. Then we went out to a man-of-war the size of the *Vagabond* and were solemnly assured there would be bombarding of Prevesa tomorrow— I go to sleep in that hope. We leave here at seven crossing the river and ride after the Greeks who are approaching Prevesa from the land side while the men-of-war bombard it from the river. At least that is what they say. I think it is the mildest war on both sides I ever heard of and I certainly mean to be a *Times* correspondent next time I play at going to war— After being insulted and frightened to death all over Cuba, this is the pleasantest picnic I was ever on— They seriously apologized for not bombarding while I was there and I said not to mention it—

With lots of love, old man, and to the family

DICK.

FLORENCE
May 16, 1897.

DEAR FAMILY:

Here I am safe and sound again in the old rooms in Florence. I was gone twenty-three days and was traveling nineteen of them, walking, riding; in sailboats, in the cars, and on steamers. I have had more experiences and adventures than I ever had before in three months and quite enough to last me for years.

After my happy ride through Turkey and the retreat of the Greek army in Arta, of which I wrote you last, I have been in Thessaly where I saw the two days' battle of Velestinos from the beginning up to the end. It was the one real battle of the war and the Greeks fought well from the first to the last. I left Athens on the 29th of April with John Bass, a Harvard graduate, and a most charming and attractive youth who is, or was, in charge of the *Journal* men; Stephen Crane being among the number. He seems a genius with no responsibilities of any sort to anyone, and I and Bass left him at Velestinos after traveling with him for four days. Crane went to Volo, as did every other correspondent, leaving Bass and myself in Velestinos. As the villagers had run away, we burglarized the house of the mayor and made it our habitation while the courier hunted for food. It was like "The Swiss Family Robinson," and we rejoiced over the discovery of soap and tablecloths and stray knives and forks, just as though we had been cast on a desert island. Bass did the cooking and I laid the table and washed up and made the beds, which were full of fleas. But we had been sleeping on chairs and on the floor for a week so we did not mind much.

The second day we were awakened by cannon and you can imagine our joy and excitement. We had it all to ourselves for eight hours, as it took the other correspondents that long to arrive. It was an artillery and infantry battle and about 20,000 men were engaged on both sides. The Greeks fought from little trenches on the hills back of the town and the Turks advanced across a great green prairie. It was very long range and only twice did they get to within a quarter of a mile of our trenches. Bass and I went all over the

Greek lines, for you were just as safe in one place as in another, which means that it wasn't safe anywhere, so we gave up considering that and followed the fight as best we could from the first trench, which was the only one that gave an uninterrupted view of the Turkish forces. It was a brilliantly clear day but opened with a hail storm, which enabled the Turks to crawl up half a mile in the sudden darkness. It also gave me the worst attack of sciatica I ever had. Fortunately, it did not come on badly until I reached Volo, when it suddenly took hold of me so that I could not walk. The trenches were wet with the rain and we had no clothes to change to, and two more showers kept us more or less wet all day. We had a fine view of everything and I learned a lot.

We were under a heavy fire for thirteen hours and certainly had some very close escapes. At times the firing was so fierce that if you had raised your arm above your head, the hand would have been instantly torn off. We had to lie on our stomachs with our chins in the dirt and not so much as budge. This was when the Turkish fire happened to be directed on our trench. At such times all the other trenches would fire so as to draw the attack away, and we would have to wait until it was over. The shells sounded like the jarring sound of telegraph wires when one hits the pole they hang from with a stone; and when the shells were close they sounded like the noise made by two trains passing in opposite directions when the wind is driven between the cars. The bullets were much worse than the shells as you could always hear them coming, and the bullets slipped up and passed you in a sneaking way with a noise like rustling silk, or if some one had torn a silk handkerchief with a sharp pull. One shell struck three feet from me and knocked me over with the dirt and stones and filled my nose and mouth with pebbles. I went back and dug it out of the ground while it was still hot and have it as a souvenir. I swore terribly at the bullets and Bass used to grin in a sickly way. It made your hair creep when they came very close. One man next me got a shot through the breast while he was ramming his cleaner down the barrel, and there were three killed within the limits of our fifty yards. We could not get back because there was a cross fire that swept a place we had to pass through, just about the way the wind comes around the City Hall in the times of a blizzard. We called it Dead Man's Curve, after that at Fourteenth Street and Union Square, because it was sprinkled with dead ammunition, mules and soldiers. We came through it the first time without knowing what we were getting into and we had no desire to go back again. So we waited until the sun set. I took some of the finest photographs and probably the only ones ever taken of a battle at such close range. Whenever the men fired, I would shoot off the camera and I expect I have some pretty great pictures. Bass took some of me so if there is any question as to whether I was at the Coronation, there will be none as to whether I was at Velestinos.

Our house was hit with two shells and bullets fell like the gentle rain from heaven all over the courtyard, so we would have been no safer there than behind the trenches. We sent off the first account of the battle written by anybody by midday, and stayed on until the next day at four when the place was evacuated in good order because, as usual, the Crown Prince was running away—from Pharsalia this time.

They say in Greece "Lewes, the peasant, won the race from Marathon, but Constantine the prince, won the race from Larissa."

I was all right until I got to Volo when my right leg refused absolutely to do its act and I had to be carried on a donkey. A Greek thought I looked funny sitting groaning on the little donkey; which I did—I looked ridiculous. So he laughed, and Bass and a French journalist batted him over the face and left me clinging to the donkey's neck and howling to them to come back and hold me up. But they preferred to fight, and a policeman came along and arrested the unhappy Greek and beat him over the head, just for luck, and marched him off to jail, just for laughing.

They took me to the hospital ship which was starting, and I came to Athens that way with one hundred and sixteen wounded; the man on my right had his ankles gone and the man on the left had a bullet in his side. They groaned all night and so did I. Then when the sun rose they sang, which was worse. I never saw anything more beautiful than the red-cross nurses, and I guess that is the most beautiful picture I shall ever see—those sweet-faced girls in blue and white bending over the dirty frightened little peasant boys and taking care of their wounds. I made love to all of them and asked three to marry me. I was in bed for two days after I got to Athens but had a fine time, as all the officers from the *San Francisco*, from the admiral down, came to see me, and the minister, consul and the rest did all that could have been done. I am now all right and was bicycling in the dear old Cascine this morning. On the whole it was a most successful trip. Sylvester Scovel and Phillips of *The*

World arrived just as it was all over, and so Bass and I are about the only two Americans who were in it.

The train from Brindisi stopped at Rome on the way back and I went to see the Pages. They took me out and showed me Rome by moonlight in one hour. It was like a cinematograph. They are here now and coming to dinner tonight. Last night the consul had all our friends to dinner to welcome me back, and maybe I was not glad. I had been living on cheese and brown bread and cold lamb for two weeks, with no tobacco, and sleeping five hours a night on floors and sofas. Sometimes the officers and men fought for food, and we never got anything warm to eat except occasionally tinned things which we cooked in my kit. It was the most satisfactory trip all round I ever had. I have been twenty years trying to be in a battle and it will be twenty years more before I will want to be in another.

On the eighteenth I start for London, stopping one day in Paris to see the Clarks and Eustises. It is going to be bigger than the Coronation for crowds, and Mother need not worry, I shall keep out of it. The Minister to Russia sent me word that the Czar's prime minister has given him my article and that the Czar said thank him very much. So that is all right. Also Hay is to present me to the Prince at the levee on the 31st of May, and I shall send him a copy, too. I am looking forward to London with such joy. Tell Mother to send me the *Bookbuyer* with her article in it. I have only read the reviews of it, and they are so enthusiastic that I must have the whole thing quick. It was such a fine thing to do about Poe, and to give those other two fetishes the coup de grâce. It reads splendidly and I want it all. What did Dad think of the Inauguration article? I send you all my dearest love and will have lots to tell you when I get back this time.

God bless you all.

DICK.

Richard left Florence the latter part of May, and went to London where he had made arrangements to report the Queen's Jubilee. He began his round of gayeties by being presented at Court. The Miss Groves and Miss Wather to whom he refers in the following letter were the clerks at Cox's hotel.

LONDON, June 2nd, 1897.

DEAR FAMILY:

I was a beautiful sight at the Levee. I wore a velvet suit made especially for me but no dearer for that and steel buttons and a beautiful steel sword and a court hat with silver on the side and silk stockings that I wore at Moscow and pumps with great buckles. I was too magnificent for words and so you would have said. I waited a long time in a long hall crowded with generals and sea captains and highlanders and volunteers and cavalry men and judges and finally was admitted past a rope and then past another rope and then rushed along into the throne room where I saw beefeaters and life guardsmen and chamberlains with white wands and I gave one my card and he read out "R. H. D. of the United States by the American Ambassador" and then I bowed to the Prince and Duke of York, Connaught and Edinburgh and to the American Ambassador and then Henry White and Spencer Eddy, the two Secretaries and the naval attache all shook hands with me and I went around in a hansom in the bright sunshine in hopes of finding some one who would know me. But no one did so I went to Cox's Hotel and showed myself to Miss Groves and Miss Wather. I went on the Terrace yesterday with the Leiters and at O'Connor's invitation brought them to tea. Labouchere was there and Dillon just out of jail and it was most interesting. I am very, very busy doing nothing and having a fine time—

DICK.

LONDON, June 21, 1897.

DEAR MOTHER:

Words cannot tell at least not unless I am well paid for it what London is like to-day. In the first place it is so jammed that no one can move and it is hung with decorations so that no one can see. Royal carriages get stuck just as do the humble drayman or Pickford's Van and royalties are lodging in cheap hotels with nothing but a couple of Grenadier's in sentry boxes to show they are any better blooded than the rest of the lodgers. I also added to the confusion by giving a lunch to the Ambassador and Miss Hay in return for the presentation. Lady Henry and Mrs. Asquith sat on either side of him and Mrs. Clark had Asquith and Lord Basil Blackwood to talk to— There was also Anthony Hope, the beautiful Julia Neilson and her husband Fred Terry and Lady Edward Cecil and Lord Lester— It went off fine and the Savoy people sent in an American Eagle of ice, decorated with American flags and dripping icy tears from its beak. It cost me five shillings a head and looked as though it cost that in pounds— To night I dine with the Goulds and then go to a musical where Melba sings, Padewreski plays and then walk the streets if I can until daybreak as I think of making the night before the procession the greater part of the story. I send you a plan showing my seat which cost me twenty-five dollars, the advertised price being $125. but there has been a terrible slump in seats. Love to dear Dad and Nora.

DICK.

LONDON.
89 Jermyn Street,
June 25th, 1897.

DEAR MOTHER:

The Jubilee turned out to be the easiest spectacle to get at and to get away from that I ever witnessed. Experience in choosing a place and police regulations made it so simple that we went straight to our seats and got away again without as much trouble as it would have taken to have gone to a matinee. The stage management of the thing almost impressed me more than anything else. For grandeur and show it about equalled the procession of the Czar and in many ways it was more interesting because it was concerned with our own people and with our own part of the world. Next to the Queen, Lord Roberts got all of the applause. He rode a little white pony that had been with him in six campaigns and had carried him on his march to Candahar. It had all the campaign medals presented to it by the War Department and wore them in a line on its forehead, and walked just as though he knew what a great occasion it was. After Roberts came in popularity a Col. Maurice Clifford with the Rhodesian Horse in sombrero's and cartridge belts and khaki suits. He had lost his arm and was easily recognized. Wilfred Laurier the French Premier of Canada and the Lord Mayor were the other favourites. The scene in front of St. Paul's was ab-

CAMPAIGNING IN CUBA AND GREECE

solutely magnificent with the sooty pillars behind the groups of diplomats, bishops and choir boys in white, University men in pink silk gowns, and soldiers, beef eaters, gentlemen at arms and the two Archbishops. The best moment was when the collected troops; negroes, Chinamen, East Indians, West Indians, African troopers, Canadian Mounted Police, Australians, Borneo police and English Grenadiers all sang the doxology together in the beautiful sunshine and under the shadow of that great facade of black and white marble. Also when the Archbishop of Canterbury without any warning suddenly after kissing the Queen's hand threw up his arm and cried out so that you could have heard him a hundred yards off "Three Cheers for Her Majesty" and the diplomats, and foreign rajahs and bishops and Salvation Army captains waved their hats and mortar boards and the soldiers ran their bearskins and helmets on their bayonets and spun them around in the air. The weather was absolutely perfect and there were no accidents. Last night the carriages were allowed to parade the streets and for hours the route was blocked with omnibuses hired by private parties, coster carts, private carriages, court carriages and the hansoms. The procession formed by these was two hours in going one mile. They passed my windows in Jermyn Street for three hours and a party of us sat inside and guyed the life out of them until one in the morning. We got very clever at it finally and very impudent and as the people were only two yards from us my windows being on a level with the tops of the buses and as we had a flaring illumination that lit up the street completely we had lots of fun with them especially with the busses, as we pretended to believe that the advertisements referred to the people on the top, and we would ask anxiously which lady was "Lottie Collins" and which gentleman had been brought up on "Mellin's Food"— We had even more fun with the swells coming home from the Gala night at the opera and hemmed in between costers and Pickford's vans loaded down with women and children.

They called on us for speeches and matches and segars and we kept the procession supplied with food and drink. Nobody got mad and they answered back but we were prepared with numerous repartees and they were apparently so surprised by finding a party of ladies and gentlemen engaged in chaffing court officials that they would forget to reply until they had moved on. One bus driver said "Oh, you can larff, cause your at 'ome. We are 'unting for Jensen on a North Pole Expedition. We won't be home for three years yet—" Charley seems very happy and he got a most hearty welcome. I shall follow him over. I do not think I shall go when he does as that would mean seeing people and getting settled and I must get the Greek war done by the 12th of July and the Jubilee by the 15th of August. I know you will not mind, but I have been terribly interrupted by the Jubilee and by so many visitors. They are running in all the time, so I shall try to get the Greek war article done before I sail and also have a little peaceful view of London. I have seen nothing of it really yet. It has been like living in a circus, and moving about on an election night. I am well as can be except for occasional twinges of sciatica but I have not had to go to bed with it and some times it disappears for a week. A little less rain and more sun will stop it. I hope you do not mind my not returning but we will all be together for many months this Fall and I really feel that I have not had a quiet moment here for pleasure and work. It has been such a rush. I do wish to see dear Dad. I am so very sorry about his being ill, and I hope he is having lots of fishing. Love to all at Marion—and God bless you.

RICHARD.

LONDON
July 13, 1897.

DEAR MOTHER:

Today Barrie gave a copyright performance of "The Little Minister" which Maude Adams is to play in the States. It was advertised by a single bill in front of the Haymarket Theater and the price of admission was five guineas. We took in fifteen guineas, the audience being Charley Frohman, Lady Craig and a man. Cyril Maude played the hero and Brandon Thomas and Barrie the two low comedy parts—two Scotchmen of Thrums. I started to play one of them, but as I insisted on making it an aged negro with songs, Barrie and Frohman got discouraged and let me play the villain, Lord Rintoul, in which character I was great. Maude played his part in five different ways and dialects so as to see which he liked best, he said. It was a bit confusing. Then one of the actors went up in the gallery and pretended to be a journalist critic who had sneaked in, and he abused the play and the actors with the exception of the man who played Whamond (himself) whom he said he thought showed great promise. Maude pretended not to know who he was and it fooled everybody. Mrs. Barrie played the gipsy and danced most of the time, which she said was her conception of the part as it was in the book. Her husband explained that this was a play, not a book, but she did not care and danced on and off. She played my daughter, and I had a great scene in which I cursed her, which got rounds of applause. Lady Lewis's daughters in beautiful Paquin dresses played Scotch lassies, and giggled in all the sad parts, and one actress who had made a great success as one of the "Two Vagabonds" made everybody weep by really trying to act. At one time there were five men on the stage all talking Scotch dialect and imitating Irving at the same time. It was a truly remarkable performance. Ethel Barrymore goes back on Saturday with Drew to play a French maid in "A Marriage of Convenience." She is announced to be engaged to Hope, I see by the papers. They are not engaged, of course, but the papers love to make matches. Look for me as sailing either on the 31st on the *St. Louis* or a week later. With lots and lots of love.

DICK.

In the late summer Richard returned to Marion and from there went to New York. However, at this time, the lure of England was very strong with my brother, and early December found him back in London.

LONDON, December 29th, 1897.

DEAR MOTHER:—

I had a most exciting Christmas, most of which I spent in Whitechapel in the London Hospital. I lunched with the Spenders and then went down with them carrying large packages for distribution to the sick. I expected to be terribly bored, but thought I would feel so virtuous that I would the better enjoy my dinner which I had promised to take with the

McCarthys— On the contrary, I had the most amusing time and much more fun than I had later. The patients seemed only to be playing sick, and some of them were very humorous and others very pathetic and I played tin soldiers with some, and distributed rich gifts, other people had paid for, with a lavish hand. I also sat on a little girl's cot and played dolls for an hour. She had something wrong with her spine and I wept most of the time, chiefly because she smiled all the time. She went asleep holding on to my middle finger like the baby in "The Luck of Roaring Camp." There were eighty babies in red flannel nightgowns buttoned up the back who had pillow fights in honor of the day and took turns in playing on a barrel organ, those that were strong and tall enough. In the next ward another baby in white was dying— Its mother was a coster girl, seventeen years old, with a big hat and plumes like those the flower girls wear at Piccadilly Circus. The baby was yellow like old ivory and its teeth and gums were blue and it died while we were watching it. The mother girl was drinking tea and crying into it out of red swollen eyes, and twenty feet off one of the red nightgowned kids was playing "Louisiana Lou" on the barrel organ. The nurse put the baby's arms under the sheets and then pulled one up over its face and took the teacup away from the mother who didn't see what had happened and I came away while three young nurses were comforting the girl. Most of the nurses were very beautiful, and I neglected my duties as Santa Claus to talk to them. They would stop talking to get down on their knees and dust up the floor, which was most embarrassing, you couldn't very well ask to be let to help. There was one coster who had his broken leg in a cage which moved with the leg no matter how much he tossed. He was like the man "who sat in jail without his boots, admiring how the world was made," he spent all his waking hours in wrapt admiration of the cage— He said to me "I've been here a fortnight now, come Monday, and I can't break my leg no how. Yer can't do it, that's all— Yer can twist, and kick, and toss, and it don't do no good. Yer jest can't do it— Now you take notice." Then he would kick violently and the cage would run around on trolleys and keep the broken limb straight. "See!" he would exclaim, "Wot did I tell you— Its no use of trying, yer just can't do it. 'ere I've been ten days a trying and it can't be done."

We had a very fine Christmas dinner just Ethel, the McCarthy's and I. Fanny, tell Charles, brought in the plum pudding with a sprig of holly in it and blazing, and after dinner I read them the Jackall— About eleven I started to take Ethel to Miss Terry's, who lives miles beyond Kensington. There was a light fog. I said that all sorts of things ought to happen in a fog but that no one ever did have adventures nowadays. At that we rode straight into a bank of fog that makes those on the fishing banks look like Spring sunshine. You could not see the houses, nor the street, nor the horse, not even his tail. All you could see were gas jets, but not the iron that supported them. The cabman discovered the fact that he was lost and turned around in circles and the horse slipped on the asphalt which was thick with frost, and then we backed into lamp-posts and curbs until Ethel got so scared she bit her under lip until it bled. You could not tell whether you were going into a house or over a precipice or into a sea. The horse finally backed

Ethel Barrymore at seventeen.

up a flight of steps, and rubbed the cabby against a front door, and jabbed the wheels into an area railing and fell down. That, I thought, was our cue to get out, so we slipped into a well of yellow mist and felt around for each other until a square block of light suddenly opened in mid air and four terrified women appeared in the doorway of the house through which the cabman was endeavoring to butt himself. They begged us to come in, and we did— Being Christmas and because the McCarthy's always call me "King" I had put on all my decorations and the tin star and I also wore my beautiful fur coat, to which I have treated myself, and a grand good thing it is, too— I took this off because the room was very hot, forgetting about the decorations and remarked in the same time to Ethel that it would be folly to try and get to Barkston Gardens, and that we must go back to the "Duchess's" for the night. At this Ethel answered calmly "yes, Duke," and I became conscious of the fact that the eyes of the four women were riveted on my fur coat and decorations. At the word "Duke" delivered by a very pretty girl in an evening frock and with nothing on her hair, the four women disappeared and brought back the children, the servants, and the men, who were so overcome with awe and excitement and Christmas cheer that they all but got down on their knees in a circle. So, we fled out into the night followed by minute directions as to where "Your Grace" and "Your Ladyship" should turn. For years, no doubt, on a Christmas Day the story will be told in that house, wherever it may be in the millions of other houses of London, how a beautiful Countess and a wicked Duke were pitched into their front door out of a hansom cab, and after having partaken of their

Christmas supper, disappeared again into a sea of fog. The only direction Ethel and I could remember was that we were to go to the right when we came to a Church, so when by feeling our way by the walls we finally reached a church we continued going on around it until we had encircled it five times or it had encircled us, we were not sure which. After the fifth lap we gave up and sat down on the steps. Ethel had on low slippers and was shivering and coughing but intensely amused and only scared for fear she would lose her voice for the first night of "Peter"— We could hear voices sometimes, like people talking in a dream, and sometimes the sound of dance music, and a man's voice calling "Perlice" in a discouraged way as if he didn't much care whether the police came or not, but regularly like a fog siren— I don't know how long we sat there or how long we might have sat there had not a man with a bicycle lamp loomed up out of the mist and rescued us. He had his mother with him and she said with great pride that her boy could find his way anywhere. So, we clung to her boy and followed. A cabman passed leading his horse with one of his lamps in his other hand and I turned for an instant to speak to him and Ethel and her friends disappeared exactly as though the earth had opened. So, I yelled after them, and Ethel said "Here, I am," at my elbow. It was like the chesire cat that kept appearing and disappearing until he made Alice dizzy. We finally found a link-boy and he finally found the McCarthy's house, and I left them giving Ethel quinine and whiskey. They wanted me to stay, but I could not face dressing in the morning. So I felt my way home and only got lost twice. The Arch on Constitution Hill gave me much trouble. I thought it was the Marble Arch, and hence— In Jermyn Street

I saw two lamps burning dimly and a voice said, hearing my footsteps "where am I? I don't know where I am no more than nothing—" I told him he was in Jermyn Street with his horse's head about twenty feet from St. James— There was a long dramatic silence and then the voice said— "Well, I be blowed! I thought I was in Pimlico! ! !"

This has been such a long letter that I shall have to skip any more. I have NO sciatica chiefly because of the fur coat, I think, and I got two Christmas presents, one from Margaret Fraser and one from the Duchess of Sutherland— Boxing Day I took Margaret to the matinee of the Pantomine and it lasted five hours, until six twenty, then I dressed and dined with the Hay's and went with them to the Barnum circus which began at eight and lasted until twelve. It was a busy day.

Lots of love.   DICK.

LONDON, March 20, 1898.

DEAR MOTHER:

The Nellie Farren benefit was the finest thing I have seen this year past. It was more remarkable than the Coronation, or the Jubilee. It began at twelve o'clock on Thursday, but at ten o'clock Wednesday night, the crowd began to gather around Drury Lane, and spent the night on the sidewalk playing cards and reading and sleeping. Ten hours later they were admitted, or a few of them were, as many as the galleries would hold. Arthur Collins, the manager of the Drury Lane and the man who organized the benefit, could not get a stall for his mother the day before the benefit. They were then not to be had, the last having sold for twelve guineas. I got *two* the morning of the benefit for three pounds each, and now people believe that I did get into the Coronation! The people who had stalls got there at ten o'clock, and the streets were blocked for "blocks" up to Covent Garden with hansoms and royal carriages and holders of tickets at fifty dollars apiece. It lasted six hours and brought in thirty thousand dollars. Kate Vaughan came back and danced after an absence from the stage of twelve years. Irving recited The Dream of Eugene Aram, Terry played Ophelia, Chevalier sang Mrs. Hawkins, Dan Leno gave Hamlet, Marie Tempest sang The Jewel of Asia and Hayden Coffin sang Tommy Atkins, the audience of three thousand people joining in the chorus, and for an encore singing "Oh, Nellie, Nellie Farren, may your love be ever faithful, may your pals be ever true, so God bless you Nellie Farren, here's the best of luck to you." In Trial by Jury, Gilbert played an associate judge; the barristers were all playwrights, the jury the principal comedians, the chorus girls were real chorus girls from the Gaiety mixed in with leading ladies like Miss Jeffries and Miss Hanbury, who could not keep in step. But the best part of it was the pantomime. Ellaline came up a trap with a diamond dress and her hair down her back and electric lights all over her, and said, "I am the Fairy Queen," and waved her wand, at which the "First Boy" in the pantomime said, "Go long, now, do, we know your tricks, you're Ellaline Terriss"; and the clown said, "You're wrong, she's not, she's Mrs. Seymour Hicks." Then Letty Lind came on as Columbine in black tulle, and Arthur Roberts as the policeman, and Eddy Payne as the clown and Storey as Pantaloon.

The rest of it brought on everybody. Sam Sothern played a "swell" and stole a fish. Louis Freear, a housemaid, and all the leading men appeared as policemen. No one had more than a line to speak which just gave the audience time to recognize him or her. The composers and orchestra leaders came on as a German band, each playing an instrument, and they got half through the Washington Post before the policemen beat them off. Then Marie Lloyd and all the Music Hall stars appeared as street girls and danced to the music of a hand-organ. Hayden Coffin, Plunkett Greene and Ben Davies sang as street musicians and the clown beat them with stuffed bricks. After that there was a revue of all the burlesques and comic operas, then the curtain was raised from the middle of the stage, and Nellie Farren was discovered seated at a table on a high stage with all the "legitimates" in frock-coats and walking dresses rising on benches around her.

The set was a beautiful wood scene well lighted. Wyndham stood on one side of her, and he said the yell that went up when the curtain rose was worse than the rebel yell he had heard in battles. In front of her, below the stage, were all the people who had taken part in the revue, forming a most interesting picture. There was no one in the group who had not been known for a year by posters or photographs: Letty Lind as the Geisha, Arthur Roberts as Dandy Dan. The French Girl and all the officers from The Geisha, the ballet girls from the pantomime, the bareback-riders from The Circus Girl; the Empire costumes and the monks from La Poupée, and all the Chinese and Japanese costumes from The Geisha. Everybody on the stage cried and all the old rounders in the boxes cried.

It was really a wonderfully dramatic spectacle to see the clown and officers and Geisha girls weeping down their grease paint. Nellie Farren's great song was one about a street Arab with the words: "Let me hold your nag, sir, carry your little bag, sir, anything you please to give—thank'ee, sir!" She used to close her hand, then open it and look at the palm, then touch her cap with a very wonderful smile, and laugh when she said, "Thank'ee, sir!" This song was reproduced for weeks before the benefit, and played all over London, and when the curtain rose on her, the orchestra struck into it and the people shouted as though it was the national anthem. Wyndham made a very good address and so did Terry, then Wyndham said he would try to get her to speak. She has lost the use of her hands and legs and can only walk with crutches, so he put his arm around her and her son lifted her from the other side and then brought her to her feet, both crying like children. You could hear the people sobbing, it was so still. She said, "Ladies and Gentleman," looking at the stalls and boxes, then she turned her head to the people on the stage below her and said, "Brothers and Sisters," then she stood looking for a long time at the gallery gods who had been waiting there twenty hours. You could hear a long "Ah" from the gallery when she looked up there, and then a "hush" from all over it and there was absolute silence. Then she smiled and raised her finger to her bonnet and said, "Thank'ee, sir," and sank back in her chair. It was the most dramatic thing I ever saw on a stage. The orchestra struck up "Auld Lang Syne" and they gave three cheers on the stage and in the house. The papers got out special editions, and said it was the greatest theatrical event there had ever been in London.

Dick.

CHAPTER XI

THE SPANISH-AMERICAN WAR

WHEN the news reached Richard that the Spanish-American War seemed inevitable he returned at once to New York. Here he spent a few days in arranging to act as correspondent for the New York *Herald*, the London *Times*, and *Scribner's Magazine*, and then started for Key West.

Off Key West—April 24th, 1898.
On Board *Smith, Herald* Yacht.

DEAR MOTHER:

I wrote you such a cross gloomy letter that I must drop you another to make up for it. Since I wrote that an hour ago we have received word that war is declared and I am now on board the *Smith*. She is a really fine vessel as big as Benedict's yacht with plenty of deck room and big bunks. I have everything I want on board and *The Herald* men are two old Press men so we are good friends. If I had had another hour I believe I could have got a berth on the flag ship for Roosevelt telegraphed me the longest and strongest letter on the subject a man could write instructing the Admiral to take me on as I was writing history. Chadwick seemed willing but then the signal to set sail came and we had to stampede. All the ships have their sailing pennants up. It is as calm as a mirror thank goodness but as hot as hell. We expect to be off Havana tomorrow at sunset. Then what we do no one knows. The crew is on strike above and the mate is wrestling with them but as it seems to be only a question of a few dollars it will come out all right. We expect to be back here on Sunday but may stay out later. Don't worry if you don't hear. It is grand to see the line of battleships five miles out like dogs in a leash puffing and straining. Thank God they'll let them slip any minute now. I don't know where "Stenie" is. I am now going to take a nap while the smooth water lasts.

DICK.

—Flagship New York—
Off Havana,
April 26, 1898.

DEAR FAMILY:

I left Key West on the morning of the 24th in the *Dolphin* with the idea of trying to get on board the flagship on the strength of Roosevelt's letter. Stenie Bonsal got on just before she sailed, not as a correspondent, but as a magazine-writer for *McClure's*, who have given him a commission, and because he could act as interpreter. I left the flagship the morning of the day I arrived. The captain of the *Dolphin* apologized to his officers while we were at anchor in the harbor of Key West, because his was a "cabin" and not a "gun" ship, and because he had to deliver the mails at once on board the flagship and not turn out of his course for anything, no matter how tempting a prize it might appear to be. He then proceeded to chase every sail and column of smoke on the horizon, so that the course was like a cat's cradle. We first headed for a big steamer and sounded "general quarters." It was fine to see the faces of the apprentices as they ran to get their cutlasses and revolvers, their eyes open and their hair on end, with the hope that they were to board a Spanish battleship. But at the first gun she ran up an American flag, and on getting nearer we saw she was a Mallory steamer. An hour later we chased another steamer, but she was already a prize, with a prize crew on board. Then we had a chase for three hours at night; after what we believed was the *Panama*, but she ran away from us. We fired three shells after her, and she still ran and got away. The next morning I went on board the *New York* with Zogbaum, the artist. Admiral Sampson is a fine man; he impressed me very much. He was very much bothered at the order forbidding correspondents on the ship, but I talked like a father to him, and he finally gave in, and was very nice about the way he did it. Since then I have had the most interesting time and the most novel experience of my life. We have been lying from three to ten miles off shore. We can see Morro Castle and houses and palms plainly without a glass, and with one we can distinguish men and women in the villages. It is, or was, frightfully hot, and you had to keep moving all the time to get out of the sun. I mess with the officers, but the other correspondents, the Associated Press and Ralph Paine of *The World* and *Press* of Philadelphia, with the middies. Paine got on because Scovel of *The World* has done so much secret service work for the admiral, running in at night and taking soundings, and by day making photographs of the coast, also carrying messages to the insurgents.

It is a wonderful ship, like a village, and as big as the *Paris*. We drift around in the sun or the moonlight, and when we see a light, chase after it. There is a band on board that plays twice a day. It is like a luxurious yacht, with none of the ennui of a yacht. The other night, when we were heading off a steamer and firing six-pounders across her bows, the band was playing the "star" song from the Meistersinger. Wagner and War struck me as the most fin de siècle idea of war that I had ever heard of. The nights have been perfectly beautiful, full of moonlight, when we sit on deck and smoke. It is like looking down from the roof of a high building. Yesterday they brought a Spanish officer on board, he had been picked up in a schooner with his orderly. I was in Captain Chadwick's cabin when he was brought in, and Scovel interpreted for the captain, who was more courteous than any Spanish Don that breathes. The officer said he had been on his way to see his wife and newly born baby at Matanzas, and had no knowledge that war had been declared. I must say it did me good to see him. I remembered the way the Spanish officers used to insult me in a language which I, fortunately for me, could not understand, and how I hated the sight of them, and I enjoyed seeing his red and yellow cockade on the table before me, while I sat in a big armchair and smoked and was in hearing of the marines drilling on the upper deck. He was invited to go to breakfast with the officers, and I sat next to him, and as it happened to be my turn to treat, I had the satisfaction of pouring drinks down his throat. I told stories about Spanish officers all the time to the rest of the mess, pretending I was telling them something else by making drawings on the tablecloth, so that the unhappy officer on his other side, who was talking Spanish to him, had a hard time not to laugh. I told Zogbaum he ought to draw a picture of him at the mess to show how we treated prisoners, and a companion one of the captain of the *Compeliton*, who came over with us on the *Dolphin*, and who showed us the marks of the ropes on his wrists and arms the Spaniards had bound him with when he was in Cabanas for nine months. The orderly messed with the bluejackets, who treated him in the most hospitable manner. He was a poor little peasant boy, half starved and hollow-eyed, and so scared that he could hardly stand, but they took great pride in the fact that they had made him eat three times of everything. They are, without prejudice, the finest body of men and boys you would care to see, and as humorous and polite and keen as any class of men I ever met.

The war could be ended in a month so far as the island of Cuba is concerned, if the troops were ready and brought over here. The coast to Havana for ten miles is broad enough for them to march along it, and the heights above could be covered the entire time by the fleet, so that it would be absolutely impossible for any force to withstand the awful hailstorm they would play on it. Transports carrying the provisions would be protected by the ships on the gulf side, and the guns at Morro could be shut up in twenty-four hours. This is not a dream, but the most obvious and feasible plan, and it is a disgrace if the Washington politicians delay. As to health, this is the healthiest part of the coast. The trade winds blow every day of the year, and the fever talk is all nonsense. The army certainly has delayed most scandalously in mobilizing. This talk of waiting a month is suicide. It is a terrible expense. It keeps the people on a strain, destroys business, and the health of the troops at Tampa is, to my mind, in much greater danger than it would be on the hills around Havana, where, as

Scovel says, there is as much yellow fever as there is snow. Tell Dad to urge them to act promptly. In the meanwhile I am having a magnificent time. I am burned and hungry and losing about a ton of fat a day, and I sleep finely. The other night the *Porter* held us up, but it was a story that never got into the papers. I haven't missed a trick so far except not getting on the flagship from the first, but that does not count now since I am on board.

I haven't written anything yet, but I am going to begin soon. I expect to make myself rich on this campaign. I get ten cents a word from *Scribner's* for everything I send them, if it is only a thousand words, and I get four hundred dollars a week salary from *The Times*, and all my expenses. I haven't had any yet, but when I go back and join the army, I am going to travel en suite with an assistant and the best and gentlest ponies; a courier and a servant, a tent and a secretary and a typewriter, so that Miles will look like a second lieutenant.

When I came out here on the *Dolphin* I said I was going to Tampa, lying just on the principle that it is no other newspaper-man's business where you are going. So, *The Herald* man at Key West, hearing this, and *not knowing I was going to the flagship*, called Long, making a strong kick about the correspondents, Bonsal, Remington and Paine, who are, or were, with the squadron. Stenie left two days ago, hoping to get a commission on the staff of General Lee. So yesterday Scovel told me Long had cabled in answer to *The Herald's* protests to the admiral as follows: "Complaints have been received that correspondents Paine, Remington and Bonsal are with the squadron. Send them ashore at once. There must be no favoritism."

THE SPANISH-AMERICAN WAR   233

Scovel got the admiral at once to cable Long on his behalf because of his services as a spy, but as Roosevelt had done so much for me, I would not appeal over him, and this morning I sent in word to the admiral that I was leaving the ship and would like to pay my respects. Sampson is a thin man with a gray beard. He looks like a college professor and has very fine, gentle eyes. He asked me why I meant to leave the ship, and I said I had heard one of the torpedo boats was going to Key West, and I thought I would go with her if he would allow it. He asked if I had seen the cable from Long, and I said I had heard of it, and that I was really going so as not to embarrass him with my presence. He said, "I have received three different orders from the Secretary, one of them telling me I could have such correspondents on board as were agreeable to me. He now tells me that they must all go. You can do as you wish. You are perfectly welcome to remain until the conflict of orders is cleared up." I saw he was mad and that he wanted me to stay, or at least not to go of my own wish, so that he could have a grievance out of it—if he had to send me away after having been told he could have those with him who were agreeable to him. Captain Chadwick was in the cabin, and said, "Perhaps Mr. Davis had better remain another twenty-four hours." The admiral added, "Ships are going to Key West daily." Then Chadwick repeated that he thought I had better stay another day, and made a motion to me to do so. So I said I would, and now I am waiting to see what is going to happen. Outside, Chadwick told me that something in the way of an experience would probably come off, so I have hopes. By this time, of course, you know all about it. I shall finish this later.

We began bombarding Matanzas twenty minutes after I wrote the above. It was great. I guess I got a beat, as *The Herald* tug is the only one in sight.

DICK.

Flagship—Off Havana
April 30th, 1898.

DEAR FAMILY:

You must not mind if I don't write often, but I feel that you see *The Herald* every day and that tells you of what I am seeing and doing, and I am writing so much, and what with keeping notes and all, I haven't much time— What you probably want to know is that I am well and that my sciatica is not troubling me at all—Mother always wants to know that. On the other hand I am on the best ship from which to see things and on the safest, as she can move quicker and is more heavily armored than any save the battle-ships— The fact that the admiral is on board and that she is the flagship is also a guarantee that she will not be allowed to expose herself. I was very badly scared when I first came to Key West for fear I should be left especially when I didn't make the flagship— But I have not missed a single trick so far— Bonsal missed the bombardment and so did Stephen Crane— All the press boats were away except *The Herald's*. I had to write the story in fifteen minutes, so it was no good except that we had it exclusively—

I am sending a short story of the first shot fired to the Scribner's and am arranging with them to bring out a book on the Campaign. I have asked them to announce it as it will help me immensely here for it is as an historian and not as a correspondent that I get on over those men who are correspondents for papers only. I have made I think my position here very strong and the admiral is very much my friend as are also his staff. Crane on the other hand took the place of Paine who was exceedingly popular with every one and it has made it hard for Crane to get into things— I am having a really royal time, it is so beautiful by both night and day and there is always color and movement and the most rigid discipline with the most hearty good feeling— I get on very well with the crew too, one of them got shot by a revolver's going off and I asked the surgeon if I might not help at the operation so that I might learn to be useful, and to get accustomed to the sight of wounds and surgery— It was a wonderful thing to see, and I was confused as to whether I admired the human body more or the way the surgeon's understood and mastered it— The sailor would not give way to the ether and I had to hold him for an hour while they took out his whole insides and laid them on the table and felt around inside of him as though he were a hollow watermelon. Then they put his stomach back and sewed it in and then sewed up his skin and he was just as good as new. We carried him over to a cot and he came to, and looked up at us. We were all bare-armed and covered with his blood, and then over at the operating table, which was also covered with his blood. He was gray under his tan and his lips were purple and his eyes were still drunk with the ether— But he looked at our sanguinary hands and shook his head sideways on the pillow and smiled— "You'se can't kill me," he said, "I'm a *New Yorker*, by God—you'se can't kill me." *The Herald* cabled for a story as to how the crew of the *New York* behaved in action. I think I shall send them that although there are a few things the people had better take for granted— Of course, we haven't been "in action" yet but the first bombardment made me nervous until it got well started. I think every one was rather nervous and it was chiefly to show them there was nothing to worry about that we fired off the U. S. guns. They talk like veterans now— It was much less of a strain than I had expected, there was no standing on your toes nor keeping your mouth open or putting wadding in your ears. I took photographs most of the time, and they ought to be excellent— what happened was that you were thrown up off the deck just as you are when an elevator starts with a sharp jerk and there was an awful noise like the worst clap of thunder you ever heard close to your ears, then the smoke covered everything and you could hear the shot going through the air like a giant rocket— The shots they fired at us did not cut any ice except a shrapnel that broke just over the main mast and which reminded me of Greece— The other shots fell short— The best thing was to see the Captains of the *Puritan* and *Cincinnati* frantically signalling to be allowed to fire too— A little fort had opened on us from the left so they plugged at that, it was a wonderful sight, the *Monitor* was swept with waves and the guns seemed to come out of the water. The *Cincinnati* did the best of all. Her guns were as fast as the reports of a revolver, a self-cocking revolver, when one holds the trigger for the whole six. We got some copies of *The Lucha* on the *Panama* and their accounts of what was going on in Havana were the best reading I ever saw— They probably reported the Matanzas bombardment as a Spanish victory— The firing yesterday was very tame. We all sat about on deck and the band played all the time— We didn't

THE SPANISH-AMERICAN WAR 237

even send the men to quarters— I do not believe the army intends to move for two weeks yet, so I shall stay here. They seem to want me to do so, and I certainly want to— But that army is too slow for words, and we love the "Notes from the Front" in *The Tribune*, telling about the troops at Chickamauga— I believe what will happen is that a chance shot will kill some of our men, and the Admiral won't do a thing but knock hell out of whatever fort does it and land a party of marines and bluejackets— Even if they only occupy the place for 24 hours, it will beat that army out and that's what I want. They'll get second money in the Campaign if they get any, unless they brace up and come over— I have the very luck of the British Army, I walked into an open hatch today and didn't stop until I caught by my arms and the back of my neck. It was very dark and they had opened it while I was in a cabin. The Jackie whose business it was to watch it was worse scared than I was, and I looked up at him while still hanging to the edges with my neck and arms and said "why didn't you tell me?" He shook his head and said, "that's so, Sir, I certainly should have told you, I certainly should"— They're exactly like children and the reason is, I think, because they are so shut off from the contamination of the world. One of these ships is like living in a monastery, and they are as disciplined and gentle as monks, and as reckless as cowboys. When I go forward and speak to one of them they all gather round and sit on the deck in circles and we talk and they listen and make the most interesting comments— The middy who fired the first gun at Matanzas is a modest alert boy about 18 years old and crazy about his work— So, the Captain selected him for the honor and also because there is such jealousy between the bow and stern guns that he decided not to risk feelings being hurt by giving it to either— So, Boone who was at Annapolis a month ago was told to fire the shot— We all took his name and he has grown about three inches. We told him all of the United States and England would be ringing with his name— When I was alone he came and sat down on a gun beside me and told me he was very glad they had let him fire that first gun because his mother was an invalid and he had gone into the navy against her wish and he hoped now that she would be satisfied when she saw his name in the papers. He was too sweet and boyish about it for words and I am going to take a snapshot at him and put his picture in *Scribner's*— "he only stands about so high—"

DICK.

I enclose a souvenir of the bombardment. Please keep it carefully for me— It was the first shot "in anger" in thirty years.

TAMPA, May 3rd, 1898.

DEAR NORA:

We are still here and probably will be. It is a merry war, if there were only some girls here the place would be perfect. I don't know what's the matter with the American girl—here am I—and Stenie and Willie Chanler and Frederick Remington and all the boy officers of the army and not one solitary, ugly, plain, pretty, or beautiful girl. I bought a fine pony to-day, her name was Ellaline but I thought that was too much glory for Ellaline so I diffused it over the whole company by re-christening her Gaiety Girl, because she is so quiet, all the Gaiety Girls I know are quiet.

THE SPANISH-AMERICAN WAR 239

She never does what I tell her anyway, so it doesn't matter what I call her. But when this cruel war is over ($6 a day with bath room adjoining) I am going to have an oil painting of her labelled "Gaiety Girl the Kentucky Mare that carried the news of the fall of Havana to Matanzas, fifty miles under fire and Richard Harding Davis." To-morrow I am going to buy a saddle and a servant. War is a cruel thing especially to army officers. They have to wear uniforms and are not allowed to take off their trousers to keep cool— They take off everything else except their hats and sit in the dining room without their coats or collars— That's because it is war time. They are terrible brave—you can see it by the way they wear bouquets on their tunics and cigarette badges and Cuban flags and by not saluting their officers. One General counted today and forty enlisted men passed him without saluting. The army will have to do a lot of fighting to make itself solid with me. They are mounted police. We have a sentry here, he sits in a rocking chair. Imagine one of Sampson's or Dewey's bluejackets sitting down even on a gun carriage. Wait till I write my book. I wouldn't say a word now but when I write that book I'll give them large space rates. I am writing it now, the first batch comes out in *Scribner's* in July.

Love to you all.

DICK.

During the early days of the war, Richard received the appointment of a captaincy, but on the advice of his friends that his services were more valuable as a correspondent, he refused the commission. The following letter shows that at least at the time my brother regretted the decision, but as events turned out he succeeded in rendering splendid service not only as a correspondent but in the field.

TAMPA—May 14, 1898.

DEAR CHAS.

On reflection I am greatly troubled that I declined the captaincy. It is unfortunate that I had not time to consider it. We shall not have another war and I can always be a war correspondent in other countries but never again have a chance to serve in my own. The people here think it was the right thing to do but the outside people won't. Not that I care about that, but I think I was weak not to chance it. I don't know exactly what I ought to do. When I see all these kid militia men enlisted it makes me feel like the devil. I've no doubt many of them look upon it as a sort of a holiday and an outing and like it for the excitement, but it would bore me to death. The whole thing would bore me if I thought I had to keep at it for a year or more. That is the fault of my having had too much excitement and freedom. It spoils me to make sacrifices that other men can make. Whichever way it comes out I shall be sorry and feel I did not do the right thing. Lying around this hotel is enough to demoralize anybody. We are much more out of it than you are, and one gets cynical and loses interest. On the other hand I would be miserable to go back and have done nothing. It is a question of character entirely and I don't feel I've played the part at all. It's all very well to say you are doing more by writing, but are you? It's an easy game to look on and pat the other chaps on the back with a few paragraphs, that is cheap patriotism. They're

THE SPANISH-AMERICAN WAR 241

taking chances and you're not and when the war's over they'll be happy and I won't. The man that enlists or volunteers even if he doesn't get further than Chickamauga or Gretna Green and the man who doesn't enlist at all but minds his own business is much better off than I will be writing about what other men do and not doing it myself, especially as I had a chance of a life time, and declined it. I'll always feel I lost in character by not sticking to it whether I had to go to Arizona or Governor's Island. I was unfortunate in having Lee and Remington to advise me. We talked for two hours in Fred's bedroom and they were both dead against it and Lee composed my telegram to the president. Now, I feel sure I did wrong. Shafter did not care and the other officers were delighted and said it was very honorable and manly giving me credit for motives I didn't have. I just didn't think it was good enough although I wanted it too and I missed something I can never get again. I am very sad about it. I know all the arguments for not taking it but as a matter of fact I should have done so. I would have made a good aide, and had I got a chance I certainly would have won out and been promoted. That there are fools appointed with me is no answer. I wouldn't have stayed in their class long.

DICK.

TAMPA, May 29, 1898.
DEAR CHAS.:

The cigars came; they are O. K. and a great treat after Tampa products. Captain Lee and I went out to the volunteer camps today: Florida, Alabama, Ohio and Michigan, General Lee's push, and it has depressed me very much. I have been so right about so many things these last five years, and was laughed at for making much of them. Now all I urged is proved to be correct; nothing our men wear is right. The shoes, the hats, the coats, all are dangerous to health and comfort; one-third of the men cannot wear the regulation shoe because it cuts the instep, and buy their own, and the volunteers are like the Cuban army in appearance. The Greek army, at which I made such sport, is a fine organization in comparison as far as outfit goes; of course, there is no comparison in the spirit of the men. One colonel of the Florida regiment told us that one-third of his men had never fired a gun. They live on the ground; there are no rain trenches around the tents, or gutters along the company streets; the latrines are dug to *windward* of the camp, and all the refuse is burned to windward.

Half of the men have no uniforms nor shoes. I pointed out some of the unnecessary discomforts the men were undergoing through ignorance, and one colonel, a Michigan politician, said, "Oh, well, they'll learn. It will be a good lesson for them." Instead of telling them, or telling their captains, he thinks it best that they should find things out by suffering. I cannot decide whether to write anything about it or not. I cannot see where it could do any good, for it is the system that is wrong—the whole volunteer system, I mean. Captain Lee happened to be in Washington when the first Manila outfit was starting from San Francisco, and it was on his representations that they gave the men hammocks, and took a store of Mexican dollars. They did not know that Mexican dollars are the only currency of the East, and were expecting to pay the men in drafts on New York.

THE SPANISH-AMERICAN WAR 243

Isn't that a pitiable situation when a captain of an English company happens to stray into the war office, and happens to have a good heart and busies himself to see that our own men are supplied with hammocks and spending money. None of our officers had ever seen khaki until they saw Lee's, nor a cork helmet until they saw mine and his; now, naturally, they won't have anything else, and there is not another one in the country. The helmets our troops wear would be smashed in one tropical storm, and they are so light that the sun beats through them. They are also a glaring white, and are cheap and nasty and made of pasteboard. The felt hats are just as bad; the brim is not broad enough to protect them from the sun or to keep the rain off their necks, and they are made of such cheap cotton stuff that they grow hard when they are wet and heavy, instead of shedding the rain as good felt would do. They have always urged that our uniforms, though not smart nor "for show," were for use. The truth is, as they all admit, that for the tropics they are worse than useless, and that in any climate they are cheap and poor.

I could go on for pages, but it has to be written later; now they would only think it was an attack on the army. But it is sickening to see men being sacrificed as these men will be. This is the worst season of all in the Philippines. The season of typhoons and rainstorms and hurricanes, and they would have sent the men off without anything to sleep on but the wet ground and a wet blanket. It has been a great lesson for me, and I have rubber tents, rubber blankets, rubber coats and hammocks enough for an army corps. I have written nothing for the paper, because, if I started to tell the truth at all, it would do no good, and it would open up a hell of an outcry from all the families of the boys who have volunteered. Of course, the only answer is a standing army of a hundred thousand, and no more calling on the patriotism of men unfitted and untrained. It is the sacrifice of the innocents. The incompetence and unreadiness of the French in 1870 was no worse than our own is now. It is a terrible and pathetic spectacle, and the readiness of the volunteers to be sacrificed is all the more pathetic. It seems almost providential that we had this false-alarm call with Spain to show the people how utterly helpless they are.

With love,   DICK.

TAMPA, June 9th, 1898.

Well, here we are again. Talk of the "Retreat from Ottawa" I've retreated more in this war than the Greeks did. If they don't brace up soon, I'll go North and refuse to "recognize" the war. I feel I deserve a pension and a medal as it is. We had everything on board and our cabins assigned us and our "war kits" in which we set forth taken off, and were in yachting flannels ready for the five days cruise. I had the devil of a time getting out to the flagship, as they call the headquarters boat. I went out early in the morning of the night when I last wrote you. I stayed up all that night watching troops arrive and lending a helping hand and a word of cheer to dispirited mules and men, also segars and cool drinks, none of them had had food for twenty-four hours and the yellow Florida people having robbed them all day had shut up and wouldn't open their miserable shops. They even put sentries over the drinking water of the

THE SPANISH-AMERICAN WAR 245

express company which is only making about a million a day out of the soldiers. So their soldiers slept along the platform and trucks rolled by them all night, shaking the boards on which they lay by an inch or two. About four we heard that Shafter was coming and an officer arrived to have his luggage placed on the Seguranca. I left them all on the pier carrying their own baggage and sweating and dripping and no one having slept. Their special train had been three hours in coming nine miles. I hired a small boat and went off to the flagship alone but the small boat began to leak and I bailed and the colored boy pulled and the men on the transports cheered us on. Just at the sinking point I hailed a catboat and we transferred the Admiral's flag to her and also my luggage. The rest of the day we spent on the transport. We left it this morning. Some are still on it but as they are unloading all the horses and mules from the other transports fifteen having died from the heat below deck and as they cannot put them on again under a day, I am up here to get cool and to stretch my legs. The transport is all right if it were not so awfully crowded. I am glad I held out to go with the Headquarter staff. I would have died on the regular press boat, as it is the men are interesting on our boat. We have all the military attachés and Lee, Remington, Whitney and Bonsal. The reason we did not go was because last night the *Eagle* and *Resolute* saw two Spanish cruisers and two torpedo boats laying for us outside, only five miles away. What they need with fourteen ships of war to guard a bottled up fleet and by leaving twenty-six transports some of them with 1,400 men on them without any protection but a small cruiser and one gun boat is beyond me. The whole thing is beyond me. It is the most awful picnic that ever happened, you wouldn't credit the mistakes that are made. It is worse than the French at Sedan a million times. We are just amateurs at war and about like the Indians Columbus discovered. I am exceedingly pleased with myself at taking it so good naturedly. I would have thought I would have gone mad or gone home long ago. Bonsal and Remington threaten to go every minute. Miles tells me we shall have to wait until those cruisers are located or bottled up. I'm tired of bottling up fleets. I like the way Dewey bottles them. What a story that would have made. Twenty-six transports with as many thousand men sunk five miles out and two-thirds of them drowned. Remember the *Maine* indeed! they'd better remember the *Maine* and brace up. If we wait until they catch those boats I may be here for another month as we cannot dare go away for long or far. If we decide to go with a convoy which is what we ought to do, we may start in a day or two. Nothing you read in the papers is correct. Did I tell you that Miles sent Dorst after me the other night and made me a long speech, saying he thought I had done so well in refusing the commission. I was glad he felt that way about it. Well, lots of love. I'm now going to take a bath. God bless you, this is a "merry war."

RICHARD.

In sight of Santiago—
June 26th, 1898.

DEAR CHAS.:

We have come to a halt here in a camp along the trail to Santiago. You can see it by climbing a hill. Instead of which I am now sitting by a fine stream on a cool rock. I have discovered that you really enjoy things more when you are not getting many comforts than you do when you have all you want. That sounds

THE SPANISH-AMERICAN WAR 247

dull but it is most consoling. I had a bath this morning in these rocks that I would not have given up for all the good dinners I ever had at the Waldorf, or the Savoy. It just went up and down my spine and sent thrills all over me. It is most interesting now and all the troubles of the dull days of waiting at Tampa and that awful time on the troopship are over. The army is stretched out along the trail from the coast for six miles. Santiago lies about five miles ahead of us. I am very happy and content and the book for Scribners ought to be an interesting one. It is really very hard that my despatches are limited to 100 words for there are lots of chances. The fault lies with the army people at Washington, who give credentials to any one who asks. To *The Independent* and other periodicals—in no sense newspapers, and they give seven to one paper, consequently we as a class are a pest to the officers and to each other. Fortunately, the survival of the fittest is the test and only the best men in every sense get to the front. There are fifty others at the base who keep the wire loaded with rumors, so when after great difficulty we get the correct news back to Daiquire a Siboney there is no room for it. Some of the "war correspondents" have absolutely nothing but the clothes they stand in, and the others had to take up subscriptions for them. They gambled all the time on the transports and are ensconced now at the base with cards and counters and nothing else. Whitney has turned out great at the work and I am glad he is not on a daily paper or he would share everything with me. John Fox, Whitney and I are living on Wood's rough riders. We are very welcome and Roosevelt has us at Headquarters but, of course, we see the men we know all the time. You get more news with the other regiments but the officers, even the Generals, are such narrow minded slipshod men that we only visit them to pick up information. Whitney and I were the only correspondents that saw the fight at Guasimas. He was with the regulars but I had the luck to be with Roosevelt. He is sore but still he saw more than any one else and is proportionally happy. Still he naturally would have liked to have been with our push. We were within thirty yards of the Spaniards and his crowd were not nearer than a quarter of a mile which was near enough as they had nearly as many killed. Gen. Chaffee told me to-day that it was Wood's charge that won the day, without it the tenth could not have driven the Spaniards back— Wood is a great young man, he has only one idea or rather all his ideas run in one direction, his regiment, he eats and talks nothing else. He never sleeps more than four hours and all the rest of the time he is moving about among the tents— Between you and me and the policeman, it was a very hot time— Maybe if I drew you a map you would understand why.

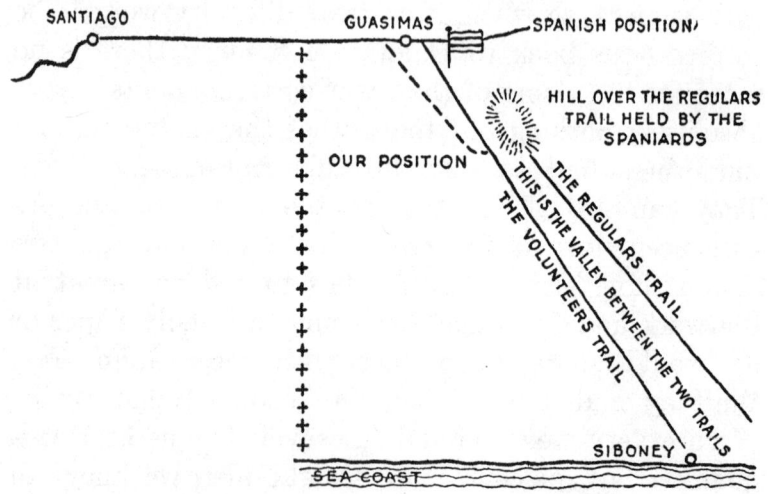

A consultation at General Wheeler's headquarters.

General Wheeler, General Wood, Colonel Dorst, Colonel Roosevelt, R. H. D., and others.

THE SPANISH-AMERICAN WAR 249

Wood and Gen. Young, by agreement the night before and without orders from anybody decided to advance at daybreak and dislodge the Spaniards from Las Guasimas. They went by two narrow trails single file, the two trails were along the crests of a line of hills with a valley between. The dotted line is the trail we should have taken had the Cubans told us it existed, if we had done so we would have had the Spaniards in the frontband rear as General Young would have caught them where they expected him to come, and we would have caught them where they were not looking for us. Of course, the Cubans who are worthless in every way never told us of this trail until we had had the meeting. No one knew we were near Spaniards until both columns were on the place where the two trails meet. Then our scouts came back and reported them and the companies were scattered out as you see them in the little dots. The Spaniards were absolutely hidden not over 25 per cent of the men saw one of them for two hours— I ran out with the company on the right of the dotted line, marked "our position." I thought it was a false alarm and none of us believed there were any Spaniards this side of Santiago. The ground was covered with high grass and cactus and vines so that you could not see twenty feet ahead, the men had to beat the vines with their carbines to get through them. We had not run fifty yards through the jungle before they opened on us with a quick firing gun at a hundred yards. I saw the enemy on the hill across the valley and got six sharp shooters and began on them, then the fire got so hot that we had to lie on our faces and crawl back to the rear. I had a wounded man to carry and was in a very bad way because I had sciatica,

Two of his men took him off while I stopped to help a worse wounded trooper, but I found he was dead. When I had come back for him in an hour, the vultures had eaten out his eyes and lips. In the meanwhile a trooper stood up on the crest with a guidon and waved it at the opposite trail to find out if the firing there was from Spaniards or Len Young's negroes. He was hit in three places but established the fact that Young was up on the trail on our right across the valley for they cheered. He was a man who had run on the Gold Ticket for Congress in Arizona, and consequently, as some one said, naturally should have led a forlorn hope. A blackguard had just run past telling them that Wood was killed and that he had been ordered to Siboney for re-inforcements. That was how the report spread that we were cut to pieces— A reporter who ran away from Young's column was responsible for the story that I was killed. He meant Marshall who was on the left of the line and who was shot through the spine— There was a lot of wounded at the base and the fighting in front was fearful to hear. It was as fast as a hard football match and you must remember it lasted two full hours; during that time the men were on their feet all the time or crawling on their hands— Not one of them, with the exception of ——, and a Sergeant who threw away his gun and ran, went a step back. It was like playing blindman's buff and you were it. I got separated once and was scared until I saw the line again, as my leg was very bad and I could not get about over the rough ground. I went down the trail and I found Capron dying and the whole place littered with discarded blankets and haversacks. I also found Fish and pulled him under cover—he was quite dead— Then I borrowed a carbine and joined Capron's troop, a second lieutenant and his Sergeant were in command. The man next me in line got a bullet through his sleeve and one through his shirt and you could see where it went in and came out without touching the skin. The firing was very high and we were in no danger so I told the lieutenant to let us charge across an open place and take a tin shack which was held by the Spaniards' rear guard, for they were open in retreat. Roosevelt ordered his men to do the same thing and we ran forward cheering across the open and then dropped in the grass and fired. I guess I fired about twenty rounds and then formed into a strategy board and went off down the trail to scout. I got lonely and was coming back when I met another trooper who sat down and said he was too hot to run in any direction Spaniard or no Spaniard. So we sat down and panted. At last he asked me if I was R. H. D. and I said I was and he said "I'm Dean, I met you in Harvard in the racquet court." Then we embraced —the tenth came up then and it was all over. My leg, thank goodness, is all right again and has been so for three days. It was only the running about that caused it. I won't have to run again as I have a horse now and there will be no more ambushes and moreover we have 12,000 men around us— Being together that way in a tight place has made us all friends and I guess I'll stick to the regiment. Send this to dear Mother and tell her I was not born to be killed. I ought to tell you more of the charming side of the life— we are all dirty and hungry and sleep on the ground and have grand talks on every subject around the headquarters tent. I was never more happy and content and never so well. It is hot but at night it is quite cool and there has been no rain only a few showers. No one is ill and there have been no cases of fever. I have not heard from you or any one since the 14th, which is not really long but so much goes on that it seems so. Lots of love to you all.

DICK.

After reading this over I ought perhaps to say that the position of the real correspondents is absolutely the very best. No one confounds us with the men at the base, and nothing they have they deny us. We are treated immeasurably better than the poor attachés who are still on the ship and who if they were spies could not be treated worse. But for Whitney, Remington and myself nothing is too good. Generals fight to have us on their staffs and all that sort of thing, so I really cannot complain, except about the fact that our real news is crowded out by the faker in the rear.

SANTIAGO.
Headquarters
Cavalry Division, U. S. Army.
Headqrs. Wood's Rough Riders.
June 29th, 1898.

DEAR DAD:

I suppose you are back from Marion now and I have missed you. I can't tell you how sorry I am. I wanted to see you coming up the street this summer in your knickerbockers and with no fish, but still happy. Never mind, we shall do the theatres this Fall, and have good walks downtown. I hope Mother will come up and visit me this September, at Marion and sit on Allen's and on the Clarks' porch and we can have Chas. too. I suppose he will have had his holiday but he can come up for a Sunday. We expect to move up on Santiago the day after to-morrow, and it's about time, for the trail will not be passable much longer. It rains every day at three o'clock for an hour and such rain you never guessed. It is three inches high for an hour. Then we all go out naked and dig trenches to get it out of the way. It is very rough living. I have to confess that I never knew how well off I was until I got to smoking Durham tobacco and I've only half a bag of that left. The enlisted men are smoking dried horse droppings, grass, roots and tea. Some of them can't sleep they are so nervous for the want of it, but to-day a lot came up and all will be well for them. I've had a steady ration of coffee, bacon and hard tack for a week and one mango, to night we had beans. Of course, what they ought to serve is rice and beans as fried bacon is impossible in this heat. Still, every one is well. This is the best crowd to be with—they are so well educated and so interesting. The regular army men are very dull and narrow and would bore one to death. We have Wood, Roosevelt, Lee, the British Attache, Whitney and a Doctor Church, a friend of mine from Princeton, who is quite the most cheerful soul and the funniest I ever met. He carried four men from the firing line the other day back half a mile to the hospital tent. He spends most of his time coming around headquarters in an undershirt of mine and a gold bracelet fighting tarantulas. I woke up the other morning with one seven inches long and as hairy as your head reposing on my pillow. My sciatica bothers me but has not prevented me seeing everything and I can dig rain gutters and cut wood with any of them. It is very funny to see Larned, the tennis champion, whose every movement at Newport was applauded by hundreds of young women, marching up and down in the wet grass. Whitney and I guy him. To-day a sentry on post was reading "As You Like It" and whenever I go down the line half the men want to know who won the boat race— To-day Wood sent me out with a detail on a pretense of scouting but really to give them a chance to see the country. They were all college boys, with Willie Tiffany as sergeant and we had a fine time and could see the Spanish sentries quite plainly without a glass. I hope you will not worry over this long separation. I don't know of any experience I have had which has done me so much good, and being with such a fine lot of fellows is a great pleasure. The scenery is very beautiful when it is not raining. I have a cot raised off the ground in the Colonel's tent and am very well off. If Chaffee or Lawton, who are the finest type of officers I ever saw, were in command, we would have been fighting every day and would probably have been in by this time. This weather shows that Havana must be put off after Porto Rico. They cannot campaign in this mud.

DICK.

SANTIAGO, July 1898.

DEAR FAMILY:

This is just to reassure you that I am all right. I and Marshall were the only correspondents with Roosevelt. We were caught in a clear case of ambush. Every precaution had been taken, but the natives knew the ground and our men did not. It was the hottest, nastiest fight I ever imagined. We never saw the enemy except glimpses. Our men fell all over the place, shouting to the others not to mind them, but

With Colonel Roosevelt in Cuba.

to go on. I got excited and took a carbine and charged the sugar house, which was what is called the key to the position. If the men had been regulars I would have sat in the rear as B—— did, but I knew every other one of them, had played football, and all that sort of thing, with them, so I thought as an American I ought to help. The officers were falling all over the shop, and after it was all over Roosevelt made me a long speech before some of the men, and offered me a captaincy in the regiment any time I wanted it. He told the Associated Press man that there was no officer in his regiment who had "been of more help or shown more courage" than your humble servant, so that's all right. After this I keep quiet. I promise I keep quiet. Love to you all.

RICHARD.

From Cuba Richard sailed with our forces to Porto Rico, where his experiences in the Spanish-American war came to an end, and he returned to Marion. He spent the fall in New York, and early in 1899 went to London.

One of the most interesting, certainly the most widely talked of, "sporting events" for which Richard was responsible was the sending of an English district-messenger boy from London to Chicago. The idea was inspired by my brother's general admiration of the London messenger service and his particular belief in one William Thomas Jaggers, a fourteen-year-old lad whom Richard had frequently employed to carry notes and run errands. One day, during a casual luncheon conversation at the Savoy with his friend Somers Somerset, Richard said that he believed that if Jaggers were asked to carry a message to New York that he could not only do it but would express no surprise at the commission. This conversation resulted in the bet described in the following letters. The boy slipped quietly away from London, but a few days later the bet became public and the newspapers were filled with speculation as to whether Jaggers could beat the mails. The messenger carried three letters, one to my sister, one to Miss Cecil Clark of Chicago, whom Richard married a few months later, and one to myself. As a matter of fact, Jaggers delivered his notes several hours before letters travelling by the same boat reached the same destinations. The newspapers not only printed long accounts of Jaggers's triumphal progress from New York to Chicago and back again, but used the success of his undertaking as a text for many editorials against the dilatory methods of our foreign-mail service. Jaggers left London on March 11, 1899, and was back again on the 29th, having travelled nearly eighty-four hundred miles in eighteen days. On his return he was received literally by a crowd of thousands, and his feat was given official recognition by a gold medal pinned on his youthful chest by the Duchess of Rutland. Also, later on, at a garden fête he was presented to the Queen, and incidentally, still later, returned to the United States as "buttons" to my brother's household.

Bachelors' Club,
Piccadilly, W.
March 15th, 1899.

DEAR CHAS.

I hope you are not annoyed about Jaggers. When he started no one knew of it but three people and I had no idea anyone else would, but the company sent it to *The Mail* without my name but describing me as

THE SPANISH-AMERICAN WAR 257

"an American gentleman"— Instantly the foreign correspondents went to them to find out who I was and to whom I was sending the letter— I told the company it was none of their damned business—that I employed the boy by the week and that I could send him where-ever I chose. Then the boy's father got proud and wrote to *The Mail* about his age and so they got the boy's name. Mine, however, is still out of it, but in America they are sure to know as the people on the steamer are crazy about him and Kinsey the Purser knows he is sent by me. After he gets back from Chicago and Philadelphia, you can do with him as you like until the steamer sails. If the thing is taken up as it is here and the fat is in the fire, then you can do as you please— I mean you can tell the papers about it or not— Somerset holds one end of the bets and I the other. There are two bets: one that he will beat the mail to Chicago, Somerset agreeing to consider the letter you give him to Bruce, as equivalent to one coming from here. The other bet is that he will deliver and get receipts from you, Nora and Bruce, and return here by the 5th of April— You and Bobby ought to be able to do well by him if it becomes, as I say, so far public that there is no possibility of further concealment— You have my permission to do what you please— He is coming into my employ as soon as he gets back and as soon as the company give him a medal.

Over here there is the greatest possible interest in the matter— At the Clubs I go to, the waiters *all* wait on me in order to have the latest developments and when it was cabled over here that the Customs' people intended stopping him, indignation raged at the Foreign office.

Lots of love,   DICK.

89 Jermyn Street, S. W.
March—1899

DEAR NORA:

This is to be handed to you by my special messenger, who is to assure you that I am in the best of health and spirits— Keep him for a few hours and then send him on to Chicago— As he is doing this on a bet, do not give him any written instructions only verbal ones. I am very well and happy and send you all my love— Jaggers has been running errands for me ever since I came here, and a most loyal servitor when I was ill— On his return I want to keep him on as a buttons. See that he gets plenty to eat— If he comes back alive he will have broken the messenger boy service record by three thousand miles. Personally, it does not cost me anything to speak of. The dramatization of the Soldiers continues briskly, and Maude is sending Grundy back the Jackal, to have a second go at it. Maude insists on its being done— so I stand to win a lot.

RICHARD.

Beefsteak Club,
9, Green Street,
Leicester Square, W. C.
Tuesday. March—1899.

DEAR MOTHER:—

The faithful Jaggers should have arrived to-day, or will do so this evening— I am sure you will make the poor little chap comfortable— I do regret having sent him on such a journey especially since the papers here made such an infernal row over it— However, neither of us will lose by it in the end—

I dined with Lady Clarke last night and met Lord Castleton there and he invited me up to Dublin for the Punchtown Races— I have a great mind to go and write a story on them— Castleton is a great sport and very popular at home and in England and it would be a pleasant experience. Kuhne Beveridge is doing a bust of me in khaki outfit for the Academy and also for a private exhibition of her own works, which includes the Prince of Wales, and the Little Queen of Holland.

Hays Hammond has invited me down to South Africa again, with a promise of making my fortune, but I am not going as it takes too long.

DICK.

CHAPTER XII

THE BOER WAR

On May 4, 1899, at Marion, Massachusetts, Richard was married to Cecil Clark, the daughter of Mr. and Mrs. John M. Clark of Chicago. After the marriage Richard and his wife spent a few weeks in Marion and the remainder of the summer in London and Aix-les-Bains.

MARION, May 28th, 1899.

DEAR MOTHER:

You sent me such a good letter about the visit of the three selected chorus girls. But what was best, was about your wishing to see me. Of course, you know that I feel that too. I would have it so that we all lived here, so that Dad could fish, and Nora and Cecil could discuss life, and you and I could just take walks and chat. But because that cannot be, we are no further away than we ever were and when the pain to see you comes, I don't let it hurt and I don't kill it either for it is the sweetest pain I can feel. If sons will go off and marry, or be war-correspondents, or managers, it does not mean that Home is any the less Home. You can't wipe out history by changing the name of a boulevard, as somebody said of the French, and if I were able to be in two places at once, I know in which two places I would be here with Cecil at Marion, and at Home in the Library with you and Dad and *The Evening Telegraph,* and Nora and Van Bibber. You will never know how much I love you

THE BOER WAR 261

all and you must never give up trying to comprehend it. God bless you and keep you, and my love to you every minute and always.

DICK.

Late in January, 1900, Richard and his wife started on their first great adventure together to the Boer War. Arriving at Cape Town, Richard left his wife there and, acting as correspondent with the British forces for the New York *Herald* and London *Mail,* saw the relief of Ladysmith. After this he returned to Cape Town, with the intention of joining Lord Roberts in his advance on Pretoria. But on arriving at Cape Town he learned that Lord Roberts did not intend to move for three weeks, and so decided to say farewell to the British army and to return to London in a leisurely and sightseeing fashion along the east coast. It was after they were well started on this return voyage that Richard conceived the idea of leaving the ship at Durban, going to Pretoria, and, as he expressed it, "watch the Boers fighting the same men I had just seen fighting them."

R. M. S. *Scot*
February 4th, 1900.

DEAR MOTHER:

A great change has come since I wrote you from Madeira. We are now on Summer seas and have regulated the days so that they pass very pleasantly—not that we do not want to be on land— I never so much wanted it— Somers is with us and is such a comfort. He is even younger than he used to be and so quick and courteous and good tempered. He is like a boy off on a holiday— I think he is very much in love with his wife, but in spite of himself he is glad to get a holiday, and like all of us he will be so much more glad when he is homeward bound. They threatened to shut us out of our only chance of putting foot on land at Madeira— In the first place, we were so delayed by the storm that we arrived at eight o'clock at night, so that we missed seeing it in its beauty of flowers and palms. And then it was so rough that they said it was most unsafe for us to attempt to go ashore. It was a great disappointment but I urged that every one loved his own life, and if the natives were willing to risk theirs to sell us photographs and wicker baskets it was probably safer than it looked— So we agreed to die together, and with Somers got our rain coats, and the three of us leaped into a row boat pulled by two Portugese pirates and started off toward a row of lamps on a quay that seemed much lower than the waves. The remainder on the ship watched us disappear with ominus warnings— We really had a most adventurous passage—towards shore the waves tossed us about like a lobster pot and we just missed being run down by a coal barge and escaped an upset over the bow anchor chain of a ship. It was so close that both Somers and I had our coats off and I told Cecil to grab the chain— But we weathered it and landed at a high gangway cut in the solid rock the first three steps of which were swamped by the waves. A rope and chain hung from the top of the wharf and a man swung his weight on this and yanked us out to the steps as the boat was on the wave. The rain beat and the wind roared and beautiful palms lashed the air with their fronds— It was grand to get on shore once again— At the end of the wharf we were hustled into a sled on steel runners, like a hearse with curtains around it and drawn by bullocks— The streets were all of mosaic, thousands of little stones being packed together like corn on a cob. Over this the heavy sledge was drawn by the bullocks while a small boy ran ahead through the narrow streets to clear the way— He had a feather duster made of horse's tail as a badge of authority and he yelled some strange cry at the empty streets and closed houses. Another little boy in a striped jersey ran beside and assured us he was a guide. It was like a page out of a fairy story. The strange cart sliding and slipping over the stones which were as smooth as ice, and the colored house fronts and the palms and strange plants. The darkness made it all the more unreal— There was a governor's palace buttressed and guarded by sentinels in a strange uniform and queer little cafe's under vines—and terraces of cannon, and at last a funny, pathetic little casino. It was such a queer imitation of Aix and Monte Carlo— There were chasseurs and footmen in magnificent livery and stucco white walls ornamented with silk *shawls*. Also a very good band and a new roulette table— Coming in out of the night and the rain it was like a theatre after the "dark scene" has just passed— There were some most dignified croupiers and three English women and a few sad English men and some very wicked looking natives in diamonds and white waistcoats. We had only fifteen minutes to spare so we began playing briskly with two shilling pieces Cecil with indifferent fortune and Somers losing— But I won every time and the croupiers gave me strange notes of the Bonco de Portugal which I put back on the board only to get more of a larger number— I felt greatly embarrassed as I was not a real member of the club and I hated to blow in out of a hurricane and take their money and sail away again— So I appealed to one of the sad eyed Englishmen and he assured me it was all right, that they welcomed the people from the passing steamers who generally left a few pounds each with the bank. But the more I spread the money the more I won until finally the whole room gathered around. Then I sent out and ordered champagne for everybody and spare gold to all the waiters and still cashed in seventy-five dollars in English money. It was pretty good for fifteen minutes and we went out leaving the people open-eyed, and hitting the champagne bottles— It was all a part of the fun especially as with all our gold we could get nothing for supper but "huevos frite" which was all the Spanish I could remember and which meant fried eggs— But we were very wet and hungry and we got the eggs and some fruit and real Madeira wine and then rowed out again rejoicing. The pirates demanded their pay half way to the boat while we were on the high seas but they had struck the very wrong men, and I never saw a mutiny quelled so abruptly— Somers and I told them we'd throw them overboard and row ourselves and they understood remarkably well— The next day we were the admired and envied of those who had not had the nerve "to dare to attempt." It was one of the best experiences altogether we had ever had and I shall certainly put Madeira on my silver cup.

RICHARD.

After their arrival at Cape Town, where Richard arranged for his wife to stay during his absence at the British front, he started for Ladysmith, sailing on the same vessel on which he had left England.

February 18th, 1900
On board *Scot*.

DEAR MOTHER:

I got off yesterday and am hoping to get to Buller before Ladysmith is relieved. I could not get to go with Roberts because Ralph has been here four months and has borne the heat and burden of the day, so although I only came in order to be with Roberts and Kitchener I could not ask to have Ralph recalled— They wanted me with Roberts and I wanted it but none of us could make up our minds to turn down Ralph. So I am going up on this side track on the chance of seeing Ladysmith relieved and of joining Roberts with Buller later. I shall be satisfied if I see Ladysmith fall. Fortunately I am to do a great deal of cabling for *The Mail* every day and that counts much more with the reading public than letters—

Cape Town is a dusty, wind ridden western town with a mountain back of it which one man said was a badly painted back drop— The only attractive thing about the town is this mountain and a hotel situated at its base in perfectly beautiful gardens. Here Cecil is settled. I got her a sitting room and a big bedroom and *The Mail* agent or Pryor pays her $150 a week and will take good care of her. It really is a beautiful and comfortable hotel and grounds and she has made many friends, and also I forced a pitch battle with a woman who was rude to her when we visited the hospital— So, as the hospital people were very keen to have me see and praise their hospital they have taken up arms against the unfortunate little bounder and championed Cecil and me. Cecil had really nothing to do with it as you can imagine— She only laughed but I gave the lady lots to remember.

On the other hand every one is as kind and interested in Cecil as can be. Mrs. Waldron whose son is Secretary to Milner and his secretary were more than polite to each of us. Milner spent the whole evening we were there talking to Cecil and not to the lady we had had the row with, which was a pleasing triumph. He sent me unsolicited a most flattering personal letter to the Governor of Natal, saying that I had come to him with my strong letters but that he had so enjoyed meeting me that he wished to pass me on on his own account. Cecil asked me what it was I had talked so much to him about and I asked her if it were possible she couldn't guess that of course I would be telling him how to run the colony. My advice was to bombard Cape Town and make martial law, for the Cape Towners are the most rotten, cowardly lot of rebels I ever imagined as being possible. He seemed so glad to find any one who appreciated that it was a queen's colony in name only and said, "Mr. Davis, it is as bad as this—I can take a stroll with you from these gardens (we were at the back of the Government House) and at the end of our stroll we will be in hostile territory."

We spent the last day after I had got my orders to join Buller (who seemed very pleased to have me) calling on the officials for passes together and they were in a great state falling into their coats and dressing guard for her and were all so friendly and hearty. The Censor seems to think I am a sort of Matthew Arnold and should be wrapped in cotton, so does Pryor *The Mail* agent who apologizes for asking me to cable, which is just what I want to do. They are very generous and are spending money like fresh air. I am to cable letters to Cape Town, only to save three days. So, now all that is needed is for something to happen. Everything else is arranged. All I want is to see three or four good fights and a big story like the relief of Ladysmith and I am ready and anxious to get home. I shall observe them from behind an ant hill—I don't say this to please you but because I mean it. This is not my war and all I want is to earn the very generous sums I have been offered and get home. We are just off Port Elizabeth. I will go on shore and post this there. With all love.

DICK.

Deal's Central Hotel, East London.
February 20th, 1900.

DEAR MOTHER:

We are stopping at every port now, as though the *Scot* were a ferry boat. We came over the side to get here in baskets with a neat door in the side and were bumped to the deck of the tender in all untenderness. This is more like Africa than any place I have seen. The cactus and palms abound and the Kaffirs wear brass anklets and bracelets. A man at lunch at this hotel asked me if I was R. H. D. and said he was an American who had got a commission in Brabants horse— He gave me the grandest sort of a segar and apparently on his representation the hotel brought me two books to sign, marked "Autographs of Celebrities of the Boer War." It seemed in my case at least to be premature and hopeful.

Good luck and God bless you. This will be the last letter you will get for ten days or two weeks, as I am now going directly away from steamers. This one reaches you by a spy gentleman who is to give it to Rene Bull of *The Graphic* and who will post it in Cape

Town— He and all the other correspondents are abandoning Buller for Roberts. Let 'em all go. The fewer the better, I say. My luck will keep I hope.

DICK.

Imperial Hotel,
Maritzburg, Natal.
Feb. 23rd, 1900.

DEAR MOTHER:—

I reached Durban yesterday. They paraded the band in my honour and played Yankee Doodle indefinitely— I had corrupted them by giving them drinks to play the "Belle of New York" nightly. The English officers thought Yankee Doodle was our national anthem and stood with their hats off in a hurricane balancing on the deck of the tender on one foot— The city of Durban is the best I have seen. It was as picturesque as the Midway at the Fair— There were Persians, Malay, Hindoo, Babu's Kaffirs, Zulu's and soldiers and sailors. I went on board the *Maine* to see the American doctors—one of them said he had met me on Walnut Street, when he had nearly run me down with his ambulance from the Penna Hospital. Lady Randolph took me over the ship and was very much puzzled when all the hospital stewards called me by name and made complimentary remarks. It impressed her so much apparently that she and the American nurses I hadn't met on board came to see me off at the station, which was very friendly. I have had a horrible day here and got up against the British officer in uniform and on duty bent— The chief trouble was that none of them knew what authority he had to do anything—and I had to sit down and tell them. I wonder with intelligence like theirs that their Intelligence Department did not tell them the Boers fought with war clubs and spears. I bought a ripping pony and my plan is to cut away from all my magnificent equipment and try to overtake Buller before he reaches Ladysmith and send back for the heavy things later. It is just a question of minutes really and it seems hard to have come 1500 miles and then to miss it by an hour— I arrive at Chievely tomorrow at five—that is only ten miles from where Buller is to night, so were it not for their d——d regulations I could ride across country and join them by midday but I bet they won't let me and I also bet I'll get there in time. Of course you'll know before you see this. Marelsburg is the capital and its chief industry is rickshaw's pulled by wild Kaffi's, with beads and snake skins around them and holes in their ears into which they stick segars and horn spoons for dipping snuff. The women wear less than the men and have their hair done up in red fungus.

Well, love to you all, to Nora and Dad and Chas, and God bless you.

DICK.

February, 1900.

DEAR DEAR MOTHER:—

I am here at last and counting the days when I shall get away. War does not soothe my savage breast. I find I want Cecil, and Jaggers, and Macklin to write, and plays to rehearse. Without Cecil bored to death at Cape Town, I would not mind it at all. I know how to be comfortable and on my second day I beat all these men who have been here three months in getting my news on the wire. For I am a news man now, and have to collect horrid facts and hosts of casualties and to find out whether it was the Dubblins or the Durbans that did it and what it was they did. I was in terrible fear that I would be too late to see the relief of Ladysmith but I was well in time and saw a fight the first few hours I arrived. It is terribly big and overwhelming like eighty of Barnum circuses all going at once in eighty rings and very hard to understand the geography. The Tugela is like a snake and crosses itself every three feet so that you never know whether you have crossed it yourself or not. Every one is most kind and I am as comfortable as can be. Indeed I like my tent so much that I am going to take it to Marion. It has windows in it and the most amusing trap doors and pockets in the walls and clothes lines and hooks and ventilators— It is colored a lovely green— I have also two chairs that fold up and a table that does nothing else and a bed and two lanterns, 3 ponies, one a Boer pony I bought for $12. from a Tommy who had stolen it. I had to pay $125 each for the other two and one had a sore back and the other gets lost in my saddle. But war as these people do it bores one to destruction. They are terribly dull souls. They cannot give an order intelligently. The real test of a soldier is the way he gives an order. I heard a Colonel with eight ribbons for eight campaigns scold a private for five minutes because he could not see a signal flag, and no one else could. It is not becoming that a Colonel should scold for five minutes. Friday they charged a hill with one of their "frontal" attacks and lost three Colonels and 500 men. In the morning—it was a night attack—when the roll was called only five officers answered. The proper number is 24. A Captain now commands the regiment. It is sheer straight waste of life through dogged stupidity. I haven't seen a Boer yet except some poor devils of prisoners but you can see every English who is on a hill. They walk along the skyline like ships on the horizon. It must be said for them that it is the most awful country to attack in the world. It is impossible to give any idea of its difficulties. However I can tell you that when I get back to the center of civilization. Do you know I haven't heard from you since I left New York on the *St. Louis*. All your letters to London went astray. What lots you will have to tell me but don't let Charley worry. I won't talk about the war this time. I never want to hear of it again.

DICK.

LADYSMITH. March 1st, 1899.
DEAR CHAS:
This is just a line to say I got in here with the first after a gallop of twelve miles. Keep this for me and the envelope. With my love and best wishes—

DICK.

LADYSMITH, March 3, 1900.
DEAR MOTHER:
The column came into town today, 2200 men, guns, cavalry, ambulances, lancers, navy guns and oxen. It was a most cruel assault upon one's feelings. The garrison lined the streets as a saluting guard of honor but only one regiment could stand it and the others all sat down on the curb only rising to cheer the head of each new regiment. They are yellow with fever, their teeth protruding and the skin drawn tight over their skeletons. The incoming army had had fourteen days hard fighting at the end of three months campaigning but were robust and tanned ragged and

caked with mud. As they came in they cheered and the garrison tried to cheer back but it was like a whisper.

Winston Churchill and I stood in front of Gen. White and cried for an hour. For the time you forgot Boers and the cause, or the lack of cause of it all, and saw only the side of it that was before you, the starving garrison relieved by men who had lost almost one out of every three in trying to help them. I was rather too previous in getting in and like every-one else who came from outside gave away everything I had so that now I'm as badly off as the rest of them. Yesterday my rations for the day were four biscuits and an ounce of coffee and of tea, with corn which they call mealies which I could not eat but which saved my horse's life. He is a Boer pony I bought from a Tommy for two pounds ten and he's worth both of the other two for which I paid $125 a piece. Tomorrow the wagon carrying my supplies will be in and I can get millions of things. It almost apalls me to think how many. Especially clean clothes. I've slept in these for four days. I got off some stories which I hope will read well. I can't complain now that I saw the raising of this siege. But I hope we don't stay still. I want to see a lot quickly and get out. This is very safe warfare. You sit on a hill and the army does the rest. My sciatica is not troubling me at all. Love to you all and God bless you.

DICK.

LADYSMITH, March 4th, 1900.

DEAR, DEAR MOTHER:

Today I got the first letter I have had from you since we left home. It was such happiness to see your

THE BOER WAR

dear sweet handwriting again. It was just like seeing you for a glimpse, or hearing you speak. I am so hungry for news of Nora and Chas and you all. I know you've written, but the letters have missed somehow. I sent yours right back to Cecil who is very lonely at present. Somerset has gone to the front and Jim—home—Blessed word! A little middy rode up to me today and began by saying "I'm going home. I'm *ordered* there. Home— To England!" He seemed to think I would not understand. He prattled on like a child saying what luck he had had, that he had been besieged in Ladysmith and seen lots of fighting and would get a medal and all the while he was "just a middy." "But isn't it awful to think of our chaps that were left on the ship" he said quite miserably. It is a beastly dull war. The whole thing is so "class" and full of "form" and tradition and worrying over "putties" and etiquette and rank. It is the most wonderful organization I ever imagined but it is like a beautiful locomotive without an engineer.

The Boers outplay them in intelligence every day. The whole army is officered by one class and that the dull one. It is like the House of Peers. You would not believe the mistakes they make, the awful way in which they sacrifice the lives of officers and men. And they let the Boers escape. I watched the Boers for four hours the other day escaping after the battle of Pieters and I asked, not because I wanted them captured but just as a military proposition "Why don't you send out your cavalry and light artillery and take those wagons?" The staff officer giggled and said "They might kill us." I don't know what he meant; neither did he. However, I'm sick of it but there's nothing else to talk of. I hate all the people about me and this dirty town and I wish I was back. And I'm going too. I'll have started by the time you get this.

I mean to cut out of this soon but don't imagine I'm in any danger. I'm taking d——d good care to keep out of danger. No one is more determined on that than I am. Dear Mother, this is such a dull letter but you must forgive me. I was never so homesick and bored in my life. It will be better when I go out tomorrow in my green tent and leave this beastly hole. I like the tent life, and the horses and being clean. I've really starved here for four days and haven't had a clean thing on me. God bless you all and dear Nora God bless her and Chas and the Lone Fisherman.

DICK.

Outside Ladysmith.
5th March, 1900.

DEAREST MOTHER:

I was a brute to write as I did last night. But I was so blue in that miserable town!!! It was so foul and dirty. The town smelt as bad as Johnstown. My room in the so called hotel stunk, the dirt was all over the floor and the servants had to be paid to do everything even to bring you a towel—and then I had no place to write or be alone, and nothing to eat— The poor souls at my table who had been in the siege, when they got a little bit of sugar or a can of condensed milk would carry it off from the table as though it were a diamond diadem— I did the same thing myself for I couldn't eat what they gave me and so I corrupted the canteen dealer and bought tin things— I've really never wanted tobacco so much and food as I have here—to give away I mean, for it was something wonderful to see what it meant to them. Three troopers came into the dining room yesterday and asked if they could buy some tea and were turned out so rudely that it seemed to hurt them much more than the fact that they were hungry: I followed them out and begged them to come back to my verandah and have tea with me but they at first would not because they knew I had witnessed what had happened in the hotel. They belonged to a very good regiment and they had been starved for four months. But in spite of their independence I got them to my porch. I had just purchased at awful prices a few delicacies like sugar and tobacco, marmalade and a bottle of whiskey. So I gave them to them and I never enjoyed anything so much— The poor yellow faced skeletons ate in absolute silence still fighting with their pride until I told them I was an American and was a canteen contractor's friend— Then I gave them segars and it was too pitiful— In our column, if you give a man something extra he says a lot and swears it's the best drink or the best segar or that you're the best chap he ever met— Just as I say it to them when they give me things. But these starved bodies tried to be very polite and conversational on every subject except food—when I offered them the segars which could only be got then at a dollar twenty-five a piece (they had not cost me that as I had bought them in Cape Town for two cents apiece!) What has Dad to say to that for economy? They accepted them quite as though it was in Havana—and then leaned back and went off into opium dreams— Imagine the first segar after three months. I am out here now on a bluff, with two trees in front and great hills with names historical of the siege of Ladysmith—names which I refuse to learn or remember—I am perfectly comfortable and were it not for Cecil perfectly content— If she were only here it would be perfectly magnificent— I have a retinue that would do credit to the Warringtons in the Virginians— Three Kaffir boys who refuse to yield to my sense of the picturesque and go naked like their less effete brothers, two oxen and three ponies, a little puppy I found starved in Ladysmith and fed on compressed beef tablets. I call her Ladysmith and she sleeps beside my cot and in my lap when I am reading—I have also a beautiful tent with tape window panes, ventilators, pockets inside, doors that loop up and red knobs; also, it is green so that the ants won't eat it. Also two tables, two chairs, a bath tub, two lanterns, and a cape cart—and a folding bed— In Cuba I had two saddle bags and was just as clean and just as happy. One boy does nothing but polish my boots and gaiters and harness, so that I look as well as the officers who are not much good at anything but that. I must tell you what I think is the saddest story of the siege— They could not feed the horses, so they kept part of them for scouting, part to eat, and drove 3,000 of them towards the Boers. Being well trained cavalry horses, they did not know how to eat grass, so at bugle call the whole 3,000 came trotting back again and sentries were placed at every street to stampede them back into the veldt— One horse from one battery met out in the prairie another horse that had been its gun mate in an artillery regiment five years before in India and the two poor things came galloping back side by side and passed the sentries and into the lines and drew up beside their battery. Another horse found its rider acting as sentry and

Kaffir boys at Ladysmith.

when the man tried to drive it away it thought he was playing with it and kept coming back and finally the man brought it in to the colonel and cried and asked if it might have half of his rations of corn. Good night and God bless you all with all my love.

DICK.

March 15th, 1900.

DEAR MOTHER:

I am on my way back to Cape Town. This seemed better than staying with Buller who will not move for two or three weeks. I shall either go straight up to Roberts, or we will return to London. I have seen the relief of Ladysmith and got a very good idea of it all, and I do not know but what I shall quit now. I started in too late to do much with it and as it is I have seen a great deal. It is neither an interesting country nor an interesting war. But I don't have to stay here to oblige anybody. If I do go up to Roberts it will only be to stay for three weeks at the most and only then if there is fighting. I won't go if he is resting as Buller is. So this will explain why we start home so soon. I am very glad I came. I would have been very sorry always if I had not, but my heart is not in it as, of course, it was in our war. Sometimes they fight all day using seven or eight regiments and kill a terrible lot of fine soldiers and capture forty Boer farmers and two women. It is not the kind of war I care to report. "Nor mean to!" I cannot make a book out of what little I've seen but I will come out about even. It has been very rough on Cecil. Today 1 went to the *Maine* and asked Lady Randolph to give me a lift down to Cape Town as the ship gets there two days ahead of the Castle

Steamer. So, they were apparently very glad to have me and I am going on Saturday. I like it on the ship where I have been spending the day as it is fun taking care of the wounded and listening to their stories. I am to write an article for her next Anglo Saxon magazine on the Passing of the War Correspondent. The idea is that he must either disappear altogether like the Vivandiere or be allowed to do his work. As it is now the Government forces him upon the Generals against their will and so they get back by taking it out of him. Either they should persuade the Government that their objections to him are weighty and suppress him altogether, or recognize him as a part of the outfit. I don't much care which as I certainly would never again go with an English army. I am sorry the letters home have been so dull but I have had rather hard luck straight through, and the distances are so very great and the time spent in covering them seems very wasteful. I shall be glad I saw it because it is the biggest thing as to scale that I ever saw of the sort, and I could not have afforded to have missed being in it. It is the first big modern war and all the conditions and weapons are new. I don't think the English have learned anything by it, because the fault lies entirely with their officers who are all or nearly all of one class.

DICK.

March 25th, 1900.
Cape Town.

This is just to explain our plans and as they take a bit of explaining this is meant for the Houses of Clark and of Davis. So, pass it on— After Ladysmith was relieved Buller decided he would not move for a month, so I came back to join Roberts. I could not do that on first arriving because there was a *Mail* man with him. I meant to do it later as a *Herald* man, and to let *The Mail* go. But on arriving here, having spent a week in coming and having sold all my outfit at a loss, I found that Roberts did not intend to move for three weeks either. So I decided I had seen enough to justify my returning. There were other reasons, the chief one being that the English irritated me and I had so little sympathy with them that I could not write with any pleasure of their work. My sporting blood refused to boil at the spectacle of such a monster Empire getting the worst of it from an untrained band of farmers— I found I admired the farmers. So we decided to chuck it and go to London. I would not have missed it for anything. I would never have been satisfied, if we had not come. I have seen much of the country and the people, and of the army and its wonderful organization and discipline. I enjoyed two battles—and the relief of Ladysmith is one of the things to have seen, almost the best, if not the best. Every officer and correspondent agrees that I got the pick of the fighting and the "best story." By the way, I beat all the London papers in getting out the news by one day. At least, so Pryor, *The Mail* manager tells me. The paper was very much pleased. We have now decided to come home by the East Coast. It was Cecil's idea and wish and I was only too glad to do it. She says we certainly will never come to this country again. God help us if we do—and that it would be criminal to spend seventeen blank days on the West coast when we could fill in the entire trip North on the East Coast at many ports. It is a rather complicated trip as one has to change frequently but it will be a great thing to have seen. Cecil has really seen nothing at Cape Town and on this trip she will be paid for all the boredom that has gone before. I have been over part of it and am sure. Durban alone is one of the most curious cities I ever saw. It is like the Midway at the Fair. I want her to have some fun out of this. She has been so unselfish and fine all through and I hope I can make the rest of the adventure to her liking— It is sure to be for after Delagoa Bay it is all real Africa not the shoddy "colonial" shopkeepers' paradise that we have here. And we are going to stop off at Zanzibar for some time where we have letters to everybody and where Cecil is to draw the Sultan and I am to play him the "Typical Tune of Zanzibar." You will see by our route that we spend two days or a day at many places and so shall get a good idea of the country. The *Konig* is a 5,000 ton ship and we have two cabins— From Port Said we will run up to Cairo to get a dinner and then over to Constantinople to see Lloyd Griscom and the city which Cecil has never visited. Then to Paris by way of the Orient Express. Then London and back with Charley to Aix. I feel sure that one more course there will cure my leg for always. As it is it has not touched me once even during the campaign when I was wet and had to climb hills, and at Ladysmith, where I had no food for a week. Of course, if we get tired on the way up we may go straight on from Port Said to Marseilles and so to London. It seems funny to look upon Port Said as being at home, but from this distance it seems as near New York as Boston— You will get this when we reach Zanzibar or later and we will cable when we can.

DICK.

It was said at the time that Richard left the British forces because the censors would not permit him to send out the truth about Buller's advance, and that the English officials resented his going to report the war from the Boer side. The first statement my brother flatly denied, and the fact that it was through the direct intervention of Sir Alfred Milner, assisted by the efforts of our consul Adelbert S. Hay at Pretoria, that Richard was enabled to reach the Boer capital seems to prove the latter charge equally false. Although throughout the war my brother's sympathies were with the Boers, and in spite of the fact that the papers he represented wanted him to report the war from the Boer side, he persisted in going at first with the British forces. His reasons were that he wished to see a great army, with all modern equipment in action, and that practically all of his English friends were with the British army. "My only reason for leaving it", he wrote, "was the fact that I found myself facing a month of idleness. Had General Buller continued his advance immediately after his relief of Ladysmith I would have gone with his column and would probably have never seen a Boer, except a Boer prisoner."

Royal Hotel,
Durban, Natal.
April 5th, 1900.

Dear Mother:

We arrived here to-day and got off in a special tug together. We did the basket trick all right, although the next time it came down a swell raised the tug and fractured every one in the basket except Sangree and Rogers, the two New York correspondents who were hanging on by the upper edges. Cecil loved the place which is the Midway Plaisance of cities and we had a good lunch and managed to get into the hotel where there are over twenty cots in the reading room, and hall. The Commandant objected to our going to Praetoria and seemed inclined to refuse us passes to leave Durban for Delagoa Bay. He also was rather fresh to Cecil, so I called him down very hard, and told him if he couldn't make up his mind whether we would go or not, I'd wire to some others who would help him to make up his mind quickly. He said I was at liberty to do that, so I went out and burned wires over all of South Africa. As he reads all the telegrams he naturally read mine and the next morning he was as humble and white as a head waiter. But by ten o'clock my wires began to bear fruit and he began to catch it. Milner wired him to send us on at once and apologized to us by another wire so all is well and we go vouched for by the High Commissioner.

DICK.

PRETORIA, May 18th, 1900.

DEAR DAD—AND OTHERS OF THE CLARK AND DAVIS FAMILIES:

I have not had time to write such a long letter as this one must be, as I have been working on my *Ledger* and *Scribner* stories.

Cecil and I started to the "front," which was then May 4th, at Brandfort with Captain Von Loosberg, a German baron who married in New Orleans and became an American citizen and who is now in command of Loosberg's Artillery in the Free State. The night we left, the English took Brandfort, so we decided to go only as far as Winburg. The next morning

THE BOER WAR

the train despatcher informed us Winburg was taken, so we decided to go to Smalldeel, but that went during the afternoon, so we stopped at Kronstad. From there, after a day's rest, we went to Ventersberg station, and rode across to Ventersberg town, about two hours away, and put up in Jones's Hotel. The next day we went down to the Boer laagers on the Sand river and met President Steyn on the way. He got out of his Cape Cart and gave Cecil a rose and Loosberg his field glasses, which Cecil took from Loosberg in exchange for her own Zeiss glass, and he gave me a drink and an interview. He also gave us a letter to St. Reid, who had established an ambulance base on Cronje's farm, telling him to give Cecil something to sleep upon. The Boers were very polite to Cecil and as she rode through the different camps every man took off his hat. We went back to Ventersberg that night and about two o'clock Cecil came to my room and woke me up with the intelligence that the British were only two hours away. She had heard the commandant informing the landlady, a grand low comedy character from Brooklyn, who had the room next to Cecil's. I interviewed the landlady who was sitting up in bed in curl papers, and with a Webley revolver. She was quite hysterical so I aroused Loosberg who was too sleepy to understand. The commandant could be heard in the distance offering his kingdom for a horse and a Cape cart. Cecil and I decided our horses were done up and that we were too ignorant of the trail to know where to run. So we decided to go to sleep. In the morning we confessed that each had been afraid the other would want to escape, and each wanted only to be allowed to go to sleep again. Loosberg's Cape Cart and five mules having arrived we packed our things on it and started again for the Sand River where we spent the night on Cronje's farm. Mrs. Cronje had taken away all the bedding but Dr. Reid gave Cecil his field mattress and I made one out of rugs and piano covers. In the morning I found that the iron straps of the mattress had marked me for life like a grilled beefsteak. There were only Reid and his assistant surgeon in the farmhouse and they were greatly excited at having a woman to look after.

We bade farewell to Loosberg who had found his artillery push, and started off in his Cape Cart which he wished us to use and take back for him for safety to Del Hay at Pretoria. Our objective point was the railroad bridge over the sand. The Boers were on one bank, the British about seven miles back on the other, the trail ran along the British side of the river which was sad of it. However, we drove on, I riding and Cecil and Christian, the Kaffir, in the Cart. We saw no one for several hours except some Kaffir Kraals and we almost ran into two herds of deer. I counted twenty-six in one herd, they were about a quarter of a mile away. We came to a cross road and I decided to put back as we had lost track of the river and were bearing straight into the English lines. Just as we found the river again and had got across a drift cannon opened on our right. We then knew we were in between the Boers and the English but we had no other knowledge of our geographical position. Such being the case we decided to outspan and lunch. Outspanning is setting the mules and horses at liberty, in-spanning trying to catch them again. It takes five minutes to out-span, and three hours to in-span. We had Armour's corned beef and Libby's canned bacon. Cecil cooked the bacon on a stick and we ate it with biscuits captured by our Boer friends at Cronje's farm from the English Tommies. About three o'clock we started off again, and were captured by three Boers. I was riding behind the cart and threw up my hands "*that* quick," but Cecil could not hear me yelling at her to stop on account of the noise of the cart. I knew if I rode after her they would shoot at me, and that if she didn't stop, as they were shouting at her to do, they would shoot her. Under these trying circumstances I sat still. It caused quite a coolness on Cecil's part. However the Boers could see I was trying to get her to halt so they only rode around and headed her off. We were so glad to see them that they could not be suspicious. Still, as we had come directly from the English lines they had doubts. We told them we had lost ourselves and the more they threatened to take us to the commandant the more satisfied we were. I insisted on taking photos of them reading Cecil's passport. It annoyed them that we refused to be serious, we assured them we had never met anyone we were so glad to see. They finally believed us, and our passports which describe Cecil as my "frau," and artist of *Harper's Weekly*, an idea of Loosberg's. We all smoked and then shook hands and they went back to their positions. We next met Christian De Vet one of the two big generals who is a grand character. Nothing could match the wonderful picturesqueness of his camp spread out over the side of a hill with the bearded fine featured old Van Dyck and Hugonot heads under great sombreros. De Vet made us a long speech saying it was only to be expected that the Great Republic would send men to help the little Republics, but he had not hoped that the women would show their sympathy by coming too. All this with the most simple earnest courtesy. He said "No English woman would dare do what you are doing." He showed us a farm house on a kopje about five miles off where he said we could get shelter and where we would be near the fighting on the morrow. We rode in the moonlight for some time but when we reached the house it was filthy and the people were in such terror that we decided to camp out in the veldt. We found a grove of trees near by and a stream of water running beside it so we made a fire there. We had only one biscuit left but several cans of bacon and tea. It was great fun and we sat up as late as we could around the fire on account of the cold. We could see the Boer fires in the moonlight on the hills and across the Sand, the English flashlights signalling all night. We put a rubber blanket on the grass and wrapped up in steamer rugs but both of us died several times of cold and even sitting on the fire failed to warm me. We were awakened out of a cold storage sort of sleep by pom-poms going off right over our heads. They sounded just as disturbing I found from the rear as when you are in front of them. They are the most effective of all the small guns for causing your nerves to riot. We climbed up the hill and saw the English coming in their usual solid formation stretching out for three miles. We went back and got the cart and drove to a nearer kopje, but just as we reached it the Boers abandoned it. Roberts's column was now much nearer. We then drove on still further in the direction of the bridge. I kept telling Cecil that the firing was all from the Boers as I did not want Christian to bolt and run away with the cart and mules. But Cecil remembered the pictures in *Harper's Weekly* showing the shrapnel smoke making rings in the air and as she saw these floating over our head, she knew the English were firing on us, but said nothing for fear of scaring Christian. I had promised to get her under fire which was her one wish so I said that she was now well under fire for the first and the last time. To which she replied "Pshaw!" I never saw any one show such self possession. We halted the cart behind a deserted farm house, and saddled her pony. The shells were now falling all over the shop, and I was scared to distraction. But she took about five minutes to see that her saddle was properly tightened and then we rode up to the hill. Again the Boers were leaving and only a few remained. They warned her to keep back but we dismounted and walked up to the hill. It was a very hot place but Cecil was quite unmoved. We showed her the shells striking back of her and around her but she refused to be impressed with the danger. She went among the Boers begging them to make a stand very quietly and like one man to another and they took it just in that way and said "But we are very tired. We have been driven back for three days. We are only a thousand, they are twenty thousand." Some of them only sat still too proud to run, too sick to fight! When the British got within five hundred yards of the artillery I told her she must run. At the same moment Botha's men a mile on our right broke away in a mad gallop, as though the lancers were after them. I finally got her on her pony and we raced for Ventersberg with Christian a good first. He had lost all desire to out-span.

At Ventersberg we found every one harnessing up in the street and abandoning everything. We again felt this untimely desire for food, and had lunch at Jones's hotel on scraps and Cecil went off to see if she could loot the cook, as everyone but her had left the hotel and as we needed one in Pretoria. A despatch-rider came running to me as I was smoking in the garden and shouted that the "Roinekes" were coming in force over the hill. I ran out in the street and saw their shells falling all over the edge of the village. They were only a quarter of an hour behind us. I yelled for Cecil who was helping the looted cook pack up her own things and anyone else's she could find in a sheet. I gathered up a dog and a kitten Cecil wanted and left a note for the next English officer who occupied my room with the inscription "I'd leave my happy home for you." We then put the cook, the kitten, the dog and Cecil in the cart and I got on the horse and we let out for Kronstad at a gallop. We raced the thirty miles in five hours without one halt. That was not our cruelty to animals but Christian's who whenever I ordered him to halt and let us rest, yelled that the Englesses were after us and galloped on. The retreat was a terribly pathetic spectacle; for hours we passed through group after group of the broken and dispirited Boers. At Kronstad President Steyn whom I went to see on arriving ordered a special car for me, and sent us off at once. We reached here the next morning, Christian arriving a day later having killed one mule and one pony in his eagerness to escape. We are going back again as soon as Roberts reaches the Vaal. There there must be a stand. Love and best wishes to you all——

DICK.

June 8th, 1900.
On board the *Kausler*.

DEAR MOTHER:

We engaged our passage on this ship some weeks ago not thinking we would have the English near

Pretoria until August. But as it happened they came so near that we did not know whether or not to wait over and see them enter the capital. I decided not, first, because after that one event, there would be nothing for us to see or do. We could not leave until the 2nd of July and a month under British martial law was very distasteful to me. Besides I did not care much to see them enter, or to be forced to witness their rejoicing. As soon as we got under way and about half the distance to the coast, it is a two days' trip. We heard so many rumors of Roberts's communication having been cut off and that the war was not over, that we thought perhaps we ought to go back— As we have no news since except that the British are in Pretoria we still do not know what to think. Personally I am glad I came away as I can do just as much for the Boers at home now as there where the British censor would have shut me off from cabling and mails are so slow. With the local knowledge I have, I hope to keep at it until it is over. But when I consider the magnitude of the misrepresentation about the burghers I feel appalled at the idea of going up against it. One is really afraid to tell all the truth about the Boer because no one would believe you— It is almost better to go mildly and then you may have some chance. But personally I know no class of men I admire as much or who to-day preserve the best and oldest ideas of charity, fairness and goodwill to men.

DICK.

June 29th, 1900.

DEAR MOTHER:

We are now just off Crete, and our next sight of the blue land will be Europe. It means so many things; being alone with Cecil again, instead of on a raft touching elbows with so many strangers, and it means a shop where you can buy collars, and where they put starch in your linen. Also many beautiful ladies one does not know and men in evening dress one does not know and green tables covered with gold and little green and red bits of ivory where one passes among the tables and wonders what they would think if they knew we two had found our greatest friends in the Boer farmers, in Dutch Station Masters who gave us a corner under the telegraph table in which to sleep, with Nelson who kept the Transvaal Steam Laundry, Col. Lynch of the steerage who comes to the dividing line to beg French books from Cecil, and that we had cooked our food on sticks, drunk out of the same cups with Kaffir servants and slept on the ground when there was frost on it. It will be so strange to find that there are millions of people who do not know Komali poort, who have thought of anything else except burghers and roor-i-neks— It seems almost disloyal to the Boers to be glad to see newspapers only an hour old instead of six weeks old, and to welcome all the tyranny of collar buttons, scarf pins, watch chains, walking sticks and gloves even. I love them both and I can hardly believe it is true that we are to go to a real hotel with a lift and a chasseur, where you cannot smoke in the dining-room. As for Aix, that I cannot believe will ever happen— It was just a part of one's honeymoon and I refuse to cheat myself into thinking that within a week I will be riding through the lanes of the little villages, drinking red wine at Burget, watching Chas spread cheese over great hunks of bread and listening to three bands at one time. And then the joy to follow of Home and America and all that is American. Even the Custom

House holds nothing but joy for me—and then "mine own people!" It has been six weeks since we have heard from you or longer, nearly two months and how I miss you and want you. It will be a happy day when Dad meets me at the wharf and I can see his blue and white tie again and his dear face under the white hat—where you and Nora will be I cannot tell, but I will seek you out. We will be happy together—so happy—It has been the longest separation we have known and such a lot of things have happened. It will be such peace to see you and hold you once again.

DICK.

AIX-LES-BAINS.
July 6th, 1900.

DEAR FAMILY:

Cecil and I arrived last night tired and about worn out—we had had a month on board ship and two days in the cars and when we got out at Aix and found our rooms ready and François waiting, we shouted and cheered. It was never so beautiful as it looked in the moonlight and we walked all over it, through the silent streets chortling with glee. They could not give us our same rooms but we got the suite just above them, which is just as good. They were so extremely friendly and glad to see us and had flowers in all the rooms. We have not heard a word about Chas yet, as our mail has not arrived from Paris, but I will cable in a minute and hear. We cannot wait any longer for news of him. I got up at seven this morning so excited that I could not sleep and have been to the baths, where I was received like the President of the Republic. In fact everybody seems to have only the kindest recollections of us and to be glad to have us back.

Such a rest as it is and so clean and bright and good—
Only I have absolutely nothing to wear except a two
pound flannel suit I bought at Lorenzo Marquez until
I get some built by a French tailor. I must wear a
bath robe or a bicycle suit until evening. We have
not been to the haunts of evil yet but we are dining
there to night and all will be well. Cecil sends her
love to you all— Goodbye and God bless you.

RICHARD.

Richard and his wife returned to America in the
early fall of 1900 and, after a visit to Mr. and Mrs.
Clark at Marion, settled for the winter in New York.
They took a house in East Fifty-eighth Street where
they did much entertaining and lived a very social
existence, but I do not imagine that either of them
regarded the winter as a success. Richard was unable
to do his usual amount of work, and both he and his
wife were too fond of the country to enjoy an entire
winter in town. In the spring they went back to
Marion.

MARION,
MASSACHUSETTS. May, 1901.

We arrived here last night in a glowing sunset which
was followed by a grand moon. The house was warm
and clean and bright, with red curtains and open
fires and everything was just as we had left it, so that
it seemed as though we had just come out of a tortuous
bad dream of asphalt and L. roads and bad air. I
was never so glad to get away from New York.

Outside it is brisk and fine and smells of earth and
melting snow and there is a grand breeze from the bay.
We took a long walk to-day, with the three dogs, and it

Mr. Davis's "workshop" at Marion.

was pitiful to see how glad they were to be free of the cellar and a back yard and at large among grass and rocks and roots of trees. I wanted to bottle up some of the air and send it to all of my friends in New York. It is so much better to smell than hot-house violets. Seaton came on with us to handle the dogs and to unpack and so to-day we are nearly settled already with silver, pictures, clothes and easels and writing things all in place. The gramophone is whirling madly and all is well— Lots and lots of love.

DICK.

The following was written by Richard to his mother on her birthday:

MARION, MASSACHUSETTS.
June 27th, 1901.

DEAR MOTHER:

In those wonderful years of yours you never thought of the blessing you were to us, only of what good you could find in us. All that time, you were helping us and others, and making us better, happier, even nobler people. From the day you struck the first blow for labor, in *The Iron Mills* on to the editorials in *The Tribune, The Youth's Companion* and *The Independent*, with all the good the novels, the stories brought to people, you were always year after year making the ways straighter, lifting up people, making them happier and better. No woman ever did better for her time than you and no shrieking suffragette will ever understand the influence you wielded, greater than hundreds of thousands of women's votes.

We love you dear, dear mother, and we *know* you and may your coming years be many and as full of happiness for yourself as they are for us.

RICHARD.

CHAPTER XIII

THE SPANISH AND ENGLISH CORONATIONS

INTERRUPTED by frequent brief visits to New York, Philadelphia, and Boston, Richard and his wife remained in Marion from May, 1901, until the early spring of 1902. During this year Richard accomplished a great deal of work and lived an ideal existence. In the summer months there were golf and tennis and an army of visitors, and during the winter many of their friends came from New York to enjoy a most charming hospitality and the best of duck shooting and all kinds of winter sports.

Late in April, they sailed for Gibraltar on their way to Madrid, where Richard was to report the coronation ceremonies, and from Madrid they went to Paris and then to London to see the coronation of King Edward. It was while on a visit to the Rudyard Kiplings that they heard the news that Edward had been suddenly stricken with a serious illness and that the ceremony had been postponed.

11, St. James's Place,
St. James's Street, S. W.
London.
June, 1902.

DEAR MOTHER:—

This is only to say that at the Kipling's we heard the news, and being two newspaper men, refused to believe it and went to the postoffice of the little village to call up Brighton on the 'phone. It was very dra-

At Marion.

matic, the real laureate of the British Empire asking if the King were really in such danger that he could not be crowned, while the small boy in charge of the grocery shop, where the postoffice was, wept with his elbows on the counter. They sent me my ticket—unasked—for the Abbey, early this morning, and while I was undecided whether to keep it—or send it back, this came. So, now, I shall frame it as a souvenir of one of the most unhappy occasions I ever witnessed. You can form no idea of what a change it has made. It really seems to have stunned every one—that is the usual and accepted word, but this time it describes it perfectly.

Goodbye,   Dick.

During the summer of 1903 my mother and father occupied a cottage at Marion, and every morning Richard started the day by a visit to them. My brother had already bought his Crossroads Farm at Mount Kisco, and the new house was one of the favorite topics of their talk. The following letter was written by my mother to Richard, after her return to Philadelphia.

September, 1903.

Here we are in the old library and breakfast over. There seemed an awful blank in the world as I sat down just now, and I said to Dad "Its Dick—he must come *this* morning."

You don't know how my heart used to give a thump when you and Bob came in that old door. It has been such a good month—everybody was so friendly—and Dad was so well and happy—but your visits were the core of it all. And our good drives! Well we'll have lots of drives at the Crossroads. You'll call at our cottage every morning and I'm going to train the peacocks to run before the trap and I'll be just like Juno.

There isn't a scrap of news. It is delightfully cool here.

M.

CHAPTER XIV

THE JAPANESE-RUSSIAN WAR

DURING the fall and early winter of 1903 Richard and his wife lingered on in Marion, but came to New York after the Christmas holidays. The success of his farce "The Dictator" had been a source of the greatest pleasure to Richard, and he settled down to playwriting with the same intense zeal he put into all of his work. However, for several years Robert J. Collier and my brother had been very close friends, and Richard had written many articles and stories for *Collier's Weekly*, so that when Collier urged my brother to go to the Japanese-Russian War as correspondent with the Japanese forces, Richard promptly gave up his playwriting and returned to his old love—the rôle of reporter. Accompanied by his wife, Richard left New York for San Francisco in February.

February, 1904.
DEAR MOTHER:

We are really off on the "long trail" bound for the boundless East. We have a charming drawing-room, a sympathetic porter and a courtly conductor descended from one of the first Spanish conquerors of California. We arranged the being late for lunch problem by having dinner at five and cutting the lunch out. Bruce and Nan came over for dinner and we had a very jolly time. They all asked after you all, and drank to our re-union at Marion in July. Later they all tried to come with us on the train. It looked so attractive with electric lights in each seat, and observation car and library. A reporter interviewed us and Mr. Clark gave us a box of segars and a bottle of whiskey. But they will not last, as will Dad's razors and your housewife. I've used Dad's razors twice a day, and they still are perfect. It's snowing again, but we don't care. They all came to the station to see us off but no one cried this time as they did when we went to South Africa. Somehow we cannot take this trip seriously. It is such a holiday trip all through not grim and human like the Boer war. Just quaint and queer. A trip of cherry blossoms and Geisha girls. I send all my love to you.

DICK.

SAN FRANCISCO, February 26th.

DEAR MOTHER:

We got in here last night at midnight just as easily as though we were coming into Jersey City. Before we knew it we had seen the Golden Gate, and were snug in this hotel. Today as soon as we learned we could not sail we started in to see sights and we made a record and hung it up high. We went to the Cliff House and saw the seals on the rocks below, to the Park, the military reservation, Chinatown, and the Poodle Dog Restaurant. We also saw the Lotta monument, the Stevenson monument, the Spreckles band stand, the place where the Vigilance Committee hung the unruly, and tonight I went to a dinner the Bohemian Club gave to the War correspondents. I made a darned good speech. Think of *me* making a speech of any sort, but I did, and I had sense enough *not* to talk about the war but the "glorious climate of

THE JAPANESE-RUSSIAN WAR 299

California" instead and of all the wonders of Frisco. So, I made a great hit. It certainly is one of the few cities that lives up to it's reputation in every way. I should call it the most interesting city, with more character back of it than any city on this continent. There are only four deck rooms and we each have one. The boat is small, but in spite of the crowd that is going on her, will I think be comfortable. I know it will be *that*, and it may be luxurious.

DICK.

On way to Japan.
March 13th, 1904.

About four this afternoon we saw an irregular line of purple mountains against a yellow sky, and it was Japan. In spite of the Sunday papers, and the interminable talk on board, the guide books and maps which had made Japan nauseous to me, I saw the land of the Rising Sun with just as much of a shock and thrill as I first saw the coast of Africa. We forgot entirely we had been twenty days at sea and remembered only that we were ten miles from Japan, only as far as New Bedford is from Marion. We are at anchor now, waiting to go in in the morning. Were it not for war we could go in now but we must wait to be piloted over the sunken mines. That and the flashlights moving from the cruisers ten miles away gave us our first idea of war. To-morrow early we will be off for Tokio, as it is only forty miles from Yokohama. Of course, I may get all sorts of news before we land, but that is what we expect to do. It *will* be good to feel solid earth, and to see the kimonos and temples and geishas and cherry blossoms. I am almost hoping the Government won't let us go to the

front and that for a week at least Cecil and I can sit in tea houses with our shoes off while the nesans bring us tea and the geishas rub their knees and make bows to us. I am sending you through Harper's, a book on Hawaii and one of Japan that I have read and like and which I think will help you to keep in touch with the wanderers. With all my love to all.
DICK.

TOKYO, March 22nd, 1904.
DEAR MOTHER:
The "situation" here continues to remain in such doubt that I cannot tell of it, as it changes hourly. There are three "columns," so far existing only in imagination. That is, so far as they concern the correspondents. The first lot have chosen themselves, and so have the second lot. But the first lot are no nearer starting than they were two weeks ago. I may be kept waiting here for weeks and weeks. I do not like to turn out Palmer, although I very much want to go with the first bunch. On the other hand I am paid pretty well to get to the front, and I am uncertain as to what I ought to do. If the second column were to start immediately after the first, we then would have two men in the field, but if it does not, then Collier will be paying $1000. a week for stories of tea houses and "festivals." Palmer threatens to resign if I take his place in the first column and that would be a loss to the paper that I do not feel I could make up. If it gets any more complicated I'll wire Collier to decide.

Meanwhile, we are going out to dinners and festivals; and we ride. I have a good pony the paper paid for, Cecil has hired another and we find it delightful to scamper out into the country. We have three rooms

THE JAPANESE–RUSSIAN WAR

in a row. One we use for a sitting room. They look very well and as it is still cold we keep them cheerful with open fires. We have a table in the dining-room to ourselves and to which we can ask our friends. The food is extremely good. Griscom and the Secretaries have all called and sent pots of flowers, and we are dining out every other night. In the day we shop and ride. But all day and all night we the correspondents plot and slave and intrigue over the places on the columns. I got mine on the second column all right but no one knows if it ever will move. So, naturally, I want to be on the first. The rows are so engrossing that I have not enjoyed the country as I expected. Still, I am everlastingly glad we came. It is an entirely new life and aspect. It completes so much that we have read and seen. In spite of the bother over the war passes I learn things daily and we see beautiful and curious things, and are educated as to the East, as no books could have done it for us. John Bass who was my comrade in arms in Greece and his wife are here. They are the very best. Also we see Lloyd daily, and the hotel is full of amusing men, who are trying to get to the front. Of course, we know less of the war than you do. None of the news from Cheefoo, none of the "unauthorized" news reaches us. Were it not for our own squabbles we would not know not only that the country was at war but not even that war existed *anywhere* in the world. We are here entirely en tourist and it cannot be helped. The men who tried to go with the Russians are equally unfortunate. Think of us as wandering around each with a copy of Murray seeing sights. That is all we really do. All my love.

DICK.

DEAR MOTHER: YOKOHAMA—April 2, 1904.

I just got your letter dated the 28th of February and the days following in which you worried over me in the ice coated trenches of Korea. I read it in a rickshaw in a warm sun on my way to buy favors for a dinner to Griscom. We have had three warm days and no doubt the sun will be out soon. The loss of the sun, though, is no great one. We have lots of pleasures and lots of troubles in spite of the Sun. Yesterday the first batch of correspondents were sent on their way. I doubt if they will get any further than Chemulpo but their going cheered the atmosphere like a storm in summer. The diplomats and Japanese were glad to get rid of them, they were delighted to be off. Some had been here 58 days, and we all looked at it as a good sign as it now puts us "next." But after they had gone it was pretty blue for some of them were as good friends as I want. I know few men I like as well as I do John Bass. Many of them were intensely interesting. It was, by all odds, the crowd one would have wished to go with. As it is, I suspect we all will meet again and that the two columns will be merged on the Yalu. None of the attaches have been allowed to go, so it really is great luck for the correspondents. Tell Chas I still am buying my Kit. It's pretty nearly ready now. I began in New York and kept on in Boston, San Francisco, and here. It always was my boast that I had the most complete kit in the world, and in spite of Charley's jeers at my lack of preparedness everybody here voted it the greatest ever seen. For the last ten days all the Jap saddlers, tent makers and tinsmiths have been copying it.

DICK.

DEAR MOTHER: TOKIO—May 2, 1904.

Today, we walked into our new house and tomorrow we will settle down there. We rented the furniture for the two unfurnished rooms; knives, forks, spoons, china for the table and extras for 35 dollars gold for two months. It took six men to bring the things in carts. They got nothing. Yesterday, I took two rickshaw men from half past twelve to half past five. Out of that time they ran and pushed me for two solid hours. Their price for the five hours was eighty cents gold. What you would pay a cabman to drive you from the Waldorf to Martin's. I wish you could see our menage. Such beautiful persons in grey silk kimonos who bow, and bow and slip and slide in spotless torn white stockings with one big toe. They make you ashamed of yourself for walking on your own carpet in your own shoes. Today we got the first news of the battle on the Yalu, the battle of April 26–30th. I suppose Palmer and Bass saw it; and I try to be glad I did what was right by *Collier's* instead of for myself. But I don't want to love another paper. I suppose there will be other fights but that one was the first, and it must have been wonderful. On the 4th we expect to be on our way to Kioto with Lloyd and his wife and John Fox. By that time we expect to be settled in the new house.

DICK.

DEAR MOTHER: TOKIO, May 22nd, 1904.

You will be glad to hear that the correspondents at the front are not allowed within two and a half miles of the firing line. This I am sure you will approve. Their tales of woe have just been received here, and they certainly are having a hard time. The one thing they all hope for is that the Japs will order them home. My temper is vile to-day, as I cannot enjoy the gentle pleasures of this town any longer and with this long trip to Port Arthur before I can turn towards home. I am as cross as a sick bear. We were at Yokohama when your last letters came and they were a great pleasure. I got splendid news of *The Dictator*. Yesterday we all went to Yokohama. There are four wild American boys here just out of Harvard who started the cry of "Ping Yang" for the "Ping Yannigans" they being the "Yannigans." They help to make things very lively and are affectionately regarded by all classes. Yesterday, they and Fox and Cecil and I went to the races, with five ricksha boys each, and everybody lost his money except myself. But it was great fun. It rained like a seive, and all the gentlemen riders fell off, and every time we won money our thirty ricksha men who would tell when we won by watching at which window we had bet, would cheer us and salaam until to save our faces we had to scatter largesses. Egan turned up in the evening and dined with John and Cecil and me in the Grand Hotel and told us first of all the story the correspondents had brought back to Kobbe for which every one from the Government down has been waiting. It would make lively reading if any of us dared to write it. To-day he made his protests to Fukushima as we mapped them out last night and the second lot will I expect be treated better. But, as the first lot were the important men representing the important syndicates the harm, for the Japs, has been done. Of course, much they do is through not knowing our points of view. To them none of us is of any con-

sequence except that he is a nuisance, and while they are conversationally perfect in politeness, the regulations they inflict are too insulting. However, you don't care about that, and neither do I. I am going to earn my money if I possibly can, and come home.
DICK.

TOKIO, June 13th, 1904.
DEAR MOTHER:

We gave a farewell dinner last night to the Ping Yannigans two of whom left on the Navy expedition and another one to-morrow for God's country. There were eight men and we had new lanterns painted with the arms of Corea and the motto of the Ping Yannigans. Also many flags. All but the Japanese flag. One of them with a side glance at the servants said, "Gentleman and Lady: I propose a toast, Japan for the Japanese and the Japanese for Japan." We all knew what he meant but the servants were greatly pleased. Jack London turned up to-day on his way home. I liked him very much. He is very simple and modest and gave you a tremendous impression of vitality and power. He is very bitter against the wonderful little people and says he carries away with him only a feeling of irritation. But I told him that probably would soon wear off and he would remember only the pleasant things. I did envy him so, going home after having seen a fight and I not yet started. Still *this time* we may get off. Yokoyama the contractor takes our stuff on the 16th, and so we feel it is encouraging to have our luggage at the front even if we are here.
DICK.

YOKOHAMA, July 26th, 1904.

DEAR MOTHER:

We gave in our passes to-day, and sail to-morrow at five. They say we are not to see Port Arthur fall but are to be taken up to Oku's army. That means we miss the "popular" story, and may have to wait around several weeks before we see the other big fight. They promised us Port Arthur but that is reason enough for believing they do not intend we shall see it at all. John and I are here at a Japanese hotel, the one Li Hung Chang occupied when he came over to arrange the treaty between China and Japan. It is a very beautiful house, the best I have seen of real Japanese and the garden and view of the harbor is magnificent. I wish Cecil could see it too, but I know she would not care for a room which is as free to the public view as the porch at Marion. It has 48 mats and as a mat is 3 x 5 you can work it out. We eat, sleep and dress in this room and it is like trying to be at home on top of a Chickering Grand. But it is very beautiful and the moonlight is fine and saddening. No one of us has the least interest in the war or in what we may see or be kept from seeing. We have been "over trained" and not even a siege of London could hold our thoughts from home. I have just missed the mail which would have told me you were at Marion. I should so love to have heard from you from there. I do not think you will find the Church house uncomfortable; and you can always run across the road when the traffic is not too great, and chat with Benjamin. I do hope that Dad will have got such good health from Marion and such lashers of fish. I got a good letter from Charles and I certainly feel guilty at putting extra work on a man as busy as he. Had I known he

THE JAPANESE-RUSSIAN WAR

was the real judge of those prize stories I would have sent him one myself and given him the name of it. Well, goodbye for a little time. We go on board in a few hours, and after that everything I write you is read by the Censor so I shall not say anything that would gratify their curiosity. They think it is unmanly to write from the field to one's family and the young princes forbade their imperial spouses from writing them until the war is over. However, not being an imperial Samaari but a home loving, family loving American, I shall miss not hearing very much, and not being able to tell you all how I love you.

DICK.

DALNY, July 27th, 1904.

DEAR MOTHER:

We left Shimonoseki three days ago and have had very pleasant going on the *Heijo Maru* a small but well run ship of 1,500 tons. Fox and I got one of the two best rooms and I have been very comfortable. We are at anchor now at a place of no interest except for its sunsets.

We have just been told as the anchor is being lowered that we can send letters back by the Island, so I can just dash this off before leaving. We have reached Dalny and I have just heard the first shot fired which was to send me home. All the others came and bid John and me a farewell as soon as we were sure it was the sound of cannon. However, as it is 20 miles away I'll have to hang on until I get a little nearer. We have had a very pleasant trip even though we were delayed two days by fog and a slow convoy. Now we are here at Dalny. It looks not at all like its pictures, which, as I remember them were all taken in winter. It is a perfectly new, good brick barracks-like town. I am landing now. The two servants seem very satisfactory and I am in excellent health. To-day Cecil has been four days at Hong Kong. Please send the gist of this letter dull as it is to Mrs. Clark. When I began it I thought I would have plenty of time to finish it on shore. Of course, after this all I write and this too, I suppose will be censored. So, there will not be much liveliness. I have no taste to expose my affections to the Japanese staff. So, goodbye.

R.

DEAR MOTHER: July 31st, 1904.

We have been met here with a bitter disappointment. We are all to be sent north, although only 18 hours away. We can hear the guns at Port Arthur the fall of which they promised us we would see. To night we are camping out in one of the Russian barracks. To-morrow we go, partly by horse and partly by train. A week must elapse before we can get near headquarters. And then we have no guarantee that we will see any fighting. This means for me a long delay. It is very disappointing and the worst of the many we have suffered in the last four months. I have written Cecil asking her to seriously think of going home but I am afraid she will not. Were it not for that and the disappointment one feels in travelling a week's journey away from the sound of guns I would be content. My horse is well and so am I. It is good to get back to drawing water, and carrying baggage and skirmishing about for yourself. The contractor gave us a good meal and the servants are efficient but I like doing things myself and skirmishing for them. We make a short ride this morning of six miles to Kin Chow and then 30 miles by rail. "Headquarters" is about a five days ride distant. Tell Chas my outfit seems nearly complete. Maybe I can buy a few things I forgot in Boston at Kin Chow. Fox and I will get out just as soon as we see fighting but before you get this you will probably hear by cable from me. If not, it will mean we still are waiting for a fight. The only mistake I made was in not going home the first time they deceived us instead of waiting for this and worst of all.

Love to you all.

DICK.

MANCHURIA, August 14, 1904.

We have been riding through Manchuria for eleven days. Nine days we rode then two days we rested. By losing the trail we managed to average about 20 miles a day. I kept well and enjoyed it very much. As I had to leave my servant behind with a sick horse, I had to take care of my mule and pony myself and hunt fodder for them, so I was pretty busy. Saiki did all he could, but he is not a servant and sooner than ask him I did things myself. We passed through a very beautiful country, sleeping at railway stations and saw two battle fields of recent fights. Now we are in a Chinese City and waiting to see what should be the biggest fight since Sedan. The Russians are about ten miles from us, so we are not allowed outside the gates of the city without a guide. Of course, we have none of that freedom we have enjoyed in other wars, but apart from that they treat us very well indeed. And in a day or two they promise us much fighting, which we will be allowed to witness from a hill. This is a very queer old city but the towns and country are all very primitive and we depend upon ourselves for our entertainment. I expect soon to see you at home. In three more days I shall have been out here five months and that is too long. Good luck to you all.

R. H. D.

MANCHURIA, August 18th, 1904.

We still are inside this old Chinese town. It has rained for five days, and this one is the first in which we could go abroad. Unless you swim very well it is not safe to cross one of these streets. We have found an old temple and some of us are in it now. It is such a relief to escape from that compound and the rain. This place is full of weeds and pine trees, cooing doves and butterflies. The temples are closed and no one is in charge but an aged Chinaman. We did not come here to sit in temples, so John and I will leave in a week, battle or no battle. The argument that having waited so long one might as well wait a little longer does not touch us. It was that argument that kept us in Tokio when we knew we were being deceived weekly, and the same man who deceived us there, is in charge here. It is impossible to believe anything he tells his subordinates to tell us, so, we will be on our way back when you get this. I am well, and only disappointed. Had they not broken faith with us about Port Arthur we would by now have seen fighting. As it is we will have wasted six months.

Love to Dad, and Chas and Nora and you.

DICK.

In writing of his decision to leave the Japanese army, Richard, after his return to the United States, said:

R. H. D. and John Fox in Manchuria, 1904.

"On the receipt of Oku's answer to the Correspondents we left the army. Other correspondents would have quit then, as most of them did ten days later, but that their work and Kuroki, so far from being fifty miles north toward Mukden, as Okabe said he was, was twenty miles to the east on our right preparing for the closing-in movement which was just about to begin. Three days after we had left the army, the greatest battle since Sedan was waged for six days.

"So, our half-year of time and money, of dreary waiting, of daily humiliations at the hands of officers with minds diseased by suspicion, all of which would have been made up to us by the sight of this one great spectacle, was to the end absolutely lost to us. Perhaps we made a mistake in judgment. As the cards fell we certainly did.

"The only proposition before us was this: There was small chance of any immediate fighting. If there were fighting we would not see it. Confronted with the same conditions again, I would decide in exactly the same manner. Our misfortune lay in the fact that our experience with other armies had led us to believe that officers and gentlemen speak the truth, that men with titles of nobility, and with the higher titles of General and Major-General, do not lie. In that we were mistaken."

Greatly disappointed at his failure to see really anything of the war, much embittered at the Japanese over their treatment of the correspondents, Richard reached Vancouver in October. As my father was seriously ill he came to Philadelphia at once and divided the next two months between our old home and Marion.

On December 14, 1904, my father died, and it was

the first tragedy that had come into Richard's life, as it was in that of my sister or myself. As an editorial writer, most of my father's work had been anonymous, but his influence had been as far-reaching as it had been ever for all that was just and fine. All of his life he had worked unremittingly for good causes and, in spite of the heavy burdens which of his own will he had taken upon his none too strong shoulders, I have never met with a nature so calm, so simple, so sympathetic with those who were weak—weak in body or soul. As all newspaper men must, he had been brought in constant contact with the worst elements of machine politics, as indeed he had with the lowest strata of the life common to any great city. But in his own life he was as unsophisticated; his ideals of high living, his belief in the possibilities of good in all men and in all women, remained as unruffled as if he had never left his father's farm where he had spent his childhood. When my father died Richard lost his "kindest and severest critic" as he also lost one of his very closest friends and companions.

During the short illness that preceded my brother's death, although quite unconscious that the end was so near, his thoughts constantly turned back to the days of his home in Philadelphia, and he got out the letters which as a boy and as a young man he had written to his family. After reading a number of them he said: "I know now why we were such a happy family. It was because we were always, all of us, of the same age."

CHAPTER XV

MOUNT KISCO

During my brother's life there were four centres from which he set forth on his travels and to which he returned to finish the articles for which he had collected the material, or perhaps to write a novel, a few short stories, or occasionally a play, but unlike most of the followers of his craft, never to rest. Indeed during the last twenty-five years of his life I do not recall two consecutive days when Richard did not devote a number of hours to literary work. The centres of which I speak were first Philadelphia, then New York, then Marion, and lastly Mount Kisco. Happy as Richard had been at Marion, the quaint little village, especially in winter, was rather inaccessible, and he realized that to be in touch with the numerous affairs in which he was interested that his headquarters should be in or near New York. In addition to this he had for long wanted a home of his very own, and so located that he could have his family and his friends constantly about him. Some years, however, elapsed between this dream and its realization. In 1903 he took the first step by purchasing a farm situated in the Westchester Hills, five miles from Mount Kisco, New York. He began by building a lake at the foot of the hill on which the home was to stand, then a water-tower, and finally the house itself. The plans to the minutest detail had been laid out on the lawn at Marion and, as the architect himself said, there was nothing left for him to do but to design the cellar.

Richard and his wife moved into their new home in July, 1905, and called it Crossroads Farm, keeping the original name of the place. In later years Richard added various adjoining parcels of land to his first purchase, and the property eventually included nearly three hundred acres. The house itself was very large, very comfortable, and there were many guest-rooms which every week-end for long were filled by the jolliest of house-parties. In his novel "The Blind Spot," Justus Miles Forman gives the following very charming picture of the place:

"It was a broad terrace paved with red brick that was stained and a little mossy, so that it looked much older than it had any right to, and along its outer border there were bay-trees set in big Italian terracotta jars; but the bay-trees were placed far apart so that they should not mask the view, and that was wise, for it was a fine view. It is rugged country in that part of Westchester County—like a choppy sea: all broken, twisted ridges, and abrupt little hills, and piled-up boulders, and hollow, cup-like depressions among them. The Grey house sat, as it were, upon the lip of a cup, and from the southward terrace you looked across a mile or two of hollow bottom, with a little lake at your feet, to sloping pastures where there were cattle browsing, and to the far, high hills beyond.

"There was no magnificence about the outlook—nothing to make you catch your breath; but it was a good view with plenty of elbow room and no sign of a neighbor—no huddling—only the water of the little lake, the brown November hillsides, and the clean blue sky above. The distant cattle looked like scenic

The terrace at Crossroads.

cattle painted on their green-bronze pasture to give an aspect of husbandry to the scene."

Although Richard was now comfortably settled, he had of late years acquired a great dread of cold weather. As soon as winter set in his mind turned to the tropics, and whenever it was possible he went to Cuba or some other land where he was sure of plenty of heat and sunshine. The early part of 1906 found him at Havana, this time on a visit to the Hon. E. V. Morgan, who was then our minister to Cuba. From Havana he went to the Isle of Pines.

ISLE OF PINES, March 26th, 1906.

DEAR MOTHER:—

We are just returning from the Isle of Pines. We reached there after a day on the water at about six on Wednesday, 22nd. They dropped us at a woodshed in a mangrove swamp, where a Mr. Mason met us with two mules. I must have said I was going to the island because every one was expecting me. Until the night before we had really no idea when we would go, so, to be welcomed wherever we went, was confusing. For four days we were cut off from the world, and in that time, five days in all, we covered the entire island pretty thoroughly— It was one of the most interesting trips I ever took and Cecil enjoyed it as much as I did. The island is a curious mixture of palm and pines, one minute it looks like Venezuela and the next like Florida and Lakewood. It is divided into two parties of Americans, the "moderates" and the "revolutionists." The Cubans are very few and are all employed by the Americans, who own nine-tenths of the Island. Of course, they all want the U. S. to take it, they differ only as to how to persuade the senators to do it. I had to change all my opinions about the situation. I thought it was owned by land speculators who did not live there, nor wish to live there, but instead I found every one I met had built a home and was cultivating the land. We gave each land company a turn at me, and we had to admire orange groves and pineapples, grapefruit and coffee until we cried for help. With all this was the most romantic history of the island before the "gringos" came. It was a famous place for pirates and buried treasures and slave pens. It was a sort of clearing house for slaves where they were fattened. I do not believe people take much interest in or know anything about it, but I am going to try and make an interesting story of it for Collier. It was queer to be so completely cut off from the world. There was a wireless but they would not let me use it. It is not yet opened to the public. I talked to every one I met and saw much that was pathetic and human. It was the first pioneer settlement Cecil had ever seen and the American making the ways straight is very curious. He certainly does not adorn whatever he touches. But never have I met so many enthusiastics and such pride in locality. To-night we reach the Hotel Louvre, thank heaven! where I can get Spanish food again, and not American ginger bread, and, "the pie like mother used to make." We now are on a wretched Spanish tug boat with every one, myself included, very seasick and babies howling and roosters crowing. But soon that will be over, and, after a short ride of thirty miles through a beautiful part of the island, we will be in Havana in time for a fine dinner, with ice. What next we will do I am not sure. After living in that beautiful palace of Morgan's, it just needed five days of the "Pinero's" to make us enjoy life at a hotel— If we can make connections, I think I will go over to Santo Domingo, and study up that subject, too. But, even if we go no where else the trip to the I. of P. was alone well worth our long journey. I don't know when I have seen anything as curious, and as complicated a political existence. Love to all of you dear ones.

Dick.

HAVANA—April 9, 1906.

ARTHUR BARTLETT MAURICE, ESQ.
MY DEAR MAURICE:

I have just read about myself, in the April *Bookman*, which I would be very ungrateful if I did not write and tell you how much it pleased me. That sounds as though what pleased me was, obviously, that what you said was so kind. But what I really mean, and that for which I thank you, was your picking out things that I myself liked, and that I would like to think others liked. *I* know that the men make "breaks," and am sorry for it, but, I forget to be sorry when you please me by pointing out the good qualities in "Laquerre," and the bull terrier. Nothing ever hurt me so much as the line used by many reviewers of "Macklin" that "Mr. Davis' hero is a cad, and Mr. Davis cannot see it." Macklin I always thought was the best thing I ever did, and it was the one over which I took the most time and care. Its failure was what as Maggie Cline used to say, "drove me into this business" of play writing. All that ever was said of it was that it was "A book to read on railroad trains and in a hammock." That was the verdict as delivered to me by Romeike from 300 reviewers, and it drove me to farces. So, I was especially glad when you liked "Royal Macklin." I tried to make a "hero" who was vain, theatrical, boasting and self-conscious, but, still likable. But, I did not succeed in making him of interest, and it always has hurt me. Also, your liking the "Derelict" and the "Fever Ship" gave me much pleasure. You see what I mean, it was your selecting the things upon which I had worked, and with which I had made every effort, that has both encouraged and delighted me. Being entirely unprejudiced, I think it is a fine article, and as soon as I stamp this, I will read it over again. So, thank you very much, indeed, for to say what you did seriously, over your own name, took a lot of courage, and for that daring, and for liking the same things I do, I thank you many times.

Sincerely yours,
RICHARD HARDING DAVIS.

In reading this over, I find all I seem to have done in it is to complain because no one, but yourself and myself liked "Macklin." What I wanted to say is, that I am very grateful for the article, for the appreciation, although I don't deserve it, and for your temerity in saying so many kind things. Nothing that has been written about what I have written has ever pleased me so much.

R. H. D.

In the spring of 1906 while Richard was on a visit to Providence, R. I., Henry W. Savage produced a play by Jesse Lynch Williams and my brother was asked to assist at rehearsals, a pastime in which he found an enormous amount of pleasure. The "McCloy" mentioned in the following letter was the city editor of *The Evening Sun* when my brother first joined the staff of that paper as a reporter.

NEW YORK, May 4, 1906.
DEAR NORA:

I left Providence Tuesday night and came on to New York yesterday. Savage and Williams and all were very nice about the help they said I had given them, and I had as much fun as though it had been a success I had made myself, and I didn't have to make a speech, either.

Yesterday I spent in the newspaper offices gathering material from their envelopes on Winston Churchill, M.P. who is to be one of my real Soldiers of Fortune. He will make a splendid one, in four wars, twice made a question; before he was 21 years old, in Parliament, and a leader in *both* parties before he was 36. In the newspaper offices they had a lot of fun with me. When I came into the city room of *The Eve. Sun*, McCloy was at his desk in his shirt spiking copy. He just raised his eyes and went on with his blue pencil. I said "There's nothing in that story, sir, the man will get well, and the woman is his wife."

"Make two sticks of it," said McCloy, "and then go back to the Jefferson police court."

When I sat down at my old desk, and began to write the copy boy came and stood beside me and when I had finished the first page, snatched it. I had to explain I was only taking notes.

At *The Journal*, Sam Chamberlain who used to pay me $500 a story, touched me on the shoulder as I was scribbling down notes, and said "Hearst says to take you back at $17 a week."

I said "I'm worth $18 and I can't come for less."

So he brought up the business manager and had a long wrangle with him as to whether I should get $18. The business manager, a Jew gentleman, didn't know me from Adam, and seriously tried to save the paper a dollar a week. When the reporters and typewriter girls began to laugh, he got very mad. It was very funny how soothing was the noise of the presses, and the bells and typewriters and men yelling "Copy!" and "Damn the boy!" I could write better than if I had been in the silence of the farm. It was like being able to sleep as soon as the screw starts.

DICK.

CHAPTER XVI

THE CONGO

DURING the winter of 1907 the world rang with the reports of the atrocities in the Congo, and Robert J. Collier, of *Collier's Weekly*, asked Richard to go to the Congo and make an investigation. I do not believe that my brother was ever in much sympathy with the commission, as he did not feel that he could afford the time that a thorough investigation demanded. However, with his wife he sailed for Liverpool on January 5, 1907, and three weeks later started for Africa. Regarding this trip, in addition to the letters he wrote to his family, I also quote from a diary which he had just started and which he conscientiously continued until his death.

From diary of January 24th, 1907.

Last day in London. Margaret Frazer offered me gun from a Captain Jenkins of Nigeria. Instead bought Winchester repeating, hoping, if need it, get one coast. Lunched Savoy-Lynch, Mrs. Lynch, her sister—very beautiful girl. In afternoon Sam Sothern and Margaret came in to say "Good bye." Dined at Anthony Hope's—Barrie and Mrs. Barrie and Jim Whigham. Mrs. Barrie looking very well, Barrie not so well. As silent as ever, only talked once during dinner when he told us about the first of his series of cricket matches between authors and artists. Did not have eleven authors, so going along road picked up utter strangers one a soldier in front of pub embracing two girls. Said he would come if girls came too—all put in brake. Mrs. Barrie said the Llewellen Davis' were the originals for the Darlings and their children in Peter Pan. They played a strange game of billiards suggested by Barrie who won as no one else knew the rules and they claimed he invented them to suit his case. Sat up until three writing and packing. The dinner was best have had this trip in London.

      Compagnie Belge Maritime Du Congo.
      S. S. February 11th, 1907.

To-morrow, we will be in Banana, which is the first port in the Congo. When I remember how far away the Congo seemed from New York and London, it is impossible to believe we are less than a day from it. I am so very glad I came. The people who have lived here for years agree about it in no one fact, so, it is a go-as-you-please for any one so far as accurate information is concerned, and I am as likely to be right as any one else. It has been a pleasant trip and for us will not be over until some days, for at Matadi, which is up the river, we will probably live on the steamer, as the shore does not sound attractive. Then I shall probably go on up the river and after a month or six weeks come back again. At Boma I am to see the Governor, one of the inspectors on board is to introduce me, and I have an idea they will make me as comfortable as possible, so that I may not see anything. Not that I would be likely to see anything hidden under a year. Yesterday was the crossing of the Equator. The night before Neptune, one of the crew, and his wife, the ship's butcher, and a kroo boy, as black as coal for the heir apparent came over the side and proclaimed that those who never before had crossed the Equator must be baptized. We had crossed but I was perfectly willing to go through it for the fun. The Belgians went at it as seriously as children, and worked up a grand succession of events. First we had gymkana races among the kroo boys. The most remarkable was their placing franc pieces in tubs of white and red flour, for which the boys dived, they then dug for more money into a big basket fitted with feathers and when they came out they were the most awful sights imaginable. You can picture their naked black bodies and faces spotted with white and pink and stuck like chickens with feathers. Then the next day we were all hauled before a court and judged, and having all been found guilty were condemned to be shaved and bathed publicly at four. Meantime the Italians, is it not the picture of them, had organized a revolution against the Tribunal, with the object of ducking them. They went into this as though it were a real conspiracy and had signs and passwords. At four o'clock, in turn they sat us on the edge of the great tank on the well deck and splashed us over with paste and then tilted us in. I tried to carry the Frenchman who was acting as barber, with me but only got him half in. But Milani, one of the Italians, swung him over his head plumb into the water. The Frenchman is a rich elephant hunter who is not very popular. When the revolution broke loose we all yelled "A bas le Tribunal," "Vive la Revolution"! and there was awful rough house. I made for the Frenchman and went in with him and nearly drowned him, and everybody was being thrown into the tank or held in front of a fire cross. After dinner there was a grand ceremony, the fourth, in which certificates were presented by an Inspecteur d'Etat who is on board, and is a Deputy Governor of a district. Then there was much champagne and a concert and Cecil and I sat with the Captain, the Bishop, in his robes and berretta and the two inspectors and they were very charming to both of us.

DICK.

Compagnie Belge Maritime Du Congo.
S. S.   February 13th, 1907.

DEAR MOTHER:

We reached Banana yesterday morning, and the mouth of the Congo, and as the soldier said when he reached the top of San Juan Hill, "Hell! well here we are!" Banana looks like one of the dozen little islands in the West Indies, where we would stop to take on some "brands of bananas," instead of the port to a country as big as Europe. We went ashore and wandered around under the palm trees, and took photos, and watched some men fishing in the lagoons, and we saw a strange fish that leaps on the top of the water just as a frog jumps on land. It is certainly hot. Milani and I went in swimming in the ocean, and got finely cool. Then we paddled the canoe back to the ship to show the blacks how good we were, and got very hot, and the blacks charged us a franc for the voyage. To-morrow we will be in Boma, the capital, which is much of a place with shops and a lawn tennis court.

BOMA, February 15th.

Boma is more or less laid out and contains the official residences of the Government. I walked all over it in an hour, and here you walk very slow. There are three or four big trading stores *and* a tennis court. It is, however, a dreary place. We called on the missionary and his wife, but she does not speak English and their point of view of everything was not cheerful or instructive. Cecil plans to remain on board while at *Matadi* and return with this same boat to Boma. I want her to go home in this boat or in some other, as I believe Boma most unhealthy and I know it to be most uncomfortable. She would have to go to a hotel which is very hot and rough, although it is clean and well run. I am undecided whether to go up the river for ten days, to where it crosses the equator, or to leave the upper Congo and go up the Kasai river. This is off the beaten track, and one may see something of interest. I will know better what I will do in an hour, when I get to Matadi.

MATADI—Feby. 21.

We are now at Matadi. The Captain invited us to stop on board and it is well he did. We dine on deck where the wind blows but the rest of the ship is being cleaned and painted for the trip North. Four hatches are discharging cargo all at once, from four in the morning until midnight. Officers and kroo boys get four hours sleep out of the twenty-four, but I sleep right through it, so does Cecil. Sometimes they take out iron rails and then zinc roofs and steel boats, 6000 cases of gin and 1000 tons of coal. Still, it is much better than in the Hotel Africa on shore. Matadi is a hill of red iron and the heat is grand. Everything in this country is grand. The river is, in places, seven miles wide, the sunsets are like nothing earthly, and the black people are like brooding shadows of lost souls, that is, if souls have shadows. Most of the blacks in this town are "prisoners" with a steel ring around the neck, and chained in long lines. I leave on the 23d to go up the Kasai River, because that is where the atrocities come from and up there there are many missionaries. I don't want you to think I say this to "calm your fears," but I say it because it is as true of this place as of every other one in the world, and that is, that it is as easy to get about here as it is in Rhode Island. It is not half as dangerous as automobiling. I have not even felt feverish, neither has Cecil. I never felt better. Cecil stays on board and goes back to Boma. There she stops a week and then takes another ship back to London. She will not wait at Boma for me, at least, I hope not and cannot imagine her doing so. In any event, after I start, there will be no way for us to communicate, and I will act on the understanding that she has started North.

I have two very good boys and both speak English, and are from Sierra Leone. I take a two-day trip of 200 miles by rail, then four days by boat up the Kasai and then I may come back by boat or walk. It depends on how I like it, how long I stay, for I can hope to see very little, as under a year it would be impossible to write with authority of this country. But I'll see more of it than some at home, and I'll hear what those who have lived here for years have to say. It is awfully interesting, absolutely different and more uncivilized than anything I ever saw. But all the time you are depressed with how little you know and can know of it. I will be here six weeks or two months and then should get up the coast to London about the middle of May or sooner.

DICK.

THE CONGO

From diary of February 22nd, 1907.

Spent about the worst night of my life. No mattress, no pillow. Not space enough for my own cot. Every insect in the world ate me. After a bath and coffee felt better. It rained heavily until three P. M. Read Pendennis, and loved it. The picture of life at Clavering and Fairoaks, and Dr. Portman and Foker are wonderful. I do not know when I have enjoyed and admired a work so much. For some reason it is all entirely new again. I will read them all now in turn. After rain cleared took my slaves and went after "supplies." Met a King. I thought he was a witch doctor, and the boys said he was a dancing man. All his suite, wives and subjects followed, singing a song that made your flesh creep. At Hatton and Cookson's bought "plenty chop" for "boys" who were much pleased. Also a sparklet bottle, some whiskey and two pints of champagne at 7 francs the pint. Blush to own it was demi Sec. Also bacon, jam, milk, envelopes, a pillow. Saw some ivory State had seized and returned. 15 Kilo's. Some taken from Gomez across street not returned until he gave up half. No reason given Taylor agent H. & C. why returned Apparently when called will come down on the ivory question. Cuthbert Malet, coffee planter, came call on me. Only Englishman still in Service State. Had much to say which did not want printed until he out of country which will be in month or two. Anstrossi has given me side of cabin where there is room for my cot, so expect to sleep.

STANLEY POOL, Feb. 22nd, 1907.

DEAR MOTHER:

When you get this, I will be on my way to London. The rest of my stay here will be on board two boats, touching at the banks of the Kasai river. One I now am on takes me up and another takes me down. I will see a great deal that is strange and it is very interesting. Yesterday, for example, only an hour before our train reached Gongolo Station, there were three elephants that wandered across the track. We were very disappointed not to have seen them. At the mission house on the way up, I brought the first ice the mission boys had seen and when I put a piece in the hand of one, he yelled and danced about as though it were a coal. The higher up you go the tougher it gets. Back in the jungle, one can only imagine what it is like. Here all the white men have black wives, and the way the whip is used on the men is very different from the lower congo. The boat is about as large as a touring car, with all the machinery exposed. I am very comfortable though, with my bed and camp chair, and, books to read, when one gets tired of this great, dirty river. I expect to see hippopotamuses and many crocodiles and to learn something of the "atrocities" by hearsay. To see for oneself, would take months. I return from the Kasai district by a boat like this one, burning wood and with a stern wheel, reaching Leopoldville, this place, about the 12th of March, and sailing on the *Albertville* for Southampton on the 19th of March. So I should be in London and so very near you by the 8th of April. Of course, if I take a later boat from here, I will be just that much later. I am perfectly well, never better. No fever, no "tired feeling" good appetite, in spite of awful tough food. From this place money cannot be used and I carry a bag of salt and rolls of cloth. For a bottle of salt you get a fowl or a turkey, for a tablespoonful an egg, or a bunch of fruit. When you write be sure and tell me

In the Congo, 1907.

all your plans for the summer; that is, after you have been to see us. My dearest love to you all.

DICK.

From diary of February 27th, 1907.

Saw two hippos. Thought Anstrossi said they were buffalo. So was glad when I found out what they were. I did not want to go home without having seen only two dead ones. In a few minutes I saw two more. Anstrossi fired at them but I did not, as thought it not the game when one could not recover them. Before noon saw six in a bunch—and then what I thought was a spit of rock with a hippo lying on the end of it, turned out to be fifteen hippos in a line! Burnham has told he had seen eleven in the Volta in one day. Before one o'clock, I had seen twenty-six, and, later in the day Anstrossi fired at another, and shot a hole in the awning. That made twenty-seven in one day. Also some monkeys.

The hippos were delightful. They seemed so aristocratic, like gouty old gentlemen, puffing and blowing and yawning, as though everything bored them.

From diary of February 28th, 1907.

When just going up for coffee, saw what was so big, looking at it against horizon, thought it must be an elephant. Was a young hippo. Captain Jensen brought boat within eighty yards of him, and both Anstrossi and I fired, apparently knocking him off his legs, for he rolled on his side as though his back was broken. I missed him the second shot, which struck the water just in front of him. The other three shots caught him in the head, in the mouth and ear. He lay quite still, and the boys rushed out a gang plank and surrounded him singing and shouting and cutting his tail to make him bleed and weaken him. They don't die for an hour but he seemed dead enough, so I went to my cabin to re-load my gun and my camera. In three minutes I came out, and found the hippo still quiet. Then he began to toss his head and I shot him again, to put him out of pain. In return for which he rolled over into the water and got away. I was mad. Later saw four more. Just at sunset while taking bath another was seen on shore. We got within sixty yards of him and all of us missed him or at least did not hurt him. He then trotted for the river with his head up and again I must have missed, although at one place he was but fifty yards away, when he entered the water, a hundred. I stepped it off later in the sand. I followed him up and hit him or some one of us hit him and he stood up on his hind legs. But he put back to land for the third time. Captain said wait until moon came out. But though we hunted up to our waists saw none. One came quite close at dinner. Seven on the day.

Congo River—March 1, 1907.

Dear Mother:

I have been up the Congo as far as the Kasai river, and up that to a place called Dima. There I found myself in a sort of cul de sac. I found that the rubber plantations I had come to see, were nine days journey distant. In this land where time and distance are so differently regarded than with us, a man tells you to go to Dima to see rubber. He means after getting to Dima, you must catch a steamer that leaves every two weeks and travel for five days. But he forgets that

that fact is important to visitors. As he is under contract to stay here three years, it does not much matter to him how he spends a month, or so. Dima was two hundred yards square, and then the jungle. In half an hour, I saw it all, and met every one in it. They gave me a grand reception, but I could not spend ten days in Dima. The only other thing I could do was to take a canoe to the Jesuit Mission where the Fathers promised me shooting, or, try to catch the boat back to England that stops at interesting ports. Sooner than stop in Boma, I urged Cecil to take that boat. So, if I catch it, we will return together. It is a five weeks journey, and rather long to spend alone. In any event my letters will go by a faster boat. I have had a most wonderfully interesting visit, at least, to me. I hope I can make it readable. But, much of its pleasure was personal.

I have just had to stop writing this, for what when I get back to New York will seem a perfectly good reason for interrupting a letter to even you. A large hippopotamus has just pushed past us with five baby hippos in front of her. She is shoving them up stream, and the papa hippo is in the wake puffing and blowing. They are very plenty here and on the way up stream, I saw a great many, and every morning and evening went hunting for them on shore. I wanted the head of a hippopotamus awfully keenly for the farm. But of the only two I saw on land, both got away from me. I did not shoot at any I saw in the water, although the other idiot on board did, because if you kill them, you cannot recover them, and it seems most unsportsmanlike. Besides, I was so grateful to them for being so proud and pompous, and real aristocrats dating back from the flood. But I was terribly disappointed at losing both of those I saw on land. One I dropped at the first shot, and the other I missed, as he was running, to get back into the water. The one I shot, and that everyone thought was dead, *after the "boys" began to cut him up,* decided he was not going to stand for that, and to our helpless dismay suddenly rolled himself into the water. If that is not hard luck, I don't know it. All I got was a bad photograph of him, and I had already decided where I would hang his head, and how much I would tip the crew for cutting him up. It was a really wonderful journey. I loved every minute of it and never was I in better health.

If I only could have known that you knew that I was all right, but instead you were worrying. The nights were bright moonlight, and the days were beautiful; full of strange people and animals, birds and views. We three sat in the little bridge of the tinpot boat, and smoked pipes and watched the great muddy river rushing between wonderful banks. There was the Danish Captain, an Italian officer and the engineer was from Finland. The Italian spoke French and the two others English, and I acted as interpreter!! Can you imagine it? I am now really a daring French linguist. People who understand me, get quick promotion. If I only could have been able to tell you all was well and not to be worried. At Kwarmouth I have just received a wire from Cecil saying she expects to leave by the slow boat but will stay if I wish it. So, now we can both go by the slow boat if I can catch it. I hope so. She must have found Boma as bad as it looked. God bless you all.

DICK.

On April 13, Richard was back in London and in his diary of that date he writes, "Never so glad to get anywhere. Went to sleep to the music of motor-cars. Nothing ever made me feel so content and comfortable and secure as their 'honk, honk.'"

From diary of April 22nd, 1907.

A blackmailer named H—— called with photos of atrocities and letters and films. He wanted 30 Pounds for the lot. I gave him 3 Pounds for three photos. One letter he showed me signed Bullinger, an Englishman, said he had put the fear of God in their hearts by sticking up the chief's head on a pole, and saying, "Now, make rubber," or you will look like that. Went to lunch with Pearson but it was the wrong day, and so missed getting a free feed. Thinking he would turn up, I ordered a most expensive lunch. I paid for it. Evening went Patience, which liked immensely and then Duchess of Sutherland's party to Premiers. Saw Churchill and each explained his share of the Real Soldiers row.

From diary of April 28th, 1907.

We went down by train to Cliveden going by Taplow to Maidenhead where Astor had sent his car to meet us. It is a wonderful place and the view of the Thames is a beautiful one. They had been making alterations, bathrooms, and putting white enamel tiles throughout the dungeons. If Dukes lived no more comfortably than those who owned Cliveden, I am glad I was not a Duke. What was most amusing was the servant's room which was quite as smart as any library or study, with fine paintings, arm chairs and writing material. Nannie and Astor were exceedingly friendly and we walked all over the place. It was good to get one's feet on turf again. They sent us back by motor, so we arrived most comfortably. I gave a dinner to the Hopes, Wyndham, Miss Mary Moore, Ashmead-Bartlett and Margaret. Websters could not come. Later, came on here, and had a chat, the Websters coming too. I read Thaw trial.

Early in May Richard and his wife returned to Mount Kisco and my brother at once started in to change his farce "The Galloper" into a musical comedy. It was produced on August 12, at the Astor Theatre, under the title of the "Yankee Tourist," with Raymond Hitchcock as the star. The following I quote from Richard's diary of that date:

Monday, August 12th, 1907.
Was to have lunched with Ned Stone but he was in court. Met Whigham in street. Impulsively asked him to lunch. Ethel and Jack turned up at Martin's; asked them to lunch. Ethel and I drove around town doing errands, mine being the purchase of tickets for numerous friends. Called on Miss Trusdale to inquire about Harden-Hickey. She wants her to go to the country. Cecil arrived at six. We had a suite of eighty-nine rooms. We dined at Sherry's with Ethel and Jack, Ethel being host. Taft was there. Hottest night ever. I sat with Jack. In spite of weather, play went well. Bonsals, Ethel, Arthur Brisbane were in Cecil's box. Booth Tarkington in Irwin's. Surprise of performance was "Hello, Bill" which Raymond had learned only that morning. Helen Hale helped him greatly with dance. People

came to supper at Waldorf, and things went all wrong. Next time I have a first Night I want no friends during or after. Missed the executive ability of Charles Belmont greatly.

CHAPTER XVII

A LONDON WINTER

From the fall of 1907 to that of 1908 Richard divided his time between Mount Kisco, Marion, and Cuba. In December of 1908 he sailed for London where he took Turner the artist's old house in Chelsea for the winter.

Cheyne Walk, Chelsea.
December 25. Christmas Day.

Dear Mother:

We are settled here in Darkest Chelsea as though we had been born here. I am thinking of putting in my time of exile by running for Mayor. Meanwhile, it is a wonderful place in which to write the last chapters of "Once Upon a Time." The house is quite wonderful. In Spring and Summer it must be rarely beautiful. It has trees in front and a yard and a garden and a squash court: a sort of tennis you play against the angles of walls covered smooth with cement. Also a studio as large as a theatre. Outside the trees beat on the windows and birds chirp there. The river flows only forty feet away, with great brown barges on it, and gulls whimper and cry, and aeroplane all day. I have a fine room, and about the only one you can keep as warm as toast *should* be, and in England never is.

Cecil has engaged a teacher, and a model and he is coming here to work. He is twenty years old, and called the "boy Sargent." So, as soon as the British

Turner's House, Chelsea, 118 Cheyne Walk, where the Davises spent the winter of 1908-9.

A LONDON WINTER

public gets sober, we will begin life in earnest, and both work hard. I need not tell you how glad I am to be at it. I was with you all in heart last night and recited as much as I could remember of "Twas the Night Before Christmas," which always means Dad to me, as he used to read it to us. How much he made the day mean to us. I wish I could just slip in for a kiss, and a hug. But tonight we will all drink to you, and a few hours later you will drink to us. God bless you all.

DICK.

December 29th.

DEAR MOTHER:

A blizzard has swept over London. The last one cost the City Corporation $25,000!! The last man who contracted to clean New York of snow was cleaned out by two days of it, to the tune of $200,000. Still, in spite of our alleged superiority in all things, one inch of snow in Chelsea can do more to drive one to drink and suicide than a foot of it "on the farm." At the farm we threw a ton of coal against it, and lit log fires and oil lamps, and were warm. Here, they try to fight it with two buckets of soft chocolate cake called Welch coal, and the result is you freeze. Cecil's studio is like one vast summer hotel at Portland Maine in January. You cannot go near it except in rubber boots, fur coats and woolen gloves. My room still is the only one that is livable. It is four feet square, heavily panelled in oak and the coal fire makes it as warm as a stoke hole. So, I am all right and can work nicely. Janet Sothern came to lunch today and Cecil and she in furs went picture gazing. Tomorrow we have Capt. Chule to dinner. He came up the West coast with us and is accustomed to a temperature of 120°.

New Year's eve we spend with Lady Lewis where we dine and keep it up until four in the morning. We will easily be able to get back here but how we can get a hansom from here to the great city, I can't imagine. I have seen none in five days. It is fine to be surrounded by busts of Carlyle, Whistler, Rosetti and Turner's own, but occasionally you wish for a taxicab. Tomorrow I am going on a spree to the great city of London. The novel goes on smoothly, and all is well. I am still running for Mayor of Chelsea.

Love to you all.
DICK.

LONDON—January 1, 1909.

DEAR MOTHER:

I drank your health and Noll's and Charley's last night and so we all came into the New Year together. I hope it will be as good for me as the last. Certainly Chas. is coming on well with another book. It is splendid. I am so very, very glad. Some of the very best stories anybody has written will be in his next book.

We dined at the Lewis's. There were 150 at dinner and as we live in Chelsea now—one might as well be in Brooklyn—we were a half hour late. Fancy feeling you were keeping 150 people hungry. I sat at Lady Lewis's table with some interesting men and one beautiful woman all dressed in glass over pink silk, and pearls, and pearls and then, pearls. She said "Who am I" and I said "You look like a girl in America, who used to stand under a green paper lamp shade up in a farm house in New Hampshire and play a violin." Whereat there was much applause, because it seemed she was that girl, the daughter of a Mrs. Van S——, who wrote short stories. Her daughter was L—— Van S—— now the wife of a baronet and worth five million dollars. The board we paid then was eight dollars a week. Now, we are dining with her next Monday and as I insisted on gold plate she said "Very well, I'll get out the gold plate." But wasn't it dramatic of me to remember her after twenty two years?

DICK.

LONDON—February 23, 1909.
DEAR MOTHER:

George Washington's health was celebrated by drinking it at dinner. I had been asked to speak at a banquet but for some strange reason could not see myself in the part. The great Frohman arrived last night and we are all agitated until he speaks. If he would only like my plays as some of the actors do, I would be passing rich. Barrie asked himself to lunch yesterday and was very entertaining. He told us of a letter he received from Guy DuMaurier who wrote "An Englishman's Home" which has made a sensation second to nothing in ten years. He is an officer stationed at a small post in South Africa. He wrote Barrie he was at home, very blue and homesick, and outside it was raining. Then came Barrie's long cable, at 75 cents a word, saying his play was the success of the year. He did not know even it had been *accepted*. He shouted to his wife, and they tried to dance but the hut was too small, so they ran out into the compound and danced in the rain. Then he sent the Kaffir boys to the mess to bring all the officers and all the champagne and they did not go to bed at all. The next day cables, still at three shillings a word came from papers and magazines and publishers, managers, syndicates. And, in his letter he says, still not appreciating what a fuss it has made, "I suppose all it needs now is to be made a question in the House," when already it has been the text of half a dozen speeches by Cabinet Ministers, and three companies are playing it in the provinces. What fun to have a success come in such a way, not even to know it was being rehearsed. Today Sargent is here to see what is wrong with Cecil's picture of Janet. He came early and said he couldn't tell until he saw Janet, so now he is back again, and both Janet and Cecil are shaking with excitement. He is the most simple, kindly genius I ever met. He says the head is very fine and I guess Cecil suspected that, before she called him in. He says she must send it to the Royal Academy. I am now going out to hear more words fall from the great man, and so farewell. Seymour and I began work yesterday on the Dictator. It went very smooth.

All my love to Noll and to you.

DICK.

Read the other letter first and then, let me tell you that when I went out to see Sargent, I found Cecil complaining that she could not understand just how it was he wanted Janet to pose. Whereat she handed him a piece of chalk and he made a sketch of Janet as exquisite as the morning and rubbed his hands of the charcoal and left it there! It's only worth a hundred pounds! Can you imagine the nerve of Cecil. I was so shocked I could only gasp. But, he was quite charming and begged her to call him next time she got in a scrape, and gave her his private telephone number.

Fancy having Sargent waiting to be called up to make sketches for you. I left Janet and Cecil giggling with happiness. Janet because she had been sketched by him and Cecil because she has the sketch. It's a three fourths length three feet high, and he did it in ten minutes. I am now going to ask her to invite the chef of the Ritz in, to give us a sketch of cooking a dinner.

DICK.

CHAPTER XVIII

MILITARY MANŒUVRES

IN August, 1909, Richard and his wife left Mount Kisco for a visit to Mr. and Mrs. Clark at Marion. While there my brother attended and later on wrote an article on the war manœuvres held at Middleboro, Massachusetts.

MARION, MASSACHUSETTS.
August 16th, 1909.

DEAR MOTHER:

We had a splendid day to day. I arranged to have Cecil meet me at eleven at Headquarters in the woods below Middleboro, and I spent the morning locating different regiments. Then, after I "met up" with her, I took her in my car. Both she and Hiller were awfully keen over it, so, we got on splendidly. And, of course, Hiller's knowledge of the country was wonderfully convenient. We had great luck in seeing the only fight of the day, the first one of the war. Indeed, I think we caused it. There was a troop of cavalry with a Captain who was afraid to advance. I chided him into doing *something*, the umpire having confided to me, he would mark him, if he did not. But, he did it *wrong*. Anyway, he charged a barn with 36 troopers and lost every fourth man. In real warfare he would have lost *all* his men and all his horses. Cecil and Hiller pursued in the car at the very heels of the cavalry, and I ran ahead with the bicycle scouts. It was most exciting. I am going out again to-morrow. Lots of Love to you all.

DICK.

MARION, MASSACHUSETTS.
August 19th, 1909.
DEAR MOTHER:

I got in last night too late to write and I am sorry. To-day, the war came to an end with our army, the Red one, with the road to Boston open before it. Indeed, when the end came, they were fighting with their backs to that City, and could have entered it to-night. I begged both Bliss and Wood to send in the cavalry just for the moral effect, but they were afraid of the feeling, that was quite strong. I had much fun, never more, and saw all that was worth seeing. I was glad to see I am in such good shape physically, but with the tramping I do over the farm, it is no wonder. I could take all the stone walls at a jump, while the others were tearing them down. I also met hundreds of men I knew and every one was most friendly, especially the correspondents. Just as I liked to be on a story with a "star" man when I was a reporter, they liked having a real "war" correspondent, take it seriously. They were always wanting to know if it were like the *Real Thing*, and as I assured them it was, they were satisfied. Some incidents were very funny. I met a troop of cavalry this morning, riding away from the battle, down a crossroad, and thinking it was a flanking manœuvre, started to follow them with the car. "Where are you going?" I asked the Captain. "Nowhere," he said, "We are dead." An Umpire was charging in advance of two troops of the 10th down a state road, when one trooper of the enemy who were flying, turned back and alone charged the two troops. "You idiot"! yelled the Umpire, "don't you know you and your horse are shot to pieces?" "Sure, I know it," yelled the trooper "but, this —— horse don't know it."

RICHARD.

Early in the fall of 1909 Richard returned from Marion to New York and went to Crossroads, where for the next three years he remained a greater part of the time. They were years of great and serious changes for him. An estrangement of long standing between him and his wife had ended in their separation early in 1910, to be followed later by their divorce. In September of that year my mother died while on a visit to Crossroads.

After my father's death life to her became only a period of waiting until the moment came when she would rejoin him—because her faith was implicit and infinite. She could not well set about preparing herself because all of her life she had done that and, so, smiling and with a splendid bravery and patience she lived on, finding her happiness in bringing cheer and hope and happiness to all who came into the presence of her wonderful personality. The old home in Philadelphia was just the same as it had been through her long married life—that is with one great difference, but on account of this difference I knew that she was glad to spend her last days with Richard at Crossroads. And surely nothing that could be done for a mother by a son had been left undone by him. Through these last long summer days she sat on the terrace surrounded by the flowers and the sunshine that she so loved. Little children came to play at her knee, and old friends travelled from afar to pay her court.

In the winter of 1910–11 my brother visited Aiken, where he spent several months. The following June he went to London at the time of King George's coronation, but did not write about it. Again, in November, 1911, he visited my sister in London, but returned to New York in January, 1912, and spent a part of the winter in Aiken and Cuba. At Aiken he found at least peace and the devotion of loving friends that he so craved, but in London and Cuba, which once had meant so much to him, he seemed to have lost interest entirely. But not once during these years did he cease working, and working hard. On almost every page of his diary at this period I find such expressions as "wrote 500 words for discipline." And again "Satisfaction in work of last years when writing for existence, has been up to any I ever wrote."

And in spite of all of the trouble of these days, he not only wrote incessantly but did some of his very finest work. Personally I have never seen a man make a more courageous fight. To quote again from his diary of this time: "Early going to my room saw red sunrise and gold moon. I seemed to stop worrying about money. With such free pleasures I found I could not worry. Every day God gives me greater delight in good things, in beauty, and in every simple exercise and amusement."

Twice during these difficult days he went to visit Gouverneur Morris and his wife at Aiken, and after Richard's death his old friend wrote of the first of these visits:

"It was in our little house at Aiken, in South Carolina, that he was with us most and we learned to know him best, and that he and I became dependent upon each other in many ways.

"Events, into which I shall not go, had made his life very difficult and complicated. And he who had given so much friendship to so many people needed a little friendship in return, and perhaps, too, he needed for a time to live in a house whose master and mistress loved each other, and where there were children. Before he came that first year our house had no name. Now it is called 'Let's Pretend.'

"Now the chimney in the living-room draws, but in those first days of the built-over house it didn't. At least, it didn't draw all the time, but we pretended that it did, and with much pretense came faith. From the fireplace that smoked to the serious things of life we extended our pretendings, until real troubles went down before them—down and out.

"It was one of Aiken's very best winters, and the earliest spring I ever lived anywhere. R. H. D. came shortly after Christmas. The spiræas were in bloom, and the monthly roses; you could always find a sweet violet or two somewhere in the yard; here and there splotches of deep pink against gray cabin walls proved that precocious peach-trees were in bloom. It never rained. At night it was cold enough for fires. In the middle of the day it was hot. The wind never blew, and every morning we had a four for tennis and every afternoon we rode in the woods. And every night we sat in front of the fire (that didn't smoke because of pretending) and talked until the next morning.

"He was one of those rarely gifted men who find their chiefest pleasure not in looking backward or forward, but in what is going on at the moment. Weeks did not have to pass before it was forced upon his knowledge that Tuesday, the fourteenth (let us say), had been a good Tuesday. He knew it the moment

With Mr. and Mrs. Morris, Aiken, 1912.

he waked at 7 A. M., and perceived the Tuesday sunshine making patterns of bright light upon the floor. The sunshine rejoiced him and the knowledge that even before breakfast there was vouchsafed to him a whole hour of life. That day began with attentions to his physical well-being. There were exercises conducted with great vigor and rejoicing, followed by a tub, artesian cold, and a loud and joyous singing of ballads.

"The singing over, silence reigned. But if you had listened at his door you must have heard a pen going, swiftly and boldly. He was hard at work, doing unto others what others had done unto him. You were a stranger to him; some magazine had accepted a story that you had written and published it. R. H. D. had found something to like and admire in that story (very little perhaps), and it was his duty and pleasure to tell you so. If he had liked the story very much he would send you instead of a note a telegram. Or it might be that you had drawn a picture, or, as a cub reporter, had shown golden promise in a half column of unsigned print, R. H. D. would find you out, and find time to praise you and help you. So it was that when he emerged from his room at sharp eight o'clock, he was wide-awake and happy and hungry, and whistled and double-shuffled with his feet, out of excessive energy, and carried in his hands a whole sheaf of notes and letters and telegrams.

"Breakfast with him was not the usual American breakfast, a sullen, dyspeptic gathering of persons who only the night before had rejoiced in each other's society. With him it was the time when the mind is, or ought to be, at its best, the body at its freshest and hungriest. Discussions of the latest plays and novels, the doings and undoings of statesmen, laughter and sentiment—to him, at breakfast, these things were as important as sausages and thick cream.

"Breakfast over, there was no dawdling and putting off of the day's work (else how, at eleven sharp, could tennis be played with a free conscience?). Loving, as he did, everything connected with a newspaper, he would now pass by those on the hall-table with never so much as a wistful glance, and hurry to his workroom.

"He wrote sitting down. He wrote standing up. And, almost you may say, he wrote walking up and down. Some people, accustomed to the delicious ease and clarity of his style, imagine that he wrote very easily. He did and he didn't. Letters, easy, clear, to the point, and gorgeously human, flowed from him without let or hindrance. That masterpiece of corresponding, the German March through Brussels, was probably written almost as fast as he could talk (next to Phillips Brooks, he was the fastest talker I ever heard), but when it came to fiction he had no facility at all. Perhaps I should say that he held in contempt any facility that he may have had. It was owing to his incomparable energy and Joblike patience that he ever gave us any fiction at all. Every phrase in his fiction was, of all the myriad phrases he could think of, the fittest in his relentless judgment to survive. Phrases, paragraphs, pages, whole stories even, were written over and over again. He worked upon a principle of elimination. If he wished to describe an automobile turning in at a gate, he made first a long and elaborate description from which there was omitted no detail, which the most observant pair of eyes in Christendom had ever noted with reference to just such a turning. Thereupon he would begin a process of omitting one by one those details which he had been at such pains to recall; and after each omission he would ask himself, 'Does the picture remain?' If it did not, he restored the detail which he had just omitted, and experimented with the sacrifice of some other, and so on, and so on, until after Herculean labor there remained for the reader one of those swiftly flashed ice-clear pictures (complete in every detail) with which his tales and romances are so delightfully and continuously adorned.

"But it is quarter to eleven, and this being a time of holiday, R. H. D. emerges from his workroom happy to think that he has placed one hundred and seven words between himself and the wolf who hangs about every writer's door. He isn't satisfied with those hundred and seven words. He never was in the least satisfied with anything that he wrote, but he has searched his mind and his conscience and he believes that under the circumstances they are the very best that he can do. Anyway, they can stand in their present order until—after lunch.

"A sign of his youth was the fact that to the day of his death he had denied himself the luxury and slothfulness of habits. I have never seen him smoke automatically as most men do. He had too much respect for his own powers of enjoyment and for the sensibilities, perhaps, of the best Havana tobacco. At a time of his own deliberate choosing, often after many hours of hankering and renunciation, he smoked his cigar. He smoked it with delight, with a sense of being rewarded, and he used all the smoke there was in it.

"He dearly loved the best food, the best champagne, and the best Scotch whiskey. But these things were friends to him, and not enemies. He had toward food and drink the continental attitude; namely, that quality is far more important than quantity; and he got his exhilaration from the fact that he was drinking champagne and not from the champagne. Perhaps I shall do well to say that on questions of right and wrong he had a will of iron. All his life he moved resolutely in whichever direction his conscience pointed; and although that ever present and never obtrusive conscience of his made mistakes of judgment now and then, as must all consciences, I think it can never once have tricked him into any action that was impure or unclean. Some critics maintain that the heroes and heroines of his books are impossibly pure and innocent young people. R. H. D. never called upon his characters for any trait of virtue, or renunciation, or self-mastery of which his own life could not furnish examples."

In June of 1912 Richard reported the Republican convention at Chicago. Shortly after this, on July 8, he married at Greenwich, Connecticut, Miss Elizabeth Genevieve McEvoy, known on the stage as Bessie McCoy, with whom he had first become acquainted in 1908 after the estrangement from his wife.

Richard and his wife made their home at Crossroads, where he devoted most of his working hours to the writing of short stories. In August of that year my brother, accompanied by his wife, returned to Chicago to report the Progressive convention. During the year 1913 he wrote and produced the farce "Who's Who," of which William Collier was the star, and in the fall of the same year spent a month in Cuba, with Augustus Thomas, where they produced a film version of "Soldiers of Fortune." In referring

At Mt. Kisco.

to this trip, Thomas wrote at the time of Richard's death:

"In 1914 a motion-picture company arranged to make a feature film of the play, and Dick and I went with their outfit to Santiago de Cuba, where, twenty years earlier, he had found the inspiration for his story and out of which city and its environs he had fashioned his supposititious republic of Olancho. On that trip he was the idol of the company. With the men in the smoking-room of the steamer there were the numberless playful stories, in the rough, of the experiences on all five continents and seven seas that were the backgrounds of his published tales.

"At Santiago, if an official was to be persuaded to consent to some unprecedented seizure of the streets, or a diplomat invoked for the assistance of the Army or the Navy, it was the experience and good judgment of Dick Davis that controlled the task. In the field there were his helpful suggestions of work and make up to the actors, and on the boat and train and in hotel and camp the lady members met in him an easy courtesy and understanding at once fraternal and impersonal.

"The element that he could not put into the account and which is particularly pertinent to this page, is the author of 'Soldiers of Fortune' as he revealed himself to me both with intention and unconsciously in the presence of the familiar scenes.

"For three weeks, with the exception of one or two occasions when some local dignitary captured the revisiting lion, he and I spent our evenings together at a café table overlooking 'The Great Square,' which he sketches so deftly in its atmosphere when Clay and the Langhams and Stuart dine there. At one end of the plaza the President's band was playing native waltzes that came throbbing through the trees and beating softly above the rustling skirts and clinking spurs of the senoritas and officers sweeping by in two opposite circles around the edges of the tessellated pavements. Above the palms around the square arose the dim, white façade of the Cathedral, with the bronze statue of Anduella the liberator of Olancho, who answered with his upraised arm and cocked hat the cheers of an imaginary populace.

"Twenty years had gone by since Dick had received the impression that wrote those lines, and now sometimes after dinner half a long cigar would burn out as he mused over the picture and the dreams that had gone between. From one long silence he said: 'I think I'll come back here this winter and bring Mrs. Davis with me—stay a couple of months.' What a fine compliment to a wife to have the thought of her and that plan emerge from that deep and romantic background.

"The picture people began their film with a showing of the 'mountains which jutted out into the ocean and suggested roughly the five knuckles of a giant's hand clenched and lying flat upon the surface of the water.' That formation of the sea wall is just outside of Santiago. 'The waves tunnelled their way easily enough until they ran up against those five mountains and then they had to fall back.' How natural for one of us to be unimpressed by such a feature of the landscape and yet how characteristic of Dick Davis to see the elemental fight that it recorded and get the hint for the whole of the engineering struggle that is so much of his book.

"We went over those mountains together, where

R. H. D. and Augustus Thomas filming "Soldiers of Fortune" in Santiago.

two decades before he had planted his banner of romance. We visited the mines and the railroads and everywhere found some superintendent or foreman or engineer who remembered Davis. He had guessed at nothing. Everywhere he had overlaid the facts with adventure and with beauty, but he had been on sure footing all the time. His prototype of MacWilliams was dead. Together we visited the wooden cross with which the miners had marked his grave."

CHAPTER XIX

VERA CRUZ AND THE GREAT WAR

LATE in April, 1914, when war between the United States and Mexico seemed inevitable Richard once more left the peace and content of Crossroads and started for Vera Cruz, arriving there on April 29. He had arranged to act as correspondent for a syndicate of newspapers, and as he had for long been opposed to the administration's policy of "watchful waiting" was greatly disappointed on his arrival at the border to learn of the President's plan of mediation. He wrote to his wife:

VERA CRUZ, April 24, 1914.

DEAREST ONE:

We left today at 5.30. It was a splendid scene, except for the children crying, and the wives of the officers and enlisted men trying not to cry. I got a stateroom to myself. With the electric fan on and the airport open, it is about as cool as a blast furnace. But I was given a seat on the left of General Funston, who is commanding this brigade, and the other officers at the table are all good fellows. As long as I was going, I certainly had luck in getting away as sharply as I did. One day's delay would have made me miss this transport, which will be the first to land troops.

April 25th.

A dreadnaught joined us today, the *Louisiana*. I wirelessed the Admiral asking permission to send a press despatch via his battleship, and he was polite in reply, but firm. He said "No." There are four transports and three torpedo boats and the battleship. We go very slowly, because we must keep up with one of the troop ships with broken engines. At night it is very pretty seeing the ships in line, and the torpedo boats winking their signals at each other. I am writing all the time or reading up things about the army I forget and getting the new dope. Also I am brushing up my Spanish. Jack London is on board, and three other correspondents, two of whom I have met on other trips, and one "cub" correspondent. He was sitting beside London and me busily turning out copy, and I asked him what he found to write about. He said, "Well, maybe I see things you fellows don't see." What he meant was that what was old to us was new to him, but he got guyed unmercifully.

April 27, 1914.

The censor reads all I write, and so do some half-dozen Mexican cable clerks and 60 (sixty) correspondents. So when I cable "love," it *means* devotion, adoration, and worship; loyalty, fidelity and truth, wanting you, needing you, unhappy for you. It means *all* that.

RICHARD.

VERA CRUZ, April 30, 1914.

This heat—humid and moist—would sweat water out of a chilled steel safe; so imagine what it does to me with all the awful winter's accumulation of fat. I hate to say it, but I *like* these Mexicans—much better than Cubans, or Central Americans. They are human, kindly; it is only the politicians and bandits like Villa who give them a bad name. But, though they ought to hate us, whenever I stop to ask my way they invite me to come in and have "coffee" and say, "My house is yours, señor," which certainly is kind after people have taken your town away from you and given you another flag and knocked your head off if you did not salute it. I now have a fine room. The Navy moved out today and I got the room of the paymaster. It faces the plaza and the cathedral. I burned a candle there today for our soon meeting. The priests all had run away, so I had to hunt up the candle, and pay the money into the box marked for that purpose, but the Lord does not run away, and He will see we soon meet.

May 2nd.

Yesterday I went out on the train that brings in refugees and saw the Mexicans. They had on three thousand cartridges, much hair, hats as high as church steeples, and lots of dirt. The Selig Moving Picture folks took many pictures of us and several "stills," in which the war correspondent was shown giving cigarettes to the brigands. Also, I had a wonderful bath in the ocean off the aviation camp. I borrowed a suit from one of the aviators, and splashed and swam around for an hour. My! it was good. It reminded me of my dear Bessie, because the last time I was in the ocean was with her.

Maybe you know what is going on, but we do not. So I just hustle around all day trying to find news as I did when I was a reporter. It is hot enough here even for me, and I have lost about eight pounds of that fat I laid in during our North Pole winter!

Rurales at the Gap on the road to Mexico City.

VERA CRUZ—May 8, 1914.

DEAR CHAS.:

Today, when Wilson ordered Huerta not to blockade Tampico which was an insult to Mediators and the act of a bully and a coward, *and* a declaration of war, we all got on our ponies to "advance." Then came word Huerta would not blockade. It is like living in a mad house. We all are hoping mediators refuse to continue negotiations. If they have self respect that is what they will do. Tonight if Wilson and Huerta ran for President, Huerta would get all our votes. He may be an uneducated Indian, but at least he is a man. However, that makes no never mind so far as to my getting back. The reason I cannot return is because I have "credentials." It is not that they want *me* here, but they want my credentials here. The administration is using, as I see it, the privilege of having a correspondent at the front as a club. It says until war is declared it won't issue any more. So those syndicates who have no correspondent and the papers forming them, are afraid to attack or to criticise the administration for fear they will be blacklisted. And those who have a correspondent with his three thousand dollar signed and sealed pass in his pocket aren't taking any chance on losing him. So, I see before me an endless existence in Vera Cruz.

RICHARD.

On May 7 Richard started for Mexico City where, if possible, he intended to interview Huerta. At Pasco de Macho he was arrested, but afterward was allowed to proceed to Mexico City. Here he was again arrested, and without being allowed to interview Heurta was sent back the day after his arrival to Vera Cruz.

Of this Vera Cruz experience John N. Wheeler, a friend of Richard's and the manager of the syndicate which sent him to Mexico, wrote the following after my brother's death:

"Richard Harding Davis went to Vera Cruz for a newspaper syndicate, and after the first sharp engagement in the Mexican seaport there was nothing for the correspondent to do but kill time on that barren, low lying strip of Gulf coast, hemmed in on all sides by Mexicans and the sea, and time is hard to kill there. Yet there was a story to be got, but it required nerve to go after it.

"In Mexico City was Gen. Huerta, the dictator of Mexico. If a newspaper could get an interview with him it would be a 'scoop,' but the work was inclined to be dangerous for the interviewer, since Americans were being murdered rather profusely in Mexico at the time in spite of the astute assurances of Mr. Bryan, and no matter how substantial his references the correspondent was likely to meet some temperamental and touchy soldier with a loaded rifle who would shoot first and afterward carry his papers to some one who could read them.

"One of the newspapers taking the stories by Mr. Davis from the syndicate had a staff man at Vera Cruz as well, and thought to 'scoop' the country by sending this representative to see Huerta, in this way 'beating' even the other subscribers to the Davis service. An interview in Mexico City was consequently arranged and the staff man was cabled and asked to make the trip. He promptly cabled his refusal, this young man preferring to take no such chances. It was then suggested that Mr. Davis should attempt it. By pulling some wires at Washington it was arranged, through the

VERA CRUZ AND THE GREAT WAR 359

Brazilian and English Ambassadors at the Mexican capital, for Mr. Davis to interview President Huerta, with safe conduct (this being about as safe as non-skid tires) to Mexico City. Mr. Davis was asked if he would make the trip. In less than two hours back came this laconic cable:

"'Leaving Mexico City to-morrow afternoon at 3 o'clock.'

"That was Richard Harding Davis—no hesitancy, no vacillation. He was always willing to go, to take any chance, to endure discomfort and all if he had a fighting opportunity to get the news. The public now knows that Davis was arrested on this trip, that Huerta refused to make good on the interview, and that it was only through the good efforts of the British Ambassador at the Mexican capital he was released. But Davis went.

"There was an echo of this journey to the Mexican capital several months later after the conflict in Europe had been raging for a few weeks. Lord Kitchener announced at one stage of the proceedings he would permit a single correspondent, selected and indorsed by the United States Government, to accompany the British army to the front. Of course, all the swarm of American correspondents in London at the time were eager for the desirable indorsement. Mr. Davis cabled back the conditions of his acceptance. Immediately Secretary of State Bryan was called in Washington on the long-distance telephone.

"'Lord Kitchener has announced,' the Secretary of State was told, 'that he will accept one correspondent with the British troops in the field, if he is indorsed by the United States Government. Richard Harding Davis, who is in London, represents a string of the strongest newspapers in the United States for this syndicate, and we desire the indorsement of the State Department so he can obtain this appointment.'

"'Mr. Davis made us some trouble when he was in Mexico,' answered Mr. Bryan. 'He proceeded to the Mexican capital without our consent and I will have to consider the matter very carefully before indorsing him. His Mexican escapade caused us some diplomatic efforts and embarrassment.' (What the Secretary of State did to bring about Mr. Davis's release on the occasion of his Mexican arrest is still a secret of the Department.)

"Mr. Bryan did not indorse Mr. Davis finally, which was well, since Lord Kitchener of Khartum kept the selected list of correspondents loafing around London on one pretext or another so long they all became disgusted and went without an official pass from 'K. of K.' As soon as Mr. Davis was told he would not be appointed he proceeded to Belgium and returned some of the most thrilling stories written on this conflict at great personal risk."

May 13, 1914.
MY DEAREST ONE:

Do not blame me for this long delay in writing. God knows I wanted every day to "talk" to you. But we were on the "suspect" list, and to make even a note was risky. The way I did it was to exclaim over the beauty of some flower or tree, and then ask the Mexican nearest me to write the name of it *himself* in *my* notebook. Then I would say, "In English that would be——" and I would pretend to write beside it the English equivalent, but really would write the word that was the key to what I wished to remember. So,

VERA CRUZ AND THE GREAT WAR   361

you see, a letter at that rate of progress was impossible. It was a case of "Can't get away to cable you today; police won't let me!" However, we are all safe at home again. As a matter of fact, I had a most exciting time, and am dying to tell you the "inside" story. But the one I sent the papers must serve. I promised myself I would give the *first* soldier, marine and sailor I met on returning a cigar, and the first *sailor* was the *chaplain of the fleet,* Father Reany. But he took the cigar and gave me his blessing. I am now burning candles to St. Rita. What worried me the *most* was how worried *you* would be; and I begged Palmer not to send the story of our first arrest. But other people told of it, and he had to forward it. You certainly made the wires *burn!* and had the army guessing. One officer said to me, "I'm awfully sorry to see you back. If you'd only have stayed in jail another day your wife would have had us all on our way to Mexico." And the censor said, "My God! I'm glad you're safe! Your wife *has made our lives hell!*" And quite right, too, bless you! None of us knows anything, but it looks to me that *nothing* will induce Wilson to go to war. But the Mexicans think we *are* at war, and act accordingly. They may bring on a conflict. That is why I am making ready in case we advance and that is why I cabled today for the rest of my kit. I have a fine little pony, and a little messenger boy who speaks Spanish, to look after the horse, and me.

And now, as to your *letters,* they came to-day, five of them, *count 'em,* and the pictures did make me laugh. I showed those of the soldier commandeering the vegetables to Funston and he laughed. And, I did love the flowers you sent no matter *how* homesick they made me! (Oh). I do not want a camera. I have one, and those fancy cameras I don't understand.

The letters you forwarded were wonderfully well selected. I mean, those from other people. One of them was from Senator Root telling me Bryan is going to reward our three heroic officers who jumped into the ocean. I know you will be glad. There are *no* mosquitoes! Haven't met up with but three and *they* are not *coming back*.

I send you a picture of my room from the outside. From the inside the view is so "pretty." Across the square is the cathedral and the trees are filled with birds that sing all night, and statues, and pretty globes. The band plays every night and when it plays "Hello, Winter Time," I *cry* for you. I paid the band-master $20 to play it, and it is *worth it*. I sit on the balcony and think of you and know just what you are doing, for there is only an hour and a half difference. That is, when with you it is ten o'clock with me it is eight-thirty. So when you and Louise are at dinner you can know I am just coming in from my horseback ride to bathe and "nap." And when at eight-thirty you are playing the Victor, I am drinking a cocktail to you, and shooing away the Colonels and Admirals who interfere with my ceremony of drinking to my dear wife.

VERA CRUZ, May 20th, 1914.

DEAREST WIFE:

I got *such* a bully letter yesterday from you, written long ago from the Webster. It said you missed me, and it said you loved me, and there were funny pictures of you reading the war and peace news each with a different expression, and you told me about Padrigh and how he runs down the road. It made me very sad and homesick, but very glad to feel I was so missed.

Also you told me cheerful falsehoods about my *Tribune* stories. I know they are no good, and as they are no good, the shorter the better, but I like to be told they are good. Anyway, I sat down at once and wrote a long screed on Vera Cruz and the sleepy people that live here.

We all live on the sidewalk under the stone porch. Every night a table is reserved and by my orders *all* chairs, except mine, are removed. So no one can sit down and bore me while I am dining. Another trick I have to be left alone is to carry a big roll of cable blanks, and I pretend to write out cables if anyone tries to talk. Then I beckon the messenger (he always sits in the plaza) and say "File that!" and he goes once around the block and reports back that it is "filed." If the bore renews the attack I write another cable, and the unhappy messenger makes another tour. The band plays from seven to eight every night. There are five bands, and I saw no reason why there should not be music every evening. After a day in this dirty hotel or dirty city a lively band helps. Funston agreed, but forgot, until after three nights with no band, I wrote him a letter. It was signed by fake names, asking if he couldn't get nineteen German musicians into a bandstand how could he hope to get ten thousand soldiers into Mexico City. So now we have a band each night. That is all my day. After dinner I sit at table and the men bring up chairs, or else I go to some other table. There are some damn fool women here who are a nuisance, and they now have dancing in the hotel adjoining, but I don't know them, except to bow, and I approve of the tango parties because it keeps them away from the sidewalk. They are "refugees," the sort of folks you meet at Ocean Grove, or rather *don't* meet!

All love to you, and give Patrigh a pat from his Uncle Richard for looking after you and looking for me, and remember me to Louise and Shu and everything at home. I love you so.

RICHARD.

VERA CRUZ, May 28, 1914.

I want to be home to see the daisy field with you. That knee you nearly busted tobogganing when the daisy field was an iceberg is now recovered.

The one and all came this morning and as I expected it was all full of love from you. I *did* get happiness out of the thought you put in it. And all done in an hour. The underclothes made me weep. I could get none here. Not because Mexicans are not as large as I am, but because no Mexican of any size would wear 'em. So I've had to wash the few that the washer-woman didn't destroy myself. And when I saw the lot you sent! It was like a white sale! Also the quinine which I tasted just for luck, and the soap in the little violet wrapper made me quite homesick. Especially was I glad to get socks and pongee suits, and shirts. I really was getting desperate. God knows what I would have done without them.

I want to see you so much, and I want to see you in the same setting of other days, I want to walk with you in the daisy field, and in the laurel blossoms, and clip roses. But to be with you I'd be willing to walk on broken glass. Not you, too. Just me.

RICHARD.

VERA CRUZ—June 4, 1914.

DEAR OLD MAN:

I am awfully sorry for your sake, you could not get away. Of course for myself I am glad that I am to see you and Dai. At least, I hope I am. God alone knows when we will get out of here. I am sick of it. Next time I go to war both armies must fight for two months before I will believe they mean it, and *before I will budge.*

It is true I am getting good money, but also there is absolutely *nothing* to write about. Bryan doesn't know that unless he talks by code every radio on sixteen ships can read every message he sends to these waters. And the State Department saying it could not understand the *Hyranga* giving up her cargo is a damn silly lie. No one is so foolish as to think the *Chester* and *Tacomah* let her land those arms under their guns unless they had been told to submit to it. And yet today, we get papers of the 29th in which Bryan says he has twice cabled Badger for information, when for a week Badger has been reading Bryan's orders to consuls to let the arms be landed. Can you beat that? This is an awful place, and if I don't write it is because I hate to harrow your feelings. It is a town of flies, filth and heat. John McCutcheon is the only friend I have seen, and he sensibly lives on a warship. I can't do that, as cables come all the time suggesting specials, and I am not paid to loaf. John is here on a vacation, and can do as he pleases. But I ride around like any cub reporter. And there is no news. Since I left home I have not talked five minutes to a woman "or mean to!" The Mexican women are a cross between apes and squaws. Of all I have seen here nothing has impressed me so as the hideousness of the women, girls, children, widows, grandmothers. And the refugees, as Collier would say it, are "terrible!" I live a very lonely existence. I find it works out that way best. And at the same time all the correspondents are good friends, and I don't find that there is one of them who does not go out of his way to *show* he is friendly. What I *can't* understand is why no one at home never guesses I might like to read some of my own stories. . . .

                                                    DICK.

Of these days in Vera Cruz John T. McCutcheon wrote the following shortly after Richard's death:

"Davis was a conspicuous figure in Vera Cruz, as he inevitably had been in all such situations. Wherever he went, he was pointed out. His distinction of appearance, together with a distinction in dress, which, whether from habit or policy, was a valuable asset in his work, made him a marked man. He dressed and looked the 'war correspondent,' such a one as he would describe in one of his stories. He fulfilled the popular ideal of what a member of that fascinating profession should look like. His code of life and habits was as fixed as that of the Briton who takes his habits and customs and games and tea wherever he goes, no matter how benighted or remote the spot may be.

"He was just as loyal to his code as is the Briton. He carried his bath-tub, his immaculate linen, his evening clothes, his war equipment—in which he had the pride of a connoisseur—wherever he went, and, what is more, he had the courage to use the evening clothes at times when their use was conspicuous. He was the only man who wore a dinner coat in Vera Cruz, and each night, at his particular table in the crowded 'Portales,' at the Hotel Diligencia, he was to be seen, as fresh and clean as though he were in a New York or London restaurant.

"Each day he was up early to take the train out to the 'gap,' across which came arrivals from Mexico City. Sometimes a good 'story' would come down, as when the long-heralded and long-expected arrival of Consul Silliman gave a first-page 'feature' to all the American papers.

"In the afternoon he would play water polo over at the navy aviation camp, and always at a certain time of the day his 'striker' would bring him his horse and for an hour or more he would ride out along the beach roads within the American lines."

. . . .

On June 15 Richard sailed on the *Utah* for New York, arriving there on the 22d. For a few weeks after his return he remained at Mount Kisco completing his articles on the Mexican situation but at the outbreak of the Great War he at once started for Europe, sailing with his wife on August 4, the day war was declared between England and Germany.

On *Lusitania*—August 8, 1914.

DEAR CHAS:

We got off in a great rush, as the Cunard people received orders to sail so soon after the Government had told them to cancel all passengers, that no one expected to leave by her, and had secured passage on the *Lorraine* and *St. Paul*.

They gave me a "regal" suite which at other times costs $1,000 and it is so darned regal that I hate to leave it. I get sleepy walking from one end of it to the other; and we have open fires in each of the three rooms. Generally when one goes to war it is in a transport or a troop train and the person of the least importance is the correspondent. So, this way of going to war I like. We now are a cruiser and are slowly being painted grey, and as soon as they got word England was at war all lights were put out and to find your way you light matches. You can imagine the effect of this Ritz Carlton idea of a ship wrapped in darkness. Gerald Morgan is on board, he is also accredited to *The Tribune,* and Frederick Palmer. I do not expect to be allowed to see anything but will try to join a French army. I will leave Bessie near London with Louise at some quiet place like Oxford or a village on the Thames. We can "take" wireless, but not send it, so as no one is sending and as we don't care to expose our position, we get no news. We are running far North and it is bitterly cold. I think Peary will sue us for infringing his copyrights.

I will try to get in touch with Nora. I am worried lest she cannot get at her money. As British subjects no other thing should upset them. Address me American Embassy, London.

I send such love to you both. God bless you.

DICK.

Richard arrived in Liverpool August 13, and made arrangements for his wife to remain in London. Unable to obtain credentials from the English authorities, he started for Brussels and arrived there in time to see the entry of the German troops, which he afterward described so graphically. Indeed this article is considered by many to be one of the finest pieces of descriptive writing the Great War has produced.

For several days after Brussels had come under the control of the Germans Richard remained there and then decided to go to Paris as the siege of the

French capital at the time seemed imminent. He and his friend Gerald Morgan, who was acting as the correspondent of the London *Daily Telegraph*, decided to drive to Hal and from there to continue on foot until they had reached the English or French armies where they knew they would be among friends. At Hal they were stopped by the German officials and Morgan wisely returned to Brussels. However, Richard having decided to continue on his way, was promptly seized by the Germans and held as an English spy. For a few days he had a most exciting series of adventures with the German military authorities and his life was frequently in danger. It was finally due to my brother's own strategy and the prompt action of our Ambassador to Belgium, Brand Whitlock, that he was returned to Brussels and received his official release.

On August 27, Richard left Brussels for Paris on a train carrying English prisoners and German wounded, and en route saw much of the burning and destruction of Louvain.

BRUSSELS, August 17, 1914.

DEAREST:

Write me soon and often! All is well here so long as I know you are all right, so do not fail to tell me all, and keep me in touch. If *I* do not write much, it is because letters do not get through always, and are read. But you know I love you, and you know twice each day I pray for you and wish for you all the time. I feel as though I had been gone a month. Gerald Morgan and I got in last night; this is a splendid new hotel; for $2.50 I get a room and bath like yours on the "royal suite," only bigger. This morning the minister did everything he could for us. There are about twenty Americans who want credentials. They say they will take no Americans, but to our minister they said they would make exception in favor of three, so I guess the three will be John McCutcheon, Palmer and myself. John and I, if anyone gets a pass, are sure. With the passes we had, Gerald and I started out in a yellow motor, covered with flags of the Allies, and saw a great deal. How I wished you were with me, you would so have loved it. The country is absolutely beautiful. We were stopped every quarter mile to show our passes and we got a working idea of how it will be. Tonight I dined with Mr. Whitlock, the minister, and John McCutcheon came in and Irving Cobb. John and I will get together and go out. All you need is a motor car and you can go pretty much everywhere, *except* near where there is fighting. So what I am to do to earn my wages I don't know. I am now going to bed and I send my darlin' all love. Today I sent you a wire. If it got to you let me know. Take such good care of yourself. Remember me to Louise, and, *write me.* All love, *dear, dear* one. My wife and my sweetheart.

Your husband,
RICHARD.

The following is the last letter that got through.

BRUSSELS, August 21, 1914.

DEAREST ONE:

I cannot say much, as I doubt if this will be opened by you. The German army came in and there was no fighting and I am very well. I am only distressed at not being able to get letters from you, and not being able to send them. I will write a long one, and hold it until I am sure of some way by which it can reach you. *You know what I would say.*

R.

Mrs. Davis had waited in London to meet Richard on his return from the war, but a misunderstanding as to the date of his return, coupled with her strong sense of duty to his interests at home, gave occasion for the letter which follows:

LONDON, August 31, 1914.

DEAREST ONE:

Not since the Herald Square days have I had such a blow as when I drove up to 10 Clarges, and found you gone! *It was nobody's fault! You* were *so right* to go; and *I could not come.* I am so distressed lest it was my cable saying I could not get back that decided you to go before the fifth. But Ashford says it was not. He tells me the cable came at *three* in the morning and that you had arranged to be called at six-thirty in order to leave for Scotland. So, for sending that cable I need not blame myself too much. I sent you so many messages I do not know which got through. But I think it must have been one saying I could not return in time to see you before the fifth. *Then*, no trains were running. The very *next day* the Germans started a troop train, and I took it. The reason I could not come by automobile was because I had a falling out with the "mad dogs" and they would not give me a pass. So Evans, with whom I was to motor to Holland, got through Friday afternoon and sent the cable. As soon as I reached Holland, I cabled I was coming and kept on telegraphing *every* step of the journey, which lasted three days.

I telegraphed last from Folkestone; even telling you what to have for my supper. As you directed, Ashford opened the cables, and when I drove up, he was at the door in tears. He had made a light in your rooms and, of course, as I looked up I thought you still were in them. When they told me I was a day late, I cried, too. It was the bitterest disappointment I ever knew. I had taken the very first train out of Brussels, the one with the wounded, and for three days had been having one hell of a time. But I kept thinking of seeing you, and hearing your dear voice. So the trip did not matter. I was only thinking of *seeing you*, and thanking God I was shut of the dirty Germans. We had nothing to eat, and we slept on the floor of the train, the Germans kept us locked in, and, all through even Holland, we were under arrest. But nothing mattered, because I was so happy at thought of meeting you. As I said neither of us was at fault. You just *had* to go, and I could *not come*. But, you can feel how I felt to learn you were at sea.

I was so glad I could use your old rooms. I went to the table where you used to write and was so glad I could at least be as near to you as that. No other place in London could have held me that night. Not Buckingham Palace. I found little things you had left. I loved even the funny pictures on the wall because we had talked of them together. It was *rotten, rotten* luck. But only the Germans and their hellish war were to blame. I drove straight to the cable office, and tried to wireless you, knowing you would feel glad to know I was well, and safe and sound. But the cable people could not send my message. You were then out of reach of wireless, on the Irish coast. And for nine days there was no way to tell you I had come back as fast as trains and boats and the dirty Germans would let me. Oh, my dear, dear one, *how I love* you. If only I could have seen you for just five minutes. As it was, I thought for five days more we would be together. What I shall do now, I don't know. I must go back with either the French or the English until my contract expires, and then, I can join you. Tomorrow I am trying to see Asquith and Churchill to get with the army. And I will at once return across the channel. But, do not worry! I will never again let a German come within *one mile* of me! After this, between me and the Germans, there will be some hundreds of thousands of English or French. So after this reaches you I will soon be on my way *home.* Don't worry. Get James back and Amelia and everyone else who can make you comfortable, and trust in the good Lord. I have your cross and St. Rita around my neck, and in spite of what the Kaiser says, God is looking after other people than Germans. Certainly he has taken good care of me. And he will guard you, and our "blessed" one. And in a little time, dear, *dear* heart, I will be back, and I will become a grocer. God love you and keep you, as he does. And you will never know *how I love you!* Good night, dearest, sweetheart and wife! I am writing this at your table, and, thanking God you are going to the farm, and to peace and happiness. *I send you all the love in all the world.*

RICHARD.

London, September 3rd.

MY DEAREST ONE:

It was a full moon again tonight and I think you were on deck and saw it, because by now, you have passed the four days at sea and should be in the St. Lawrence. So I knew you saw the moon, too, and I sent you a kiss, via it. It was just over St. James Palace but also it was just over you.

Today has been a day of worries. Wheeler cabled that the papers wanted me to be "neutral" and not write against the Germans. As I am not interested in the German vote, or in advertising of German breweries (such a hard word to *say*) I thought, considering the *exclusive* stories I had sent them, instead of kicking, they ought to be sending me a few bouquets. Especially, as I got cables from Gouvey, Whigham, *Scribner's* and others congratulating me on the anti-German stories. So I cabled Wheeler to tell papers of his syndicate, dictation from them as to what I should write was "unexpected," that they could go to name-of-place censored and that if he wished I would release him from his contract tonight. Considering that without credentials I was with French, Belgian and German armies and saw entry of Germans into Brussels and sacking of Louvain and got arrested as a spy, they were a bit ungrateful. I am now wondering *what* I would have seen *had I had* credentials.

I saw Anthony Hope at the club last night. He had to go back to the country, so I dined alone on English oysters. Fancy anyone being *neutral* in this war! Germany dropping bombs in Paris and Antwerp on women and churches and scattering mines in the channel where they blow up fishermen and burning the cathedrals! A man who now would be neutral would be a coward. Good night, *near, dear, dear* one. It has been several weeks since I had sleep, so if I rave and wander in my letters forgive me. You know how I am thinking of you. God bless you. God keep you for me.

Your husband who loves you *so!*

LONDON, September 7th.

DEAREST:

I just got your cable saying you were at the farm, and well! *How happy it made me!* I cabled you to Quebec, and to Mt. Kisco, and when two days passed and I heard nothing, today I was scared, so I cabled Gouvey to look after you, and also to Wheeler. I went to the Brompton Oratory today, which is the second most important church here (the cardinal lives at Westminster) and burned the *biggest candle* they had for you and the "blessing." A big woman all in black was kneeling in the little chapel and when I could not get the candle to stand up, she beckoned to one of the priests, and he ran and fixed it. Then she went on praying. And *who* do you think she was? Queen Amelie of Portugal, you see her pictures in the *Tattler* and *Sphere* opening bazaars. So she must be very good or she would not be saying her prayers all alone with the poor people and seeing that my Bessie's candle was burning. I have been waiting here hoping to get some sort of credentials from Kitchener. But though Winston Churchill has urged him, and tomorrow is going to urge him again, they give me no hope. So I'll just go over "on my own" and I bet I'll see more than anyone else. I have fine papers, anyhow. I am now writing for the morning *Chronicle* over here. Today I finished the *Scribner* article, so *that* is off my mind. And now that you are home, I have no "worries." I wish I had got your cable earlier. I would have had *oysters* and champagne in *bath tubs.* Give my love to all the flowers, and to Shea and Paedrig, and Tom, and Louise, and Gouvey and the lake. And take *such* good care of yourself, and love me, and be happy for I do so love you dear one. *I do so love you.*

Your Husband.

September 15th.

Dearest:

Tonight I got your cable in answer to mine asking if you were well. All things considered twenty-four hours was not so long for them to get the answer to me. You *bet* I will be careful. I don't want to get nearer to a German than twenty miles. At the battle-field I collected five German spiked helmets but at the Paris gate they took *all* of them from me. I *was* mad! I wanted to keep them in my "gym," and pound them with Indian clubs. I wrote all day yesterday, so today I did not work. There is nothing more here to do. And as soon as my contract is up October 1st, I will make towards YOU! Seeing the big battle was great luck. So far I have seen more than anyone. I have had no credentials; and yet have been with *all* the armies. Now I am just beating time, until I can get home. The fighting is too far away even if I could go to it. But I can't without being arrested. And I am fed up on being arrested. Today all the little children came out of doors. They have been locked up for fear of airships. It was fine to see them playing in the Champs Elysees and making forts out of pebbles, and rolling hoops.

God loves you, dear one, and I trust in Him. But I am awful sick for a sight of you. What a lot we will have to tell each other. One thing I never have to tell you, but it makes me happy when I can. It is this: I *love you!* And every minute I think of you. With all my love.

Your
RICHARD.

PARIS, September 15th, 1914.
DEAR CHAS.:

I got this morning your letter of August 25th. In it you say kind things about my account of the Germans entering Brussels. Nothing so much pleases me as to get praise from you or to know my work pleases you. Since the Germans were pushed in every one here is breathing again. But for me it was bad as now the armies are too far to reach by taxicab, and if you are caught anywhere outside the city you are arrested and as a punishment sent to Tours. Eight correspondents, among them two *Times* men and John Reed and Bobby Dunn, were sent to Tours Sunday. I had another piece of luck that day with Gerald Morgan. I taxicabed out to Soissons and saw a wonderful battle. So, now I can go home in peace. Had I been forced to return without seeing any fighting I never would have lived it down. I am in my old rooms of years ago. I got the whole imperial suite for eight francs a day. It used to be 49 francs a day. Of course, Paris that closes tight at nine is hardly Paris, but the beauty of the city never so much impressed me. There is no fool running about to take your mind off the gardens and buildings. What *most* makes me know I am in Paris, though, are the packages of segars lying on the dressing table. Give my love to Dai, and tell her I hope soon to see you. The war correspondent is dead. My only chance was to get with the English who will take one American and asked Bryan to choose, he passed it to the Press Association and they chose Palmer. But I don't believe the official correspondents will be allowed to see much. I saw the Germans enter Brussels, the burning of Louvain and the Battle of Soissons and had a very serious run in with the Germans and nearly got shot. But now if you go out, every man is after you, and even the gendarmes try to arrest you. It is sickening. For never, of course, was there such a chance to describe things that everyone wants to read about. Again my love to Dai and you. I will see you soon.

RICHARD.

In October Richard returned to the United States and settled down to complete his first book on the war. During this period and indeed until the hour of his death my brother devoted the greater part of his time to the cause of the Allies. He had always believed that the United States should have entered the war when the Germans first outraged Belgium, and to this effect he wrote many letters to the newspapers. In addition to this he was most active in various of the charities devoted to the causes of the Allies, wrote a number of appeals, and contributed money out of all proportion to his means. The following appeal he wrote for the Secours National:

"You are invited to help women, children and old people in Paris and in France, wherever the war has brought desolation and distress. To France you owe a debt. It is not alone the debt you incurred when your great grandfathers fought for liberty, and to help them, France sent soldiers, ships and two great generals, Rochambeau and La Fayette. You owe France

VERA CRUZ AND THE GREAT WAR 379

for that, but since then you have incurred other debts.

"Though you may never have visited France, her art, literature, her discoveries in Science, her sense of what is beautiful, whether in a bonnet, a boulevard or a triumphal arch, have visited you. For them you are the happier; and for them also, to France you are in debt.

"If you have visited Paris, then your debt is increased a hundred fold. For to whatever part of France you journeyed, there you found courtesy, kindness, your visit became a holiday, you departed with a sense of renunciation; you were determined to return. And when after the war, you do revisit France, if your debt is unpaid, can you without embarrassment sink into debt still deeper? What you sought Paris gave you freely. Was it to study art or to learn history, for the history of France is the history of the world; was it to dine under the trees or to rob the Rue de la Paix of a new model; was it for weeks to motor on the white roads or at a cafe table watch the world pass? Whatever you sought, you found. Now, as in 1776 we fought, to-day France fights for freedom, and in behalf of all the world, against militarism that is 'made in Germany.'

"Her men are in the trenches; her women are working in the fields, sweeping the Paris boulevards, lighting the street lamps. They are undaunted, independent, magnificently capable. They ask no charity. But from those districts the war has wrecked, there are hundreds of thousands of women and little children without work, shelter or food. To them throughout the war zone the Secours National gives instant relief. In one day in Paris alone it provides 80,000 free meals. Six cents pays for one of these meals. One dollar from you will for a week keep a woman or child alive.

"The story is that one man said, 'In this war the women and children suffer most. I'm awfully sorry for them!' and the other man said, 'Yes I'm five dollars sorry. How sorry are you?'

"If ever you intend paying that debt you owe to France do not wait until the war is ended. Now, while you still owe it, do not again impose yourself upon her hospitality, her courtesy, her friendship.

"But, pay the debt now.

"And then, when next in Paris you sit at your favorite table and your favorite waiter hands you the menu, will you not the more enjoy your dinner if you know that while he was fighting on the Aisne, it was your privilege to help a little in keeping his wife and child alive."

The winter of 1914–15 Richard and his wife spent in New York, and on January 4, 1915, their baby, Hope, was born. No event in my brother's life had ever brought him such infinite happiness, and during the short fifteen months that remained to him she was seldom, if ever, from his thoughts, and no father ever planned more carefully for a child's future than Richard did for his little daughter.

On April 11 my brother and his wife took Hope to Crossroads for the first time. In his diary of this time he writes, "Only home in the world is the one I own. Everything belongs. It is so comfortable and the lake and the streams in the woods where you can get your feet wet. The thrill of thinking a stump is a trespasser! You can't do that on ten acres."

A cause in which Richard was enormously interested

at this time was that of the preparedness of his own country, and for it he worked unremittingly. In August, 1915, he went to Plattsburg, where he took a month of military training.

PLATTSBURG, N. Y.
August, 1915.

DEAR OLD MAN:

This is a very real thing, and *strenuous*. I know now why God invented Sunday. The first two days were mighty hard, and I had to work extra to catch up. I don't know a darned thing, and after watching soldiers for years, find that I have picked up nothing that they have to learn. The only things I have learned don't count here, as they might under marching conditions. My riding I find is quite good, and so is my rifle shooting. As you could always beat me at that you can see the conditions are not high. But being used to the army saddle helps me a lot. I have a steeple chaser on one side and a M. F. H. on the other, and they can't keep in the saddle, and hate it with bitter oaths. The camp commander told me that was a curious development; that the best gentlemen jockeys and polo players on account of the saddle, were sore, in every sense. Yesterday I rose at 5-30, assembled for breakfast at six, took down tent to ventilate it, when a cloud meanly appeared, and I had to put it up again. Then in heavy marching order we drilled two hours as skirmishers, running and hurling ourselves at the earth, like falling on the ball, and I always seemed to fall where the cinder path crossed the parade ground. We got back in time to clean ourselves for dinner at noon. And then practised firing at targets. At two we were drilled as cavalry in extended order. We galloped to a point, advanced on foot, were driven back by an imaginary enemy, and remounted. We galloped as a squadron, and the sight was really remarkable when you think the men had been together only four days. But the horses had been doing it for years. All I had to do to mine was to keep on. He knew what was wanted as well as did the Captain. After that we put on our packs and paraded at retreat to the band. Then had supper and listened to a lecture. I ache in every bone, muscle, and joint. But the riding has not bothered me. It is only hurling the damned rifle at myself. At nine I am sound asleep. It certainly is a great experience, and, all the men are helping each other and the spirit is splendid. The most curious meetings come off and all kinds of men are at it from college kids to several who are great grand fathers. Russell Colt turned up and was very funny over his experiences. He said he saluted everybody and one man he thought was a general and stood at attention to salute was a Pullman car conductor. The food is all you want, and very good. I've had nothing to drink, but sarsaparilla, but with the thirst we get it is the best drink I know. I have asked to have no letters forwarded and if I don't write I hope you will understand as during the day there is not a minute you are your own boss and at night I am too stiff and sleepy to write.

All love to you.

DICK.

Friday.

DEAREST:

It is now seven-thirty, and I have had twelve busy hours. They made me pass an examination as though for Sing Sing, then a man gave me a gun that at first weighed eight pounds and then twenty. He made me

From a photograph copyright by Underwood and Underwood.

At Plattsburg.

do all sorts of things with it, such as sentries used to do to me. Then I was given the gun to keep, and packs, beds, blankets, and I made myself at home in a tent; then I was moved to another tent with five other men. Then I got a horse and they galloped us up and down a field for two hours. I lost ten pounds. Then we were marched around to a band. I had a sergeant on either side of me, so I did not go wrong, *often.* Then, aching in every bone and with my head filled with orders and commands, I got into the lake and escaped. You can believe I enjoyed that bath. It certainly is a fine thing, and I am glad I enrolled (for every one has been as nice as could be), but I miss you and Hope terribly. It seems years since I saw you. I am going to my cot quick. It is now eight o'clock, and I feel like I had been beaten in a stone crusher. Kiss Hope's foot for me.

Your loving husband,   DICK.

Monday.

DEAREST ONE:

I got such a beautiful letter from you! With pictures of Hope playing with the Bunny. It is the best picture yet. I carry it next to my heart because you made it, because it is of her. And she sits up now? Well, I will miss the big clothes-basket. I loved to see her in it. Years ago, when I left home, she was trying to crawl out of it. What you tell me of her—knowing what you mean when you say "Kitty" and "Bunny"—is wonderful. How good it will be! You must come close under my arm, and tell me every little thing. I feel so much better now that we have broken into the last week, and are on the home stretch. We have broken the backbone of the long absence, and, the first thing you know, I'll be telephoning to have you meet me at White Plains.

This is me sewing up a hole in my breeches. The socks are drying on the line, my rubber bath is on the right. I am now going to Canada. But I'll be back in half an hour; it's only 200 yards distant. All the folks here are French, and the signs are in French. Last place we halted I bought lumberman's socks to wear at night. I sleep very well, for I buy my raincoat full of hay from the nearest farmer, and sleep on that. Today we had another "battle." It began at 7.30 and ended at one o'clock. We were kept going all that time, taking "cover" behind railroad embankments and stone walls and in plowed fields, finally ending with a bayonet charge. I killed so many I stopped counting.

Don't let Hope forget her father. Better put on a wrist-watch and my horn spectacles, and hold her the wrong way, so she will be reminded of her Dad.

Good-night, my dearest one. You will never know how terribly I miss you and love you, and want you in my arms, and you holding Hope so that I can have all my happiness in one big armful of all that is good.

Your Loving Husband.

Wednesday.

Dearest One:

The Vitagraph people came today. They have a great film to stir people to preparedness called "The Battle Cry of Peace." It shows New York destroyed by Germans. They took pictures of several of the better-known men showing "them" preparing. I was taken cleaning my rifle, and, as the captain was passing, I asked him to get in the picture with me and be shown instructing me. He was delighted, but right in the middle of the picture he "inspected" my barrel. I had not cleaned it, and he forgot the camera, and gave me the devil. You can imagine how the crowd roared, and the camera director man was delighted. I wanted it retaken showing the captain patting me on the back.

Roosevelt turned up today, and was very nice. Martin Egan came with him and the British Naval Attaché, and they have asked me to dine at a real table at Hotel Champlain with two other men. It will be fine to eat off china. The "hike" begins Friday, and we sleep each night on the ground, but the country we march through is beautiful. All that counts is getting the days behind me and getting you in my arms. Doing one's "bit" for one's country is right, but as the man said, "God knows I love my country and want to fight for her, but I hope to God I never love another country." Good-night, dear, dear one! How wonderful it will be to see and hear you again. Kiss Hope for her Dad.

RICHARD.

Saturday.

DEAREST:

This is writing with all the love, but with difficulties. I am sitting on a log and the light is a candle. Today we had our first fight. It happened the squad of eight men I am in was sent in advance, and I was 100 yards in front, so I was the first to come in touch with the scouts of the Red Army, and I killed a lot. My squad was so brave that we all got killed *three times*. But as soon as the umpire rode away we would come to life, and go on fighting. Finally, he took us prisoners, and made us sit down and look on at the battle. As we had been running around and each carrying a forty-pound pack, we were glad to remain dead. But we have declared that nothing can kill us tomorrow but asphyxiating gas. I have terrible nightmares for fear something has happened to one of you, and then I trust in the good Lord, and pray him to make the time pass swiftly.

Good-night, and all the love and kisses for you both.

RICHARD.

On October 19, 1915, Richard sailed on the *Chicago* for France and his second visit to the Great War. He arrived at Paris on October 30, and shortly afterward visited the Western front at Amiens and Artois. He also interviewed Poincaré, and through him the French President sent a message to the American people. At this time my brother had received permission from the authorities to visit all of the twelve sectors of the French front under particularly advantageous conditions, and was naturally most anxious to do so. However, through a misunderstanding between the syndicate he represented and certain of the newspapers using its service, he found it advisable, even although against his own judgment, to go to Greece, and to postpone his visit to the sectors of the French front he had not already seen. On November 13 he left Paris bound for Salonica.

On Way to France, Oct. 18, 1915.

DEAREST ONE:

You are much more brave than I am. Anyway, you are much better behaved. For all the time you were talking I was crying, not with my eyes only, but

R. H. D. and Captain Gabriel Puaux of the General Headquarters Staff at the ruined village of Gerbéviller.

with *all* of me. I am so sad. I love you so, and I will miss you so. I want you to keep saying to yourself all the time, "This is the most serious effort he ever made, because the chances of seeing anything are so *small*, and because never had he such a chance to *help*. But, all the time, every minute he thinks of me. He wants me. He misses my voice, my eyes, my presence at his side when he walks or sleeps. He never loved me so greatly, or at leaving me was so unhappy as he is now."

Goodby, dear heart. My God-given one! Would it not be wonderful, if tonight when I am up among the boats on the top deck that girl in the Pierrot suit, and in her arms Hope, came, and I took them and held them both? You will walk with her at five, and I will walk and think of you and love you and long for you.

God keep you, dearest of wives, and mothers.

RICHARD.

October 24.

MY DEAR DAUGHTER:

So many weeks have passed since I saw you that by now you are able to read this without your mother looking over your shoulder and helping you with the big words. I have six sets of pictures of you. Every day I take them down and change them. Those your dear mother put in glass frames I do not change. Also, I have all the sweet fruits and chocolates and red bananas. How good of you to think of just the things your father likes. Some of them I gave to a little boy and girl. I play with them because soon my daughter will be as big. They have no mother like you, *of course;* they have no mother like *yours*—for except my mother there never was a mother like yours; so loving, so tender, so unselfish and thoughtful. If she is reading this, kiss her for me. These little children have a little father. He dresses them and bathes them himself. He is afraid of the cold; and sits in the sun; and coughs and shivers. His children and I play hide-and-seek, and, as you will know some day, for that game there is no such place as a steamer, with boats and ventilators and masts and alleyways. Some day we will play that game hiding behind the rocks and trees and rose bushes. Every day I watch the sun set, and know that you and your pretty mother are watching it, too. And all day I think of you both.

Be very good. Do not bump yourself. Do not eat matches. Do not play with scissors or cats. Do not forget your dad. Sleep when your mother wishes it. Love us both. Try to know how we love you. *That* you will never learn. Good-night and God keep you, and bless you.

Your Dad.

Paris, November 1.
Dearest One:

Today is "moving" day, and I feel like —— censored word, at the thought of your having the moving to direct and manage by yourself. I can picture Barney and Burke loading, and unloading, and coal and wood being stored, and provisions and ice, and finally Hope brought down to take her third—no—fourth motor ride. And God will see she makes it all safely, and that in her new house you are comfortable.

Last night I dreamed about Hope and you, a long dream, and it made me so happy. Something happened today that you will like to hear. When the war came the French students at the Beaux Arts had to go to fight. The wives and children had nothing to live on. So, the American students, about a dozen of them, organized a relief league. The Beaux Arts is in a most wonderful palace built by Cardinal Richelieu and decorated later by Napoleon. In this they were gathering socks, asphyxiating masks, warm clothes. They were hand painting postcards for fifty cents apiece. The "masters" as they call their teachers, also were painting them. I gave them some money which was received politely, but, as it would not go far, without much enthusiasm. As I was going, I said, "I'll be back tomorrow to get some facts and I'll write a story about what you're doing." This is the part that is embarrassing to write, but you will understand. They gave a cheer and a yell just as though I had said, "Peace is declared" or "I will give you Carnegie's fortune." And they danced around, and shook hands, and Whitney Warren, who is at the head of it, all but cried. Later, he told me the letter I had written for his wife's fund for orphans by the war had brought in $5000, that was why they were so pleased. So we, you and I, will try to look at it that way, and try to believe that from this separation, which is cruel for us, others may get some benefit. Tomorrow, I am to be received at the Elysée by the President, and I am going to try to make him say something that will draw money from America for the French hospitals. If he will only ask, I know our people will give. In a day or two, I think I will be allowed to see something, but, that you will know best by reading *The Times*.

Your loving husband is lonely for you, and so it will be always.
RICHARD.

Dear Sweetheart: November 17th.

My last letter was such a complaining one that I am ashamed. But, not leaving me to decide what was best for the papers, made me mad. Since I wrote, I ought to be madder, for I have been to the trenches outside of Rheims in Champagne; and, had they not deviled the spirit out of me with cables, I believe I could have written such a lot of stories of France that no one else has had the opportunity to write. Believe me no one has yet told the story of the trench war. Anyway, in spite of all the photographs and articles, to me it was all new. I was allowed to go alone, and given *carte blanche* to see whatever I wished. I saw everything, but it would not be possible to write of it yet. It was wonderful. I was in the three lines, reaching the *first* line by moonlight. No one spoke above a whisper. The Germans were only 300 to 400 yards distant. But worst of all were the rats. They ran over my feet and I was a darned sight more afraid of them than the Germans. I saw the Cathedral, and the only hotel open (from which I sent you and Hope a postal) was the same one in which we stopped a year ago. I had sent the hotel my book in which I said complimentary things, and I got a great welcome. They even gave me a room with a fire in it, and so I was warm for the first time since I left the Crossroads. And this morning it *snowed*. On my way back to Paris, I stopped to tell the General what I had seen and to thank him. He said, "Oh, that is nothing. When you return, I will take you out myself, and I will show you something worth while." I am going to carry a rat-trap, and two terriers on a leash. Tonight, when I got back, there was a letter from you, but no writing, but there was a photo of Her, and me holding her. How is it possible that any living thing is so beautiful as my child? How fat, and wonderful, and dear, and lovable, and how terribly I want to hold her as I am holding her in the picture, and how much better (as I really don't need my left arm to hold such a mite), if I had you close to me in it. I miss you so, and love you so! I told Wheeler before I left as I was not going to waste time traveling I would not go to Servia. So, as soon as I arrived, I was fretted with cables to go. I cabled to stop giving me advice, that I had a much better chance in France than anyone could have anywhere else. Maybe, before I arrive, the Greeks will have joined the Germans, in which case, *I won't leave the ship.* I'll come straight back on her to the Allies.

RICHARD.

November 20th.

This is the way Hope's cat looks, "My whiskers!" she says, "I never knew I was to be let in for anything like this!" When I told her about the big rats in the trenches she wanted to go with me next time, but, today when I told her that the Crown Prince of Servia made his servants eat live mice (he is no longer Crown Prince), she looked just as she does in the picture. "Then, what do *I* eat in Servia?" she said, and I told her both of us would live on goat's milk.

You will be glad when I tell you I have been warm. We came pretty far south in two days, and, the damp chill of Paris is gone. On the train a funny thing happened. An English officer and I got talking and he was press censor at Salonica where I am going after Athens. I asked him to look over the many letters I had and tell me if any of them would be likely to get me in bad, being addressed to pro-Germans, for example. He said, "Well, *this* chap is all right anyway. I'll vouch for him, because this letter is ad-

SEE THE CAT!
HOPE GAVE THE CAT TO HER DAD.
IS THE CAT SAD?
YES
IS THE DAD SAD?
VERY!!
WHY IS THE CAT AND THE DAD SAD?
THEY WANT HOME AND HOPE.
DO THEY LOVE HOPE?
DON'T MAKE THEM LAUGH!

dressed to me." We leave, the Basses, the English officer and I, in a small tub of a boat for Patras, and train to Athens. I will try to go at once to Servia. Harjes, who are the Paris house of J. P. Morgan, gave me a "mission" to try and organize for the Servians the same form of relief as has been arranged for the Belgians. He gave me permission if I saw the need for help was imminent (and it will be) to cable him for whatever I thought the Serbs most needed. So, it is a chance to do much. To get out news will be impossible. However, here I am and tomorrow I'll be good and seasick.

I have your charm around my neck, and all the pictures, and the luck-bringing cat, and the scapular, and the love you give me to keep me well and bring us soon together. That is the one thing I want. God bless you both, Hope's dad and your husband.

ATHENS,
November 26th.

DEAR HEART:

I am off tonight for Salonica. I am not very cheerful for I miss you very, very terribly, and the further I go, the worse I feel. But now I am nearly as far as I can get, and when you receive this I will—thank God—be turned back to Paris, and London, and *home!* I thought so often of you this morning when I took a holiday and climbed the Acropolis. On the top of it I picked a dandelion for you. It was growing between the blocks of marble that have been there since 400 years before our Lord: before St. Paul preached to the Athenians. I was all alone on the rock, and could see over the Ægean Sea, Corinth, Mount Olympus, where the Gods used to sit, and the Sphinx lay in wait for travelers with her famous riddle. It takes two days and one night to go to Salonica, and the boats are so awful no one undresses but sleeps in his clothes on top of the bed.

Goodby, sweetheart, and give *such* a kiss to my precious daughter. How beautiful she is. Even the waiter who brought me a card stopped to exclaim about her picture. So, of course, being not at all proud I showed him her in my arms. I want you both so and I love you both *so*. And, I wanted you so this morning as I always do when there is a beautiful landscape, or flowers, or palms. I know how you love them. The dandelion is very modest and I hope the censor won't lose it out, for she has a long way to go and

carries a burden of love. I wish I was bringing them in the door of the Scribner cottage at this very minute.
RICHARD.

VOLO, November 27.

I got here today, after the darnedest voyage of two days in a small steamer. We ran through a snow storm and there was no way to warm the boat. So, I *died*. You know how cold affects me—well—this was the coldest cold I ever died of. I poured alcohol in me, and it was like drinking iced tea. Now, I am on shore in a café near a stove. We continue on to Salonica at midnight. There are 24 men and one woman, Mrs. Bass, on board. I am much too homesick to write more than to say I love you, and I miss you and Hope so, that I don't look at the photos. Did you get the cable I sent Thanksgiving — from Athens, it read: "Am giving thanks for Hope and you." I hope the censor let that get by him. The boat I was on was a refrigerator ship; it was also peculiar in that the captain dealt baccarat all day with the passengers. It was a sort of floating gambling house. This is certainly a strange land. Snow and roses and oranges, all at once. I must stop. I'm froze. Give the kiss I want to give to Her, and know, oh! how I love and love and love her mother—*never so much as now*.

SALONICA November 30th, 1915.

DEAR OLD MAN:

I got here to night and found it the most picturesque spot I ever visited. I am glad I came. It was impossible to get a room but I found John McCutcheon and two other men occupying a grand suite and they have had a cot put in for me. To-morrow I hope to get a room. The place is filled with every nation except Germans and even they are here out of uniforms. We had a strange time coming. The trip from Athens should have taken two nights and a day but we took four. The Captain of the boat anchored and played baccarat whenever he thought there were enough passengers not seasick to make it worth his while. He played from eleven in the morning until four in the morning. I don't know now who ran the ship. It is so cold when you bathe, the steam runs off you. I never have suffered so. But, it looked as though every one else was singing "Its going to be a hard, hard winter" from the way they dress. To-morrow I am going to buy fur pants. You can't believe what a picture it is. Servians, French, Greeks, Scots in kilts, London motor cars, Turks, wounded and bandaged Tommies and millions of them fighting for food, for drink, for a place at the "movies," and more "rumors" than there are words in the directory. To-morrow, I present my letters and hope to get to the "front." I only hope the front doesn't come to us. But, it ought to be a place for great stories. All love to you old man, and bless you both. How I look forward to our first lunch in your wonderful home! And to sit in front of your fire, and hear all the news. All love to you both.

RICHARD.

December 6, 1915.

DEAREST ONE:

I have been away so could not write. They took us to the French and English "front" and away from Greece; we were in Bulgaria and Servia. It was at a place where the three boundaries met. We saw remarkable mountain ranges and deep snow, and some fine artillery. But throwing shells into that bleak, white jumble of snow and rocks—there was fifty miles of it—was like throwing a baseball at the Rocky Mountains. Still, it was seeing something. Now, I have a room, and a very wonderful one. I had to bribe everyone in the hotel to get it; and I have something to write and, no more moving about I hope, for at least a week. I am able to see the ships at anchor for miles, and the landing stage for all the warships is just under my window. As near as McCoy Rock from the terrace. It is like a moving picture all the time. I bought myself an oil stove and a can of Standard oil, and, instead of trying to warm the hotel with my body, I let George do it. But it is a very small stove, and to really get the good of it, I have to sit with it between my legs. Still, it is such a relief to be alone, and not to pack all the time. McCutcheon and Bass, Hare and Shepherd are fine, but I felt like the devil, imposing on them, and working four in a room is no joke. We dine together each night. Except them, I see no one, but have been writing. Also, I have been collecting facts about Servian relief. Harjes, Morgan's representative in Paris, gave me *carte blanche* to call on him for money or supplies; but I waited until today to cable, so as to be sure where help was most needed. It is still cold, but that *awful* cold spell was quite unprecedented and is not likely to come again. I *never* suffered so from cold, and, as you know, I suffer considerable. All the English officers who had hunted in cold places, said neither had they ever felt such cold. Seven hundred Tommies were frost bitten and toes and fingers fell off. I do not say anything about how awful it is not to hear. But, if I had had your letters forwarded to this dump of the Levant, I *never* would have got them. Now, I have to wait for them until I get to Paris, but there I will surely get them. Cables, of course, can reach me, but no cables mean to me that you are all right. Nor do I want to "talk" about Christmas. You know how I feel about that, and about missing the first one *she* has had. But it will be the *last* one we will know apart. Never again!

I want you in my arms and to hear you laugh and see your eyes. I am in need of you to make a fuss over me. McCutcheon and Co. don't care whether I have cold hands or not. You do. Your ointment and gloves saved my fingers from falling off like the soldiers' did. And your "housewife" I use to put on buttons, and, your scapular and medal keep me well. But your love is what really lifts me up and consoles me. When I think how you and I care for each other, then, I am scared, for it is very beautiful. And we must not ever be away from each other again. God keep you my beloved, and both my blessings. I cannot bear it—when I think of all I am missing of her, and, all that she is doing. God guard you both. My darling and dear wife and mother of Hope.

Your husband,
RICHARD.

SALONICA, December 18th.

DEAREST WIFE AND SWEETHEART:

I am very blue tonight, and *never* was so homesick. Yesterday just to feel I was in touch with you I sent a cable through the fog, it said, "Well, homesick, all love to you both." I did not ask if you and Hope were well, because I *know* the good Lord will not let any harm come to you. I am certainly caught by the heels this time. And it will be the last time. As you know, I meant only to go to France where no time would be wasted in travel, and I would be able to get back soon. But the blockade held up the ship and on the other one the captain stayed at anchor, and, then when I got here, the Allies retreated, and I had to stay on to cover what is to come next. What that is, or whether nothing happens, you will know by the time this reaches you. So, here I am. For *ten* days until this morning we have never seen the sun. In sixty years nothing like it has happened. The Salonicans said the English transports brought the fog with them. Anyway, I got it. My room is right on the harbor. I never thought I would *love* an oil stove. I always thought they were ill-smelling, air-destroying. But this one saved my life. I wrote with it between my knees, I dry my laundry on it, and use the tin pan on top of it to take the dampness out of the bed. The fog kept everything like a sponge. Coal is thirty dollars a ton. To get wood for firewood the boatmen row miles out, and wait below the transports to get the boxes they throw overboard. I go around asking *everybody* if this place is not now a dead duck for news. But they all give me no encouragement. They say it is the news center of the world. I hope it chokes. I try to comfort myself by thinking you are happy, because you have Hope, and I have nobody, except John McCutcheon and Bass and Jimmie Hare, and they are as blue as I am, and no one can get any money. I cabled today to Wheeler for some via the State Department. I went to the Servian camp for the little orphans whose fathers have been killed, and they all knelt and kissed my hands. It was awful. I thought of Hope, and hugged a few and carried them around in my arms and felt much better. Today for the first time, I quit work and went to see an American film at the cinema to cheer me. But when I saw the streetcars, and "ready to wear" clothes, and the policemen I got suicidal. I went back and told the others and they all rushed off to see "home" things, and are there now. This is a yell of a letter, but it's the only kind I can write. My stories and cables are rotten, too. I have seen nothing—just traveled and waited for something to happen. Goodnight, dearest one. I love you so. You will never know how much I love you. Kiss my darling for me, and, think only of the good days when we will be together again. Such good days. Goodnight again—all love.

RICHARD.

HARBOR SALONICA, December 19th.

I am a happy man tonight! And that is the first time I have been able to say so since I left you. The backbone of the trip is broken! and my face is turned West—toward you and Hope. John McCutcheon gave me a farewell dinner tonight of which I got one half, as the police made me go on board at nine, although we do not sail until five in the morning. So there was time for only one toast, as I was making for the door. Was it to your husband? It was not. It was to Hope Davis, two weeks yet of being one year old, and being toasted by the war correspondents in Salonica. They knew it would please me. And I went away very choken and happy. *Such* a boat as this is! I have a sofa in the dining-room, and at present it is jammed with refugees and all smoking and not an air port open. What a relief it will be to once more get among clean people. We must help the

Servians, and God knows they need help. But, if they would help each other, or themselves, I would like them better. I am now on deck under the cargo light and, on the top floor of the Olympus Hotel, can see John's dinner growing gayer and gayer. It is like the man who went on a honeymoon alone. I am so happy tonight. You seem so near now that I am coming West.

How terribly I have missed you, and wanted you, and longed for your voice and *laugh*, and to have you open the door of my writing room, and say, "A lady is coming to call on you," and then enter the dearest wife and dearest baby in the world!

God bless you, and all my love.

RICHARD.

ROME,
Christmas Eve,
1915.

MY DEAREST, DEAREST, DEAREST:

I planned to get to Paris late Christmas night. I cabled Frazier at the Embassy, to have all my letters at the Hotel de l'Empire. I *meant* to spend the night reading of you and Hope. I made a record trip from Salonica. By leaving the second steamer at Messina and taking an eighteen-hour trip across Italy I saved ten hours. But when I got here I found the French Consul had taken a holiday, *and was out buying Christmas presents!* So, I could not get permission to enter France. With some Red Cross Americans, I raged around the French Consulate, but it was no use. So I am here, and cannot leave *until midnight Christmas.* When I found I could not get away, I told Cook's to give me their rapid-fire guide, and I set out to *see Rome.* The Manager of Cook's was the same man

Latest photograph of Richard Harding Davis.

who, 19 years ago, sold me tickets to the Greek war in Florence, when the American Consulate was in the same building with Cook's, and Charley was Consul. So he gave me a great guide. We began at ten this morning and we stopped at six. They say it takes five years to see Rome, but when I let the rapid-fire guide escape, he said he had to compliment me; we climbed more stairways and hills than there are in all New York and Westchester County; and there is just one idea in my mind, and that is that you and I must see this sacred place together. On all this trip I have wanted *you*, but *never* so as today. And I particularly inquired about the milk. It is said to be excellent. So we will come here, and you, with all your love of what is fine and beautiful, will be very happy, and Hope will learn Italian, and to know what is best in art, and statues and churches. I have seen 2900 churches, and all of them built by Michael Angelo and decorated by Raphael; and it was so wonderful I cried. I bought candles and prayers, and I am afraid Christian Science had a dull day. Tomorrow we start at nine, and go to high mass at St. Peter's, and then into the country to the catacombs, where the early Christians hid from the Romans. It is not what you would call an English Christmas, but it is so beautiful and wonderful that you *both are very near*.

I sent you a cable, the second one, because it is not sure they are forwarded, and I hung up a stocking for Hope. One of the peasant women made in Salonica. I am bringing it with me. And the *cat* is on my window—still looking out on the Romans. The green leaf I got in the forum, where Mark Antony made his speech over Cæsar's body. It is the plant that gave Pericles the idea of the Corinthian column. You remember. It was growing under a tile some one had laid over it—and the yellow flower was on my table at dinner, so I send it, that we may know on Christmas Eve we dined together. Good-night, now, and God bless you. I am off to bed now, in a bed with *sheets*. The first in six days. How I *love* you, and *love* you. Such good wishes I send you, and such love to you both. May the good Lord bless you as he has blessed me—with the best of women, with the best of daughters. I am a proud husband and a proud father; and soon I will be a *happy* husband and a *happy* father.

Good-night, dear heart.

RICHARD.

PARIS, December 28th, 1915.

DEAR OLD MAN:

Hurrah for the Dictator! He has been a great good friend to me. I will know to-day about whether I can go back to the French front. If not I will try the Belgians and then London, and home. I spent Christmas day in Rome in the catacombs. I could not wear my heart upon my sleeve for duchesses to peck at. It is just as you say, Dad and Mother made the day so dear and beautiful. I did not know how glad I would be to be back here for while the trip East led to no news value, to me personally it was interesting. But I am terribly tired after the last nine days, sleeping on sofas, decks, a different deck each night and writing all the time and such poor stuff. But, oh! when I saw Paris I knew how glad I was! *What* a beautiful place, what a kind courteous people. We will all be here some day. Tell Dai she must be my interpreter. All love to her, and you, and good luck to the syndicate. *Your* syndicate. I have not heard from *mine* for six

VERA CRUZ AND THE GREAT WAR 403

weeks. They have not sent me a single clipping of anything, so I don't know whether anything got through or not, and I have nothing to show these people here that might encourage them to send me out again. They certainly have made it hard hoeing. Tell Guvey his letter about the toys was a great success here, and copied into several papers.

Goodbye, and God bless you, and good luck to you.

DICK.

PARIS, December 31st, 1915.

DEAR OLD MAN:

To wish you and Dai a Happy New Year. It will mean a lot to us when we can get together, and take it together, good and bad. I am awfully pleased over the novel coming out by the Harper's and, in landing so much for me out of *The Dictator*. You have started the New Year for me splendidly. I expect I will be back around the first of February. I am now trying to "get back," but, I need more time. I can only put the trip down to the wrong side of the ledger. Personally, I got a lot out of it, but I am not sent over here to improve my knowledge of Europe, but to furnish news and stories and that has not happened.

I am constantly running against folks who knew you in Florence, and I regret to say most of them are in business at the Chatham bar. What a story they make; the M——'s and the like, who know Paris only from the cocktail side. One of our attaches told me to-day he had been lunching for the last 18 months at the grill room of the Chatham, where the "mixed grill" was as good as in New York. He had no knowledge of any other place to eat. The Hotel de l'Empire is a terrible tragedy. They are so poor, that I believe

it is my eight francs a day keeps them going; nothing else is in sight. But, it is the exception. Never did a people take a war as the French take this worst of all wars. They really are the most splendid of people. I only wish I could have had one of them for a grandfather or grandmother. Bessie writes that Hope is growing wonderfully and beautifully, and I am sick for a sight of her, and for you. Good night and God bless you and the happiest of New Years to you both.
Your loving brother,
Dick.

These postcards are "originals" painted by students of the Beaux-Arts to keep alive, and to keep those students in the trenches. They are for Dai.

Paris, December 31, 1915.
Dearest One:
The old year, the dear, old year that brought us Hope, is very near the end. I am not going to watch him go. I have drunk to the New Year and to my wife and daughter, and before there is "a new step on the floor, and a new face at the door," I will be asleep. Of all my many years, the old year, that is so soon to pass away, has been the *best*, for it has brought you to me with a closer tie, has added to the love I have for every breath you breathe, for your laugh and your smile, and deep concern, that comes if you think your worthless husband is worried, or cross, or dismayed. Each year I love you more; for I know you more, and to know more of the lovely soul you are, is to love more. Just now we are in a hard place. I am sure you cannot comprehend how her father, her "Dad" and your husband can keep away. Neither do I understand.

From a photograph by Walter Scott Shinn.

Hope Davis.

VERA CRUZ AND THE GREAT WAR

But, for both your sakes, I want, before I own up that this adventure has been a failure, to try and pull something out of the wreck. If the government says I *can*, then I still may be able to do something. If it says, "*no*," then it's Home, boys, Home, and that's where I want to be. It's home, boys, home, in the old countree. 'Neath the ash, and the oak, and the spreading maple tree, it's home, boys, home, to mine own countree! This is Hope and you. So know, that in getting to you I have not thrown away a minute. I have been a slave-driver, to others as well as to myself. But you cannot get favors with a whip; and, the French war office has other matters to occupy it, that it considers of more importance than an impatient war correspondent. So long as you understand, it will not matter. Nothing hurts, except that you may not understand. The moment I see you, and you see me, you *will* understand. So, goodnight, and God bless you, you, my two blessings. Here is to our own year of 1915, your year and Hope's year, and, because I have you both, my year. I send you all the love in all the world.

RICHARD.

MY DEAREST ONE: January 5, 1916.

What pictures! What happiness. What a proud Richard! On top of my writing yesterday that I had had no sketches of yours, and no kodaks of Hope, eight came to-night, and oh! I am so proud, so homesick. What a wonderful nurse and mother you are! Was ever there anything so lovable? And that she should be ours, to hold and to love, and to make happy. These last eight days in Paris, in and out, have made me so homesick for those I love, that you will never know what the delays meant. I felt just the way poor women feel who kidnap babies. In the parks I know the nurse-maids are afraid of me. I stick my head under the hoods of the baby carriages, and stop and stand watching them at play. And tonight when all these beautiful pictures came, I was the happiest father anywhere.

The delay was no one's fault, not mine anyway, nor can I blame anyone. These people are splendid. They are willing to do anything for one, but it takes time. When they are fighting for their lives and have not seen their own babies in a year, that you want to see yours is only natural and to oblige you they can't see why they should upset the whole war. But now it looks less as though I would have to call it a failure. And Hope may be proud of me, and you may be proud of me, and I will have enough ammunition to draw on for many articles and letters, and another book.

It has been a cruel time; and when I tell you how I worked to get it over, and to be back with you, you will understand many things. The most important of all will be how I love you. Only wait until I can lay eyes on you, you will just take one look and know that it couldn't be helped, that the delay was the work of others, that, all I wanted was my Bessie and my Hope.

How heavy she will be, if she is anything like the picture of her on the coverlet, she is a prize baby. And if she is anything like as beautiful as in the baby carriage she is an angel straight from God. I want to sit in the green chair and have you on one knee and her majesty on the other, and have her climb over me, and pull my hair and bang my nose, and in time to know how I love you both.

Goodnight, dear heart, I wish you had had yourself in the picture. I have three in the summer time with you holding her and that is the way I like to see you, that is the way I think of you. I love you, and I love her for making you so happy, and I love her for her sake, and because she is *ours:* and has tied us tighter and closer even than it has ever been. I love you so that I can't write about it, and I am going to do nothing all spring but just sit around, and be in everybody's way, watching you together.

How jealous I am of you, and homesick for you. Of course, she knows "mamma" is *you;* and to look at you when they ask, "Where's mother?" Who else could be her mother *but the dearest woman in the world*, and the one who loves her so, and in so wonderful a way. She is beautiful beyond all things human I know. If ever a woman deserved a beautiful daughter, *you do*, for you are the best of mothers, and you know how "to care greatly."

Good-night, my precious, dear one, and God keep you, as He will, and help me to keep you both happy. What you give me you never will know.

RICHARD.

CHAPTER XX

THE LAST DAYS

AFTER a short visit to London, Richard returned to New York in February, 1916. During his absence his wife and Hope had occupied the Scribner cottage at Mount Kisco, about two miles from Crossroads. Here my brother finished his second book on the war, and wrote numerous articles and letters urging the immediate necessity for preparedness in this country. As to Richard's usefulness to his country at this time, I quote in part from two appreciations written after my brother's death by the two most prominent exponents of preparedness.

Theodore Roosevelt said:

"He was as good an American as ever lived, and his heart flamed against cruelty and injustice. His writings form a text-book of Americanism which all our people would do well to read at the present time."

Major-General Leonard Wood said:

"The death of Richard Harding Davis was a real loss to the movement for preparedness. Mr. Davis had an extensive experience as a military observer, and thoroughly appreciated the need of a general training system like that of Australia or Switzerland and of thorough organization of our industrial resources in order to establish a condition of reasonable preparedness in this country. A few days before his death he came to Governors Island for the purpose of ascertaining in what line of work he could be most useful in

THE LAST DAYS 409

building up sound public opinion in favor of such preparedness as would give us a real peace insurance. His mind was bent on devoting his energies and abilities to the work of public education on this vitally important subject, and few men were better qualified to do so, for he had served as a military observer in many campaigns.

"Throughout the Cuban campaign he was attached to the headquarters of my regiment in Cuba as a military observer. He was with the advanced party at the opening of the fight at Las Guasimas, and was distinguished throughout the fight by coolness and good conduct. He also participated in the battle of San Juan and the siege of Santiago, and as an observer was always where duty called him. He was a delightful companion, cheerful, resourceful, and thoughtful of the interests and wishes of others. His reports of the game were valuable and among the best and most accurate.

"The Plattsburg movement took a very strong hold of him. He saw in this a great instrument for building up a sound knowledge concerning our military history and policy, also a very practical way of training men for the duties of junior officers. He realized fully that we should need in case of war tens of thousands of officers with our newly raised troops, and that it would be utterly impossible to prepare them in the hurry and confusion of the onrush of modern war. His heart was filled with a desire to serve his country to the best of his ability. His recent experience in Europe pointed out to him the absolute madness of longer disregarding the need of doing those things which reasonable preparedness dictates, the things which cannot be accomplished after trouble is upon us. He had in mind at the time of his death a series of articles to be written especially to build up interest in universal military training through conveying to our people an understanding of what organization as it exists to-day means, and how vitally important it is for our people to do in time of peace those things which modern war does not permit done once it is under way.

"Davis was a loyal friend, a thoroughgoing American devoted to the best interests of his country, courageous, sympathetic, and true. His loss has been a very real one to all of us who knew and appreciated him, and in his death the cause of preparedness has lost an able worker and the country a devoted and loyal citizen."

Although suffering from his strenuous experiences in France, and more particularly from those in Greece, Richard continued to accomplish his usual enormous amount of work, and during these weeks wrote his last short story, "The Deserter."

The following letter was written to me while I was in the Bahamas and was in reference to a novel which I had dedicated to Hope:

MOUNT KISCO—February 28, 1916.

DEAR OLD MAN:

No word yet of the book, except the advts. I enclose. I will send you the notices as soon as they begin to appear. I am so happy over the dedication, and, very proud. So, Hope will be when she knows. As I have not read the novel it all will come as a splendid and pleasant surprise. I am looking forward to sitting down to it with all the pleasure in the world.

You chose the right moment to elope. Never was weather so cold, cruel and bitter. Hope is the only one who goes out of doors.

From a photograph by Walter Scott Shinn.

Mrs. R. H. Davis and Hope Davis.

I start the fires in the Big House tomorrow and the plumbers and paper hangers, painters enter the day after. The attack on Verdun makes me sick. I was there six weeks ago in one of the forts but of course could not then nor can I now write of it. I don't believe the drive ever can get through. For two reasons, and the unmilitary one is that I believe in a just God. Give my love to Dai, and for you always

DICK.

P. S. I am happy you are both so happy, but those post cards with the palms were cruelty to animals.

On the 21st of March, 1916, Richard and his wife and daughter moved from the Scribner cottage to Crossroads, and a few days later he was attacked by the illness that ended in his death on April 11. He had dined with his wife and afterward had worked on an article on preparedness, written some letters and telegrams concerning the same subject and, while repeating one of the latter over the telephone, was stricken. Within a week of his fifty-third year, just one year from the day he had first brought his baby daughter to her real home, doing the best and finest work of his career in the cause of the Allies and preparedness, quite unconscious that the end was near, he left us. In those fifty-two years he had crowded the work, the pleasures, the kind, chivalrous deeds of many men, and he died just as I am sure he would have wished to die, working into the night for a great cause, and although ill and tired, still fretful for the morning that he might again take up the fight.

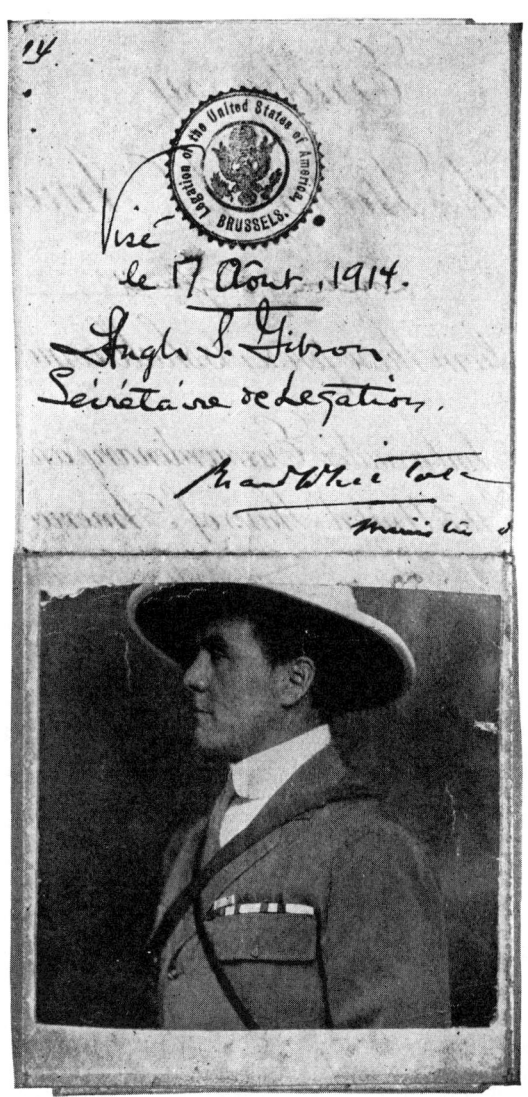

The passport and photograph which, though indorsed by Mr. Whitlock and Mr. Gibson, led to the arrest of Mr. Davis.

Mr. Davis's ticket of leave.

The pencil writing is the German "ticket of leave," requiring Mr. Davis to report in forty-eight hours or "be as a spy treated."

Reverse side of ticket of leave.
The ink writing (lower half) is the visé stating he is "not at all" to be treated as a spy.

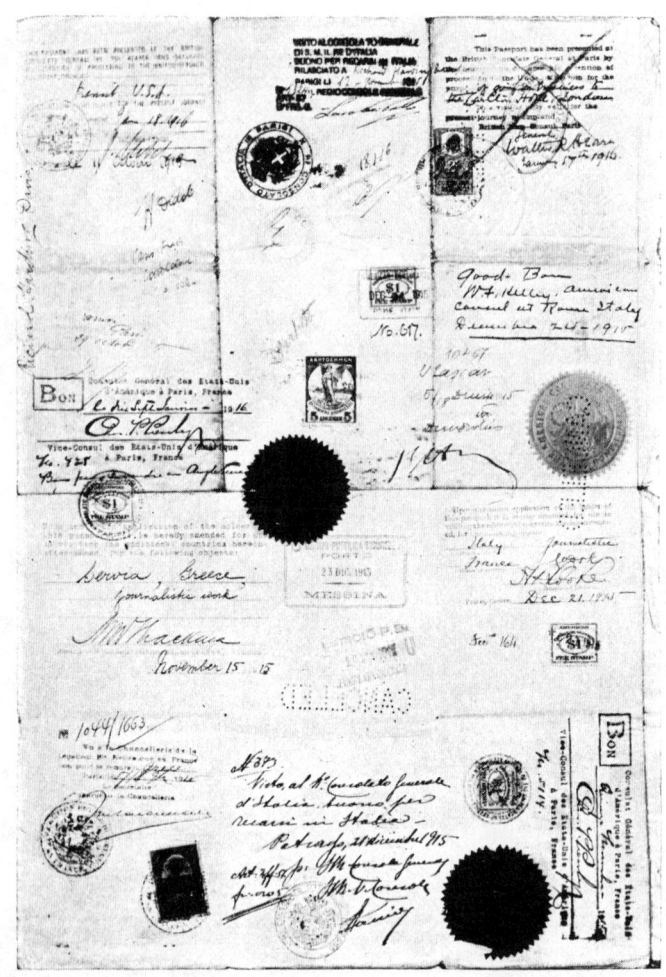

Mr. Davis's passport on his last trip to Europe, 1915–16.

INDEX

Abbey, E. A., 129.
Adams, Maude, 59, 167, 168, 217.
Allen, G. P., 17, 29.
Arnold, Edwin, 181.
Asquith, H. H., 213, 373.
Asquith, Mrs. H. H., 213.
Astor, Waldorf, 333.
Astor, Mrs. Waldorf, 333.

Badger, C. J., 365.
Balfour, A. J., 88.
Barrie, J. M., 200, 217, 321, 322.
Barrie, Mrs. J. M., 217, 321, 322, 339.
Barrymore, Ethel, 8, 9, 59, 167, 218, 220, 221, 222, 334.
Barrymore, John, 334.
Barrymore, Maurice, 60, 172.
Barrymore, Mrs. Maurice, 8.
Bartlett, Ashmead, 334.
Bartol, Dr., 19.
Bass, John F., 207, 209, 210, 211, 301, 302, 303, 398.
Bass, Mrs. John, 394.
Bayard, T. F., 187.
Benedict, E. C., 227.
Benedict, Helen (see Mrs. Thomas Hastings).
Bernardi, Spirito, 174.
Bernhardt, Mme., 138, 139.
Beveridge, Kuhne, 259.
Bisland, Elizabeth, 165.
Blackwood, Lord Basil, 213.
Blavatsky, Mme. H. P., 8.
Bliss, T. L., 343.
Bogran, General, 145, 147.
Bonilla, Manuel, 144, 150, 151, 154, 162.
Bonsal, Stephen, 106, 107, 130, 165, 228, 232, 234, 238, 245, 246, 334.
Boone, Lieut., 238.
Booth, Edwin, 9, 11.

Boucicault, Dion, 11.
Bourget, Paul, 169.
Breckinridge, G. R., 178, 182.
Brisbane, Arthur, 42, 44, 48, 50, 51, 59, 334.
Brodhead, J. Davis, 16.
Brownlow, Lady, 89, 90.
Bryan, W. J., 358, 359, 360, 365, 378.
Buckle, Captain, 108.
Buckle, Miss, 103, 104.
Bull, Rene, 267.
Buller, General, 265, 266, 268, 269, 277, 278, 281.
Burnett, Frances Hodgson, 8.
Burnham, F. R., 329.

Cable, G. W., 18.
Camp, Walter, 65.
Capron, Captain, 250, 251.
Carmencita, 52, 103.
Carnot, President, 137, 138.
Castleton, Lord, 258, 259.
Cecil, Lady Edward, 213.
Chadwick, F. E., 227, 230, 233.
Chaffee, A. R., 248, 254.
Chamberlain, Mrs. J., 84.
Chamberlain, S., 188, 319.
Chanler, W. A., 108, 165, 238.
Chevalier, Albert, 109, 121, 224.
Childs, G. W., 66.
Chule, Captain, 337.
Church, Dr., 253.
Churchill, Lady Randolph, 268, 277.
Churchill, Winston Spencer, 272, 319, 333, 373, 375.
Claiborne, J. H., 152.
Clark, Bruce, 257.
Clark, J. M., 93, 211, 260, 292, 298, 342.
Clark, Mrs. J. M., 213, 260, 292, 308, 342.

413

INDEX

Clark, J. S., 9, 11.
Clarke, Lady, 258.
Clemens, Samuel L., 132, 133.
Cleveland, Grover, 54, 66, 92, 110, 171, 180.
Cleveland, Mrs. Grover, 54, 93.
Clifford, Colonel Maurice, 214.
Cline, Maggie, 317.
Cobb, Irvin S., 7, 370.
Coffin, Hayden, 224, 225.
Cohen, Isaac, 142.
Coleridge, Lady, 86, 87.
Coleridge, Lord, 86.
Collier, R. J., 297, 300, 316, 321.
Collier, William, 350, 365.
Collins, Arthur, 223.
Colt, Russell G., 382.
Coquelin, B. C., 128, 129.
Coward, E. F., 158.
Crabtree, Lotta, 9.
Craig, Lady, 217.
Crane, Stephen, 200, 207, 234, 235.
Creelman, James, 165.
Crespo, Joaquin, 163.
Cromer, Lord, 115, 118.
Cronje, Mrs., 284.
Crute, Jennings, 38, 39.
Cumnock, Arthur, 61, 65.
Curtis, G. W., 57.
Curzon, George N., 199.
Cushing, H. G., 61, 90, 91, 129.
Cust, Henry I. C., 88, 89, 90, 91.

Daly, Augustin, 12, 13.
Daschoff, Count, 177, 178, 180.
Davies, Ben, 225.
Davis, Llewellen, 322.
De Koven, Mrs. Reginald, 168.
Deland, Margaret, 61.
de Tnas, Duke, 101.
De Vet, Christian, 285.
Dewey, George, 246.
Dixey, H. E., 20.
Dorst, J. H., 246.
Douglas, H. B., 24.
Drew, John, 12, 131, 136, 137, 166, 167, 218.
Drew, Mrs. John, 167.

Drew, Sr., Mrs. John, 8, 9.
Dufferin, Lord, 130.
Du Maurier, Guy, 339.
Dunn, Robert, 377.
Dunne, F. P., 15.
Dunraven, Earl of, 172.

Eddy, Spencer, 212.
Edison, Thomas, 178.
Egan, Martin, 304, 385.
Eliot, George, 55.
Eustis, James B., 125, 211.
Eustis, Jr., J. B., 125.
Eustis, Newton, 125.
Eustis, Tina, 125, 130.

Fairchild, S., 63.
Farren, Nellie, 223, 225.
Ferrondeux, Comtesse de la, 129.
Field, Dr. H. M., 98, 99, 102, 105.
Fish, Hamilton, 250.
Fletcher, Charles, 9.
Flint, Grover, 188.
Forbes, Archibald, 199.
Forman, J. M., 314.
Forrest, Edwin, 10.
Fox, Jr., John, 247, 303, 304, 306, 307, 310.
Fraser, Margaret, 223, 321, 334.
Frazier, Kenneth, 125.
Frederic, Harold, 200.
Frederick, Lord William, 90.
Freear, Louise, 224.
Freye, Louise, 370, 376.
Frohman, Charles, 217, 339.
Frohman, Daniel, 169, 172.
Funston, Frederick, 354.
Furness, H. H., 8.
Furness, 3rd, W. H., 143.

Gardner, Mrs. John, 61.
Garza, General, 69, 74.
Gibson, Charles Dana, 59, 93, 125, 138, 196.
Gibson, Mrs. C. D., 196.
Gilbert, Mrs., 12.
Gilbert, W. H., 224.
Gilder, R. W., 54, 92, 132.
Gilder, Mrs. R. W., 54.

INDEX 415

Gomez, Maximo, 187, 188.
Goodnough, W. T., 24.
Gosse, Edmund, 49.
Gould, G. J., 213.
Gower-Browne, Lady, 118.
Greene, Plunkett, 225.
Griscom, L. C., 140, 141, 142, 147, 148, 151, 152, 155, 157, 162, 163, 164, 165, 166, 167, 280, 301, 302, 303.
Guilbert, Yvette, 123, 130, 168, 169, 172.

Haines, C. O., 29.
Hale, Helen, 334.
Hammond, John Hays, 259.
Hanbury, Lilly, 224.
Hardie, F. H., 70, 71, 72, 73.
Harding, H. W., 15, 17.
Hare, James, 398.
Hare, John, 169.
Hastings, Mrs. Thomas, 59, 105, 165, 167, 168, 171.
Hawkins, Anthony Hope, 200, 213, 218, 321, 334, 374.
Hay, Adelbert, S., 281, 284.
Hay, Helen, 213.
Hay, John, 211, 213, 223.
Hearst, W. R., 170, 181, 194, 319.
Hicks, Seymour, 60, 169, 170, 200, 340.
Hicks, Mrs. Seymour, 60, 169, 170, 172, 224, 238.
Hilliard, Robert, 60.
Hitchcock, Raymond, 334.
Holland, J. G., 33.
Holmes, O. W., 19, 61.
Hopper, De Wolfe, 45, 46, 51.
Howe, Julia Ward, 61.
Howe, Jr., M. A. De W., 25, 27, 29.
Howells, M., 63.
Howells, W. D., 60, 63, 132, 199.
Huerta, V., 357, 358, 359.
Hutton, L., 132.

Irving, Henry, 12, 132, 133, 138, 139, 167, 172, 224.
Irwin, Wallace, 334.

Jaggers, W. T., 255, 256, 258.
Jefferson, Joseph, 8, 9, 11, 69, 92.
Jefferson, Mrs. Joseph, 8, 11.
Jeffries, Ellis, 224.

Kelly, Commander, 165.
Kipling, Rudyard, 49, 64, 294.
Kitchener, Lord, 118, 265, 359, 360, 375.
Kuroki, General, 311.

Laffan, W. M., 50.
Lambdin, George, 8.
Lamont, D. G., 187.
La Montagne, Albert, 59.
Larned, W. A., 253.
Laurier, Wilfrid, 214.
Lawton, General, 254.
Lee, Arthur H., 241, 242, 243, 245, 253.
Lee, General, 232.
Leno, Dan, 224.
Lester, Lord, 213.
Lewes, George, 55.
Lewis, James, 12, 98.
Lewis, Lady, 338.
Lind, Letty, 224, 225.
Little, E. C., 111, 113, 114.
Lloyd, Marie, 225.
Logan, Jr., John A., 180.
London, Jack, 305, 355.
Long, J. D., 232, 233.

McCarthy, J. H., 200, 219, 220, 221, 222.
McCloy, W. C., 318, 319.
McClure, S. S., 49, 50.
McCullough, John, 9.
McCutcheon, J. T., 365, 366, 370, 394, 397, 398, 399, 400.
McMichael, 3rd, Morton, 40, 41, 123.
Malet, Cuthbert, 327.
Mannce, A. B., 317.
Marlowe, Julia, 12.
Marshall, Edward, 250, 254.
Maude, Cyril, 217, 258.
Meade, Admiral, 165.
Melba, Mme., 168, 213.

Merrill, Bradford, 50.
Michaelson, Charles, 187, 188, 189, 190, 192.
Miles, Gen. N. A., 232, 246.
Millet, F. D., 132.
Milner, Sir Alfred, 266, 281, 282.
Moloney, Sir Arthur, 140.
Moore, Mary, 334.
Morgan, Commissioner, 79.
Morgan, E. V., 315, 316.
Morgan, Gerald, 368, 369, 377.
Morris, Gouverneur, 93, 345, 374, 375, 376.
Morrow, R. T., 26.

Neilson, Adelaide, 9.
Neilson, Julia, 213.
Nordica, Mme., 168.

Oku, General, 306.
Olcott, W. K., 8.
Olney, Richard, 187.
Osgood, J. R., 64.

Paderewski, Ignace, 213.
Page, T. N., 211.
Paine, R. D., 229, 232, 235.
Palmer, A. M., 132.
Palmer, Frederick, 303, 368, 370, 378.
Payne, Edward, 224.
Pembroke, Lord, 88.
Pennell, Joseph, 129.
Phillips, Percival, 210.
Plancon, Pol, 168.
Poe, E., 65.
Poincaré, President, 386.
Pollen, Arthur, 86.
Porter, H. H., 132.
Powers, J. T., 20.
Purnell, F. C., 24, 29.

Ralph, Julian, 170, 181, 200, 265.
Ramsay, Milne, 8.
Reany, Father, 361.
Reed, John, 377.
Reeves, A. S., 29.
Rehan, Ada, 12, 13.
Reid, Whitelaw, 132.

Rejane, Mme., 138, 139.
Remington, Frederic, 186, 187, 189, 190, 191, 192, 193, 194, 196, 232, 238, 241, 245, 246, 252.
Roberts, Arthur, 224, 225.
Roberts, Lord, 214, 261, 265, 268, 277, 279, 286, 288, 289.
Roosevelt, Theodore, 227, 233, 247, 248, 251, 253, 254, 255, 408.
Rothenstein, W., 128, 129.
Ruff, John D., 17, 22, 24, 25, 26.
Ruff, Margaret, 8.
Russell, John, 98.
Russell, Lillian, 162.
Russell, Robert Howard, 59, 152, 165, 166, 170, 187, 196, 257.
Rutland, Duchess of, 256.

St. Cyres, Viscount, 85.
Salisbury, Lord, 171.
Sampson, Admiral, 229, 233.
Sangree, Allen, 281.
Sargent, J. S., 340, 341.
Savage, H. W., 318, 319.
Scovel, Sylvester, 210, 229, 230, 232, 233.
Shafter, General, 241, 245.
Smith, Ballard, 200.
Somerset, Lady Henry, 169, 213.
Somerset, Somers, 140, 141, 142, 146, 148, 152, 154, 157, 161, 164, 165, 169, 170, 255, 257, 261, 262, 263, 264, 273.
Sothern, E. A., 10.
Sothern, E. H., 59, 60, 144, 172.
Sothern, Janet, 337, 340.
Sothern, Sam., 59, 165, 170, 172, 224, 321.
Spender, Earl, 88.
Stanley, H. M., 133.
Stanley, Mrs., 88.
Stevenson, R. L., 6, 7, 41.
Steyn, M. T., 283, 288.
Stone, Jr., M. E., 334.
Storey, Fred, 224.
Stuart, Murray, 25.
Sullivan, Sir Arthur, 51.
Sutherland, Duchess of, 223.

INDEX 417

Taft, W. H., 334.
Tarkington, Booth, 58, 334.
Tempest, Marie, 224.
Terriss, Ellaline (*see* Mrs. Seymour Hicks).
Terry, Ellen, 12, 139, 172, 220, 224.
Terry, Fred, 213, 226.
Terry, Willis, 65.
Thaw, H. K., 334.
Thomas, Augustus, 36, 350.
Thomas, Brandon, 217.
Thurston, W. W., 16, 35.
Tiffany, W., 254.
Tnas, Duke de, 101.
Tolman, C. M., 25.
Trowbridge, Augustus, 173, 177, 178, 180, 182.
Twain, Mark (*see* S. L. Clemens).
Tyler, Trooper, 70, 71, 72, 73.

Van Loosberg, Captain, 282, 283, 284.
Vaughan, Kate, 224.

Waldron, Mrs., 266.
Walsh, Blanche, 171.
Warner, C. D., 132.
Warren, Whitney, 389.
Watrous, A., 39, 40.

Webster, Ben, 334.
Webster, Mrs. Ben, 334.
Weyler, General, 196.
Wheeler, J. N., 358, 374, 375.
Whigham, H. J., 82, 321, 334, 374.
Whistler, J. McN., 129.
White, General, 272.
White, Henry, 212.
White, Stanford, 113.
Whitlock, Brand, 369, 370.
Whitman, Mrs., 61.
Whitman, Walt., 41.
Whitney, Caspar, 245, 247, 248, 252, 253, 254.
Wilde, Oscar, 129.
Williams, J. L., 318, 319.
Wilson, Francis, 45, 46.
Wilson, Hugh, 17.
Wilson, Woodrow, 357.
Wood, Sir Evelyn, 200.
Wood, Leonard, 247, 248, 249, 250, 253, 254, 343, 400.
Wyndham, Charles, 225, 226, 334.

Young, J. R., 132.
Young, S. B. M., 249, 250.

Zogbaum, R. F., 229, 230.

PS 1523.A43 1974